THE LOW, LOW WOODS

THE LOW, LOW WOODS

CARMEN MARIA MACHADO WRITER

DANI ARTIST

TAMRA BONVILLAIN COLORIST **STEVE WANDS** LETTERER

SAM WOLFE CONNELLY COVER ARTIST

J.A.W. COOPER COVER ARTIST *THE LOW, LOW WOODS #1*

THE LOW, LOW WOODS CREATED BY
CARMEN MARIA MACHADO AND **DANI**

CURATED FOR **HILL HOUSE COMICS** BY **JOE HILL**

THE LOW, LOW WOODS

PUBLISHED BY DC COMICS. COMPILATION AND ALL
NEW MATERIAL COPYRIGHT © 2020 CARMEN MARIA
MACHADO AND DORION BUSINESS SERVICES LTD. ALL
RIGHTS RESERVED. ORIGINALLY PUBLISHED IN SINGLE
MAGAZINE FORM IN *THE LOW, LOW WOODS* 1-6.
COPYRIGHT © 2019, 2020 CARMEN MARIA MACHADO
AND DORION BUSINESS SERVICES LTD. ALL RIGHTS
RESERVED. ALL CHARACTERS, THEIR DISTINCTIVE LIKE-
NESSES, AND RELATED ELEMENTS FEATURED IN THIS
PUBLICATION ARE TRADEMARKS OF CARMEN MARIA
MACHADO AND DORION BUSINESS SERVICES LTD.
HILL HOUSE COMICS IS A TRADEMARK OF DC COMICS.
THE STORIES, CHARACTERS, AND INCIDENTS FEATURED
IN THIS PUBLICATION ARE ENTIRELY FICTIONAL. DC
COMICS DOES NOT READ OR ACCEPT UNSOLICITED
SUBMISSIONS OF IDEAS, STORIES, OR ARTWORK.
DC – A WARNERMEDIA COMPANY.

DC COMICS, 2900 WEST ALAMEDA AVE., BURBANK,
CA 91505

PRINTED BY TRANSCONTINENTAL INTERGLOBE,
BEAUCEVILLE, QC, CANADA. 8/21/20.

ISBN: 978-1-77950-452-4

LIBRARY OF CONGRESS CATALOGING-IN-
PUBLICATION DATA IS AVAILABLE.

AMEDEO TURTURRO EDITOR – ORIGINAL SERIES
JEB WOODARD GROUP EDITOR – COLLECTED EDITIONS
ERIKA ROTHBERG EDITOR – COLLECTED EDITION
STEVE COOK DESIGN DIRECTOR – BOOKS
AMIE BROCKWAY-METCALF PUBLICATION DESIGN
SUZANNAH ROWNTREE PUBLICATION PRODUCTION

BOB HARRAS SENIOR VP – EDITOR-IN-CHIEF, DC COMICS
MARK DOYLE EXECUTIVE EDITOR, DC BLACK LABEL

JIM LEE PUBLISHER & CHIEF CREATIVE OFFICER
BOBBIE CHASE VP – GLOBAL PUBLISHING INITIATIVES & DIGITAL STRATEGY
DON FALLETTI VP – MANUFACTURING OPERATIONS & WORKFLOW MANAGEMENT
LAWRENCE GANEM VP – TALENT SERVICES
ALISON GILL SENIOR VP – MANUFACTURING & OPERATIONS
HANK KANALZ SENIOR VP – PUBLISHING STRATEGY & SUPPORT SERVICES
DAN MIRON VP – PUBLISHING OPERATIONS
NICK J. NAPOLITANO VP – MANUFACTURING ADMINISTRATION & DESIGN
NANCY SPEARS VP – SALES
JONAH WEILAND VP – MARKETING & CREATIVE SERVICES
MICHELE R. WELLS VP & EXECUTIVE EDITOR, YOUNG READER

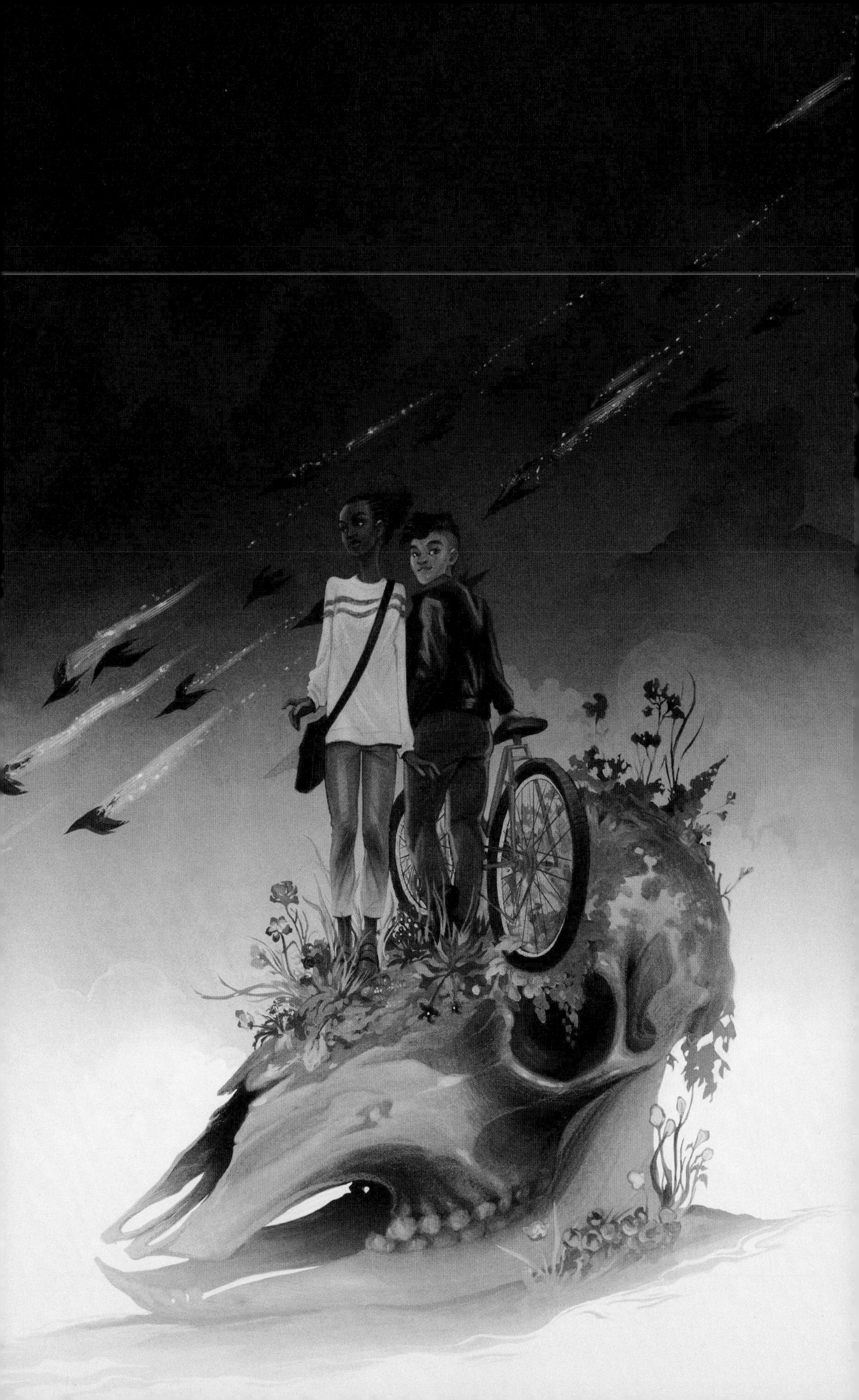

Bottomless

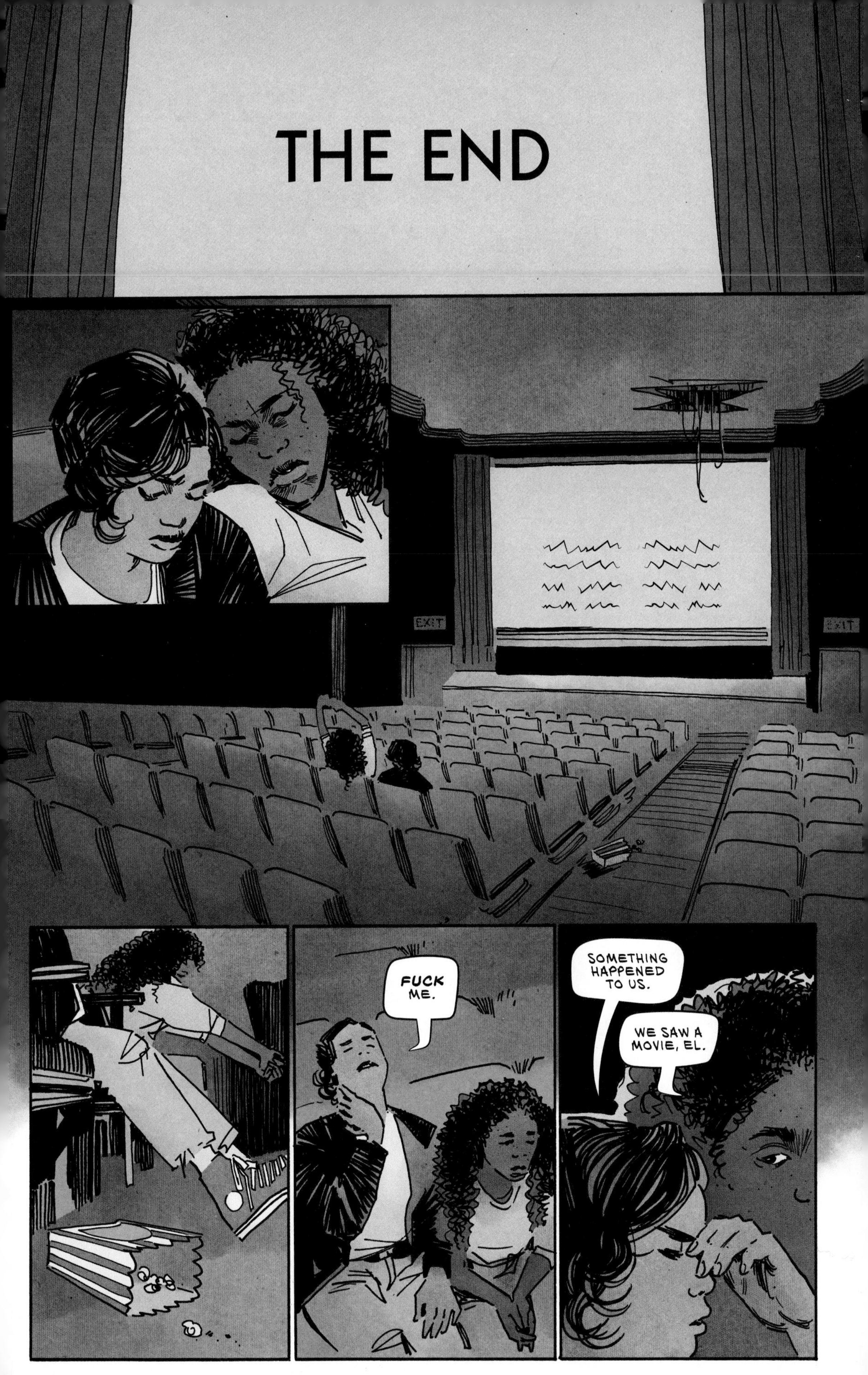
THE END
EXIT
EXIT
FUCK ME.
SOMETHING HAPPENED TO US.
WE SAW A MOVIE, EL.

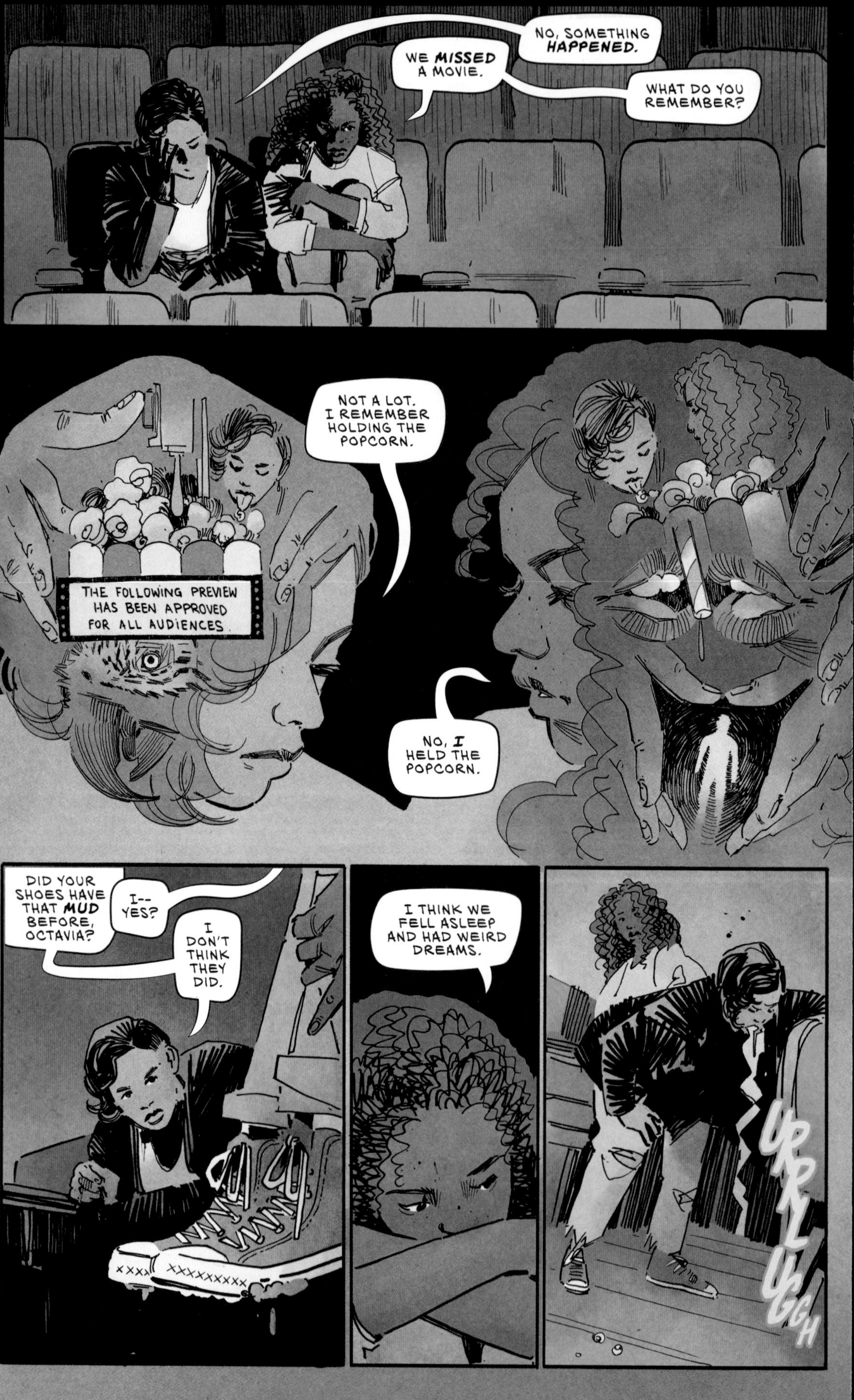
WE **MISSED** A MOVIE.
NO, SOMETHING **HAPPENED.**
WHAT DO YOU REMEMBER?
NOT A LOT. I REMEMBER HOLDING THE POPCORN.
THE FOLLOWING PREVIEW HAS BEEN APPROVED FOR ALL AUDIENCES
NO, **I** HELD THE POPCORN.
DID YOUR SHOES HAVE THAT **MUD** BEFORE, OCTAVIA?
I-- YES?
I DON'T THINK THEY DID.
I THINK WE FELL ASLEEP AND HAD WEIRD DREAMS.
URRLUGGH

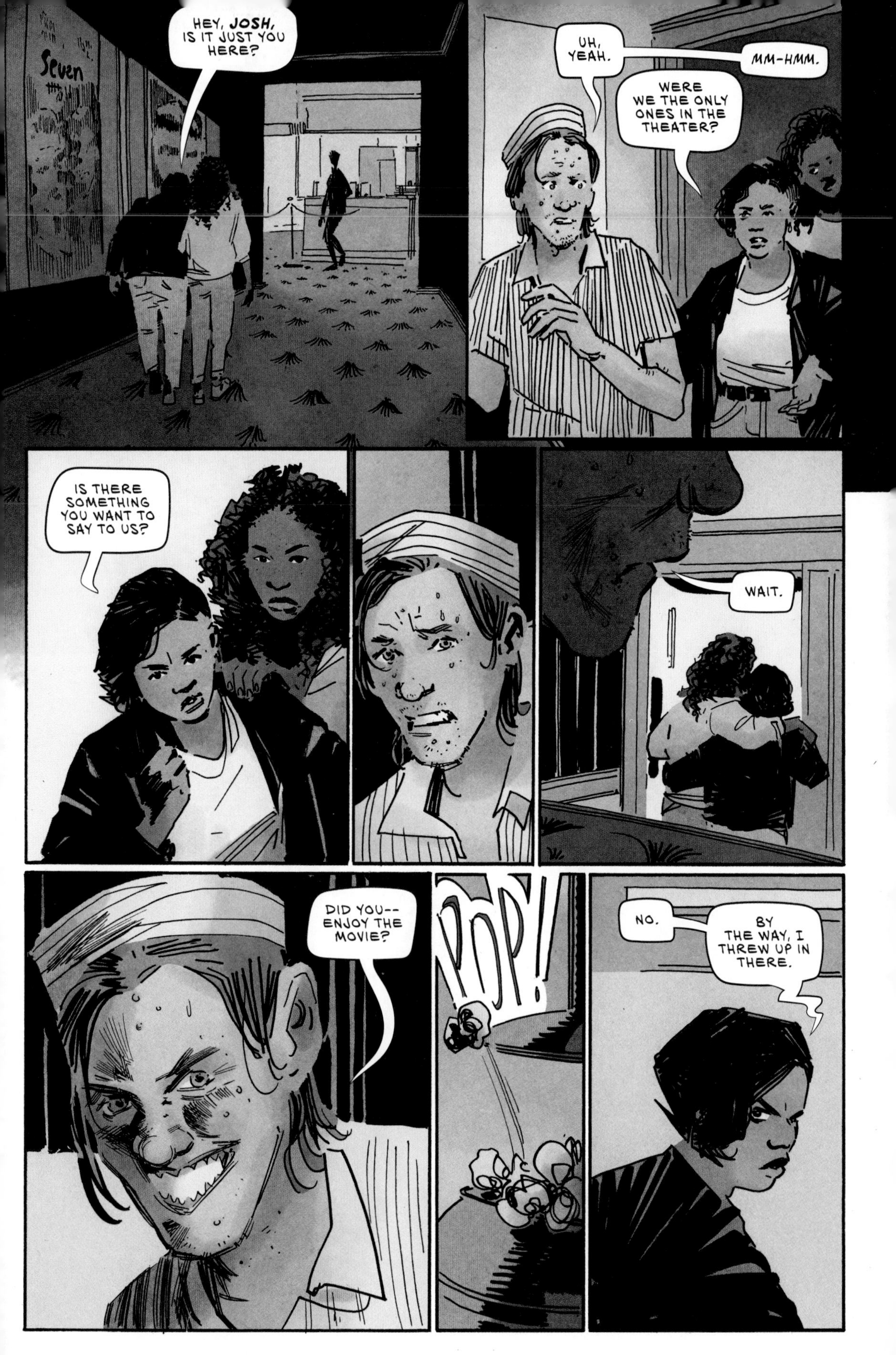
Seven
HEY, JOSH, IS IT JUST YOU HERE?
UH, YEAH.
MM-HMM.
WERE WE THE ONLY ONES IN THE THEATER?
IS THERE SOMETHING YOU WANT TO SAY TO US?
WAIT.
DID YOU-- ENJOY THE MOVIE?
POP!
NO.
BY THE WAY, I THREW UP IN THERE.

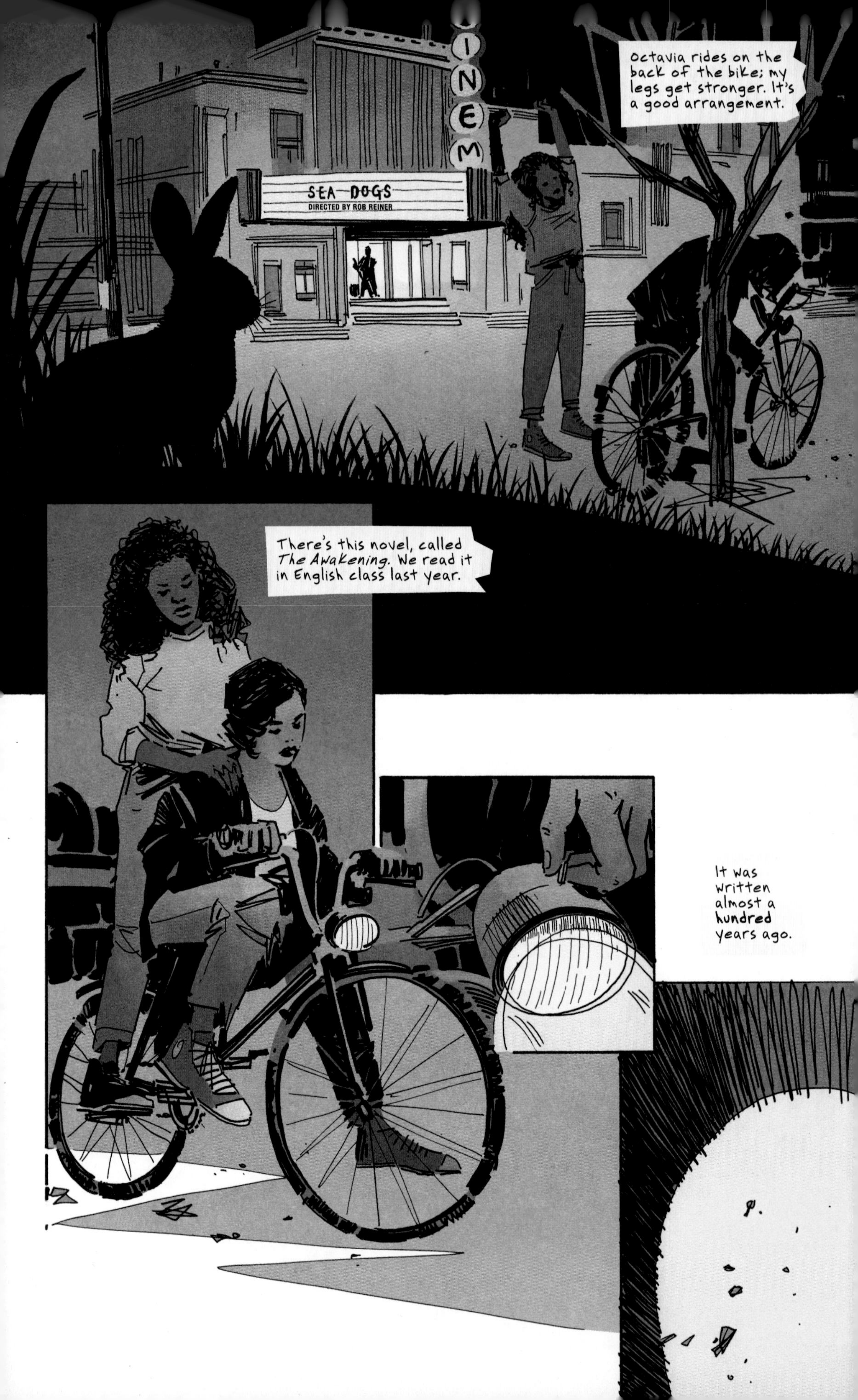

INEM
SEA DOGS
DIRECTED BY ROB REINER
Octavia rides on the back of the bike; my legs get stronger. It's a good arrangement.
There's this novel, called *The Awakening*. We read it in English class last year.
It was written almost a hundred years ago.

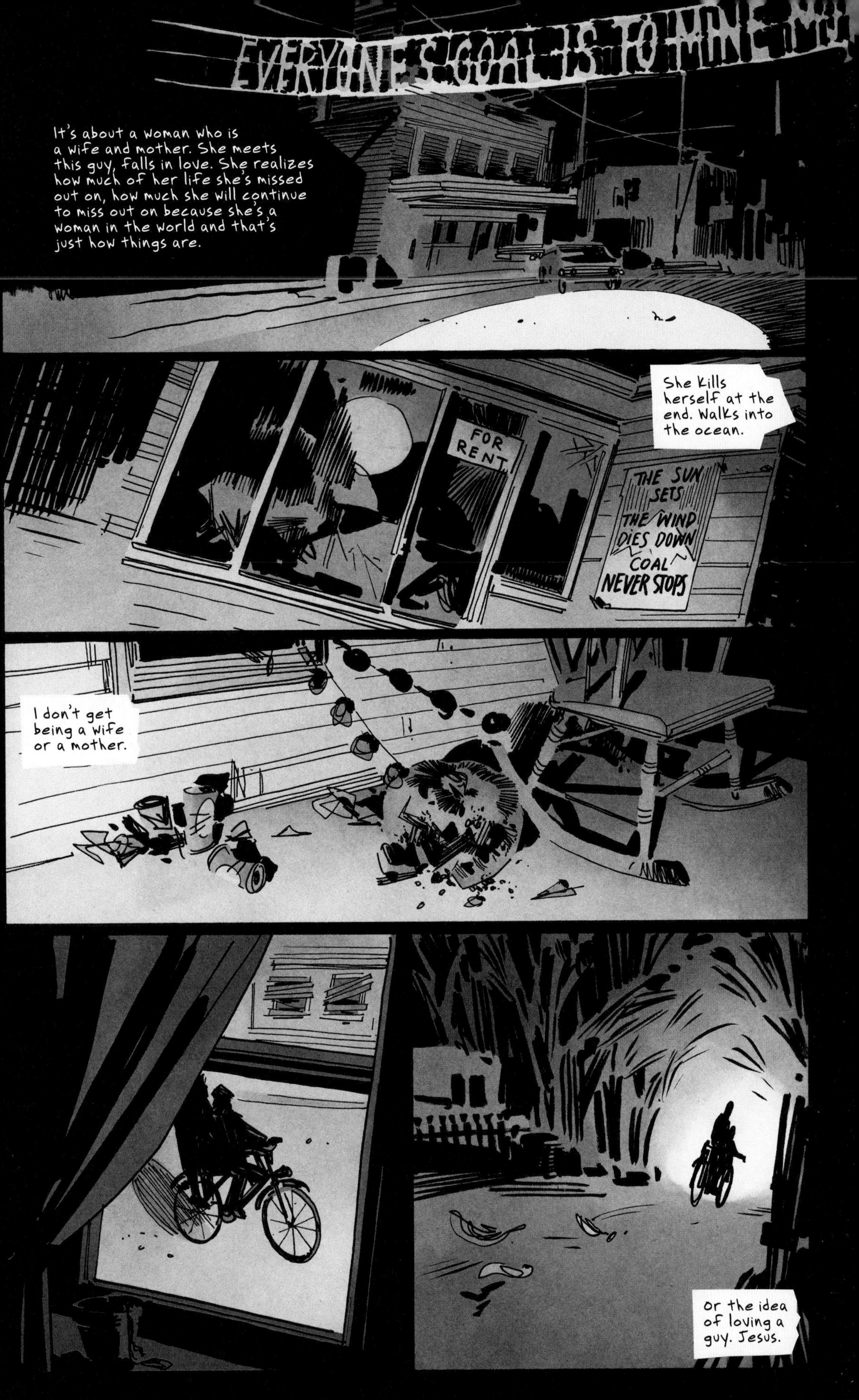
It's about a woman who is a wife and mother. She meets this guy, falls in love. She realizes how much of her life she's missed out on, how much she will continue to miss out on because she's a woman in the world and that's just how things are.
She kills herself at the end. Walks into the ocean.
FOR RENT
THE SUN SETS THE WIND DIES DOWN COAL NEVER STOPS
I don't get being a wife or a mother.
Or the idea of loving a guy. Jesus.

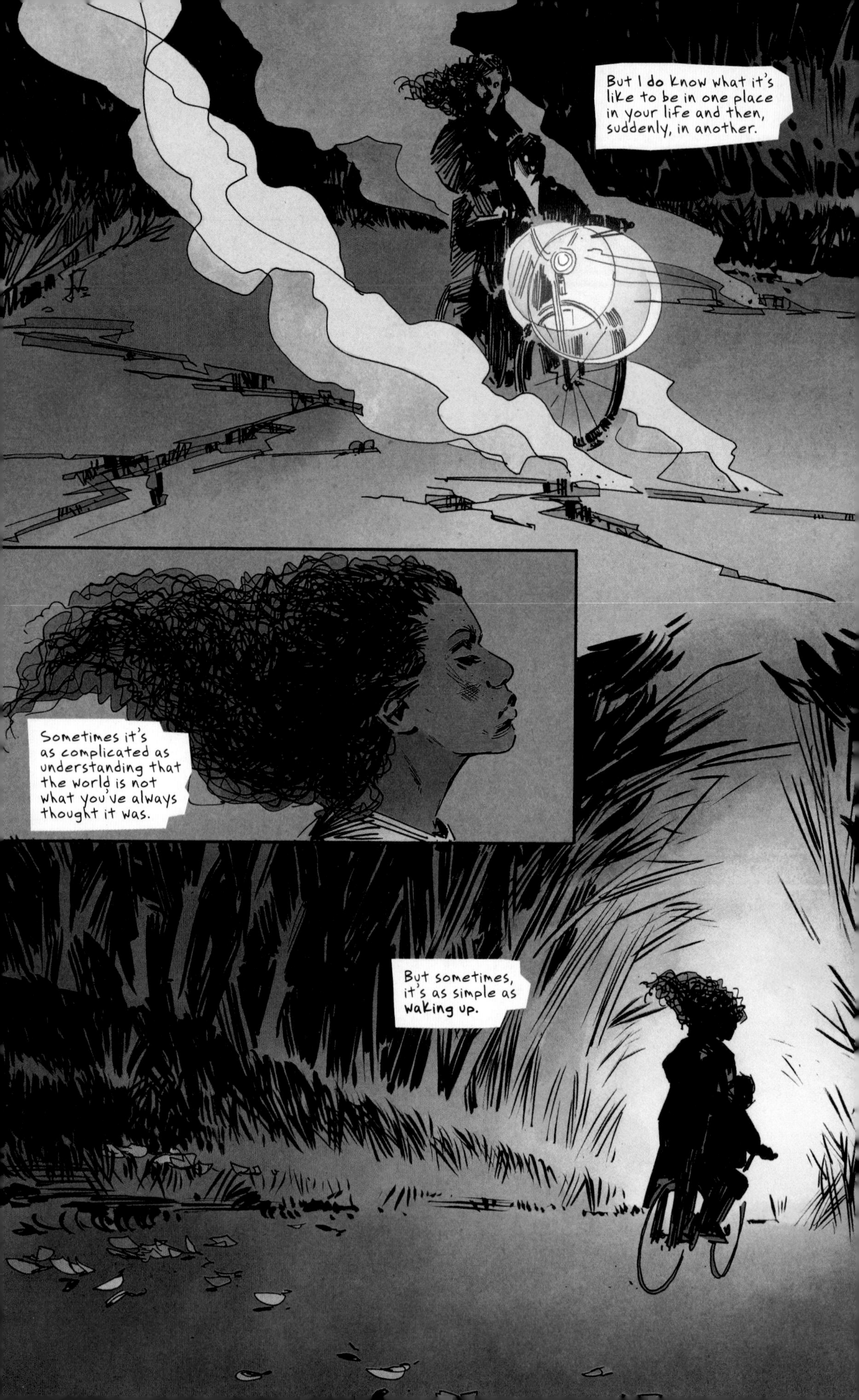
But I do know what it's like to be in one place in your life and then, suddenly, in another.
Sometimes it's as complicated as understanding that the world is not what you've always thought it was.
But sometimes, it's as simple as **waking up.**

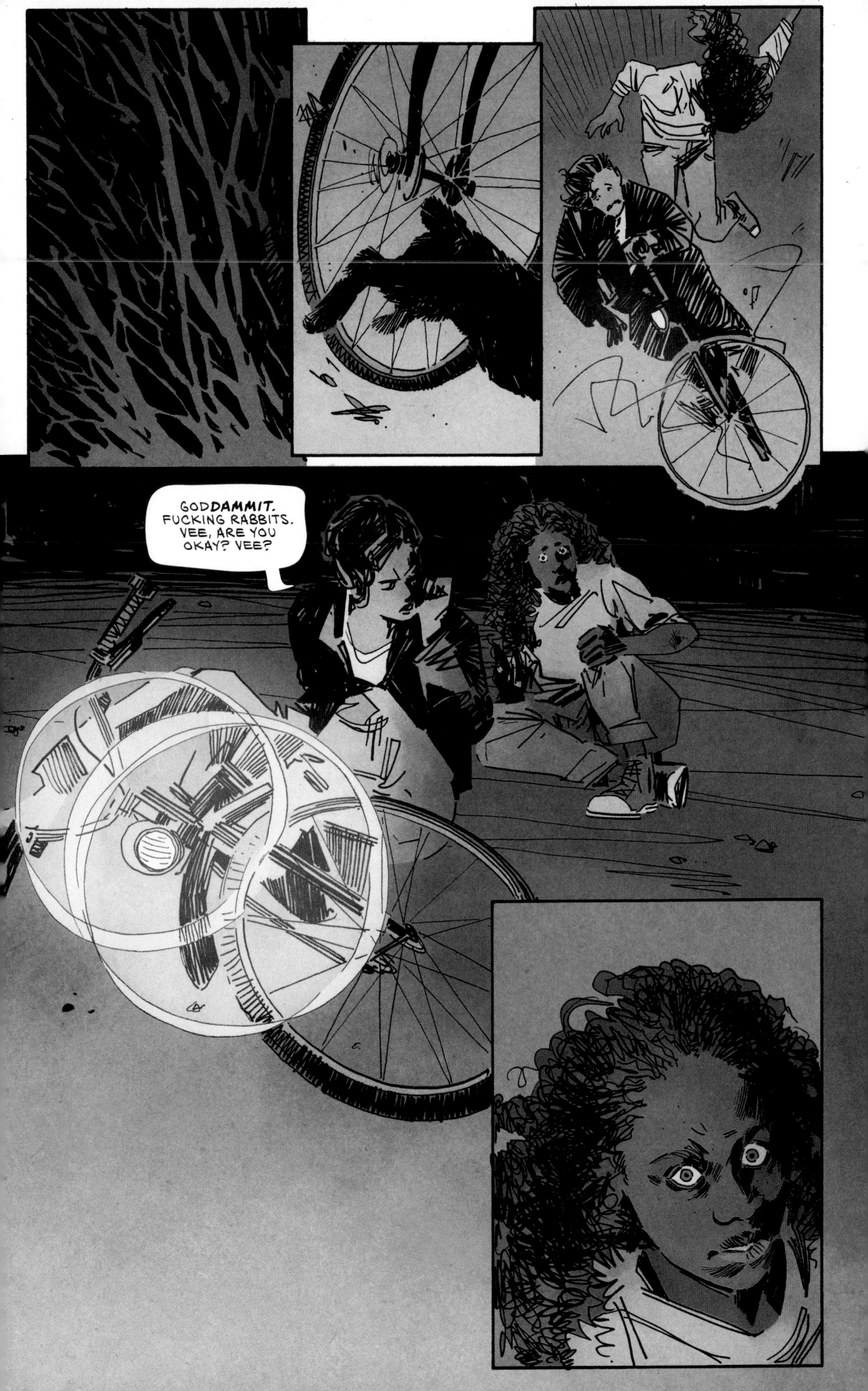
GODDAMMIT. FUCKING RABBITS. VEE, ARE YOU OKAY? VEE?

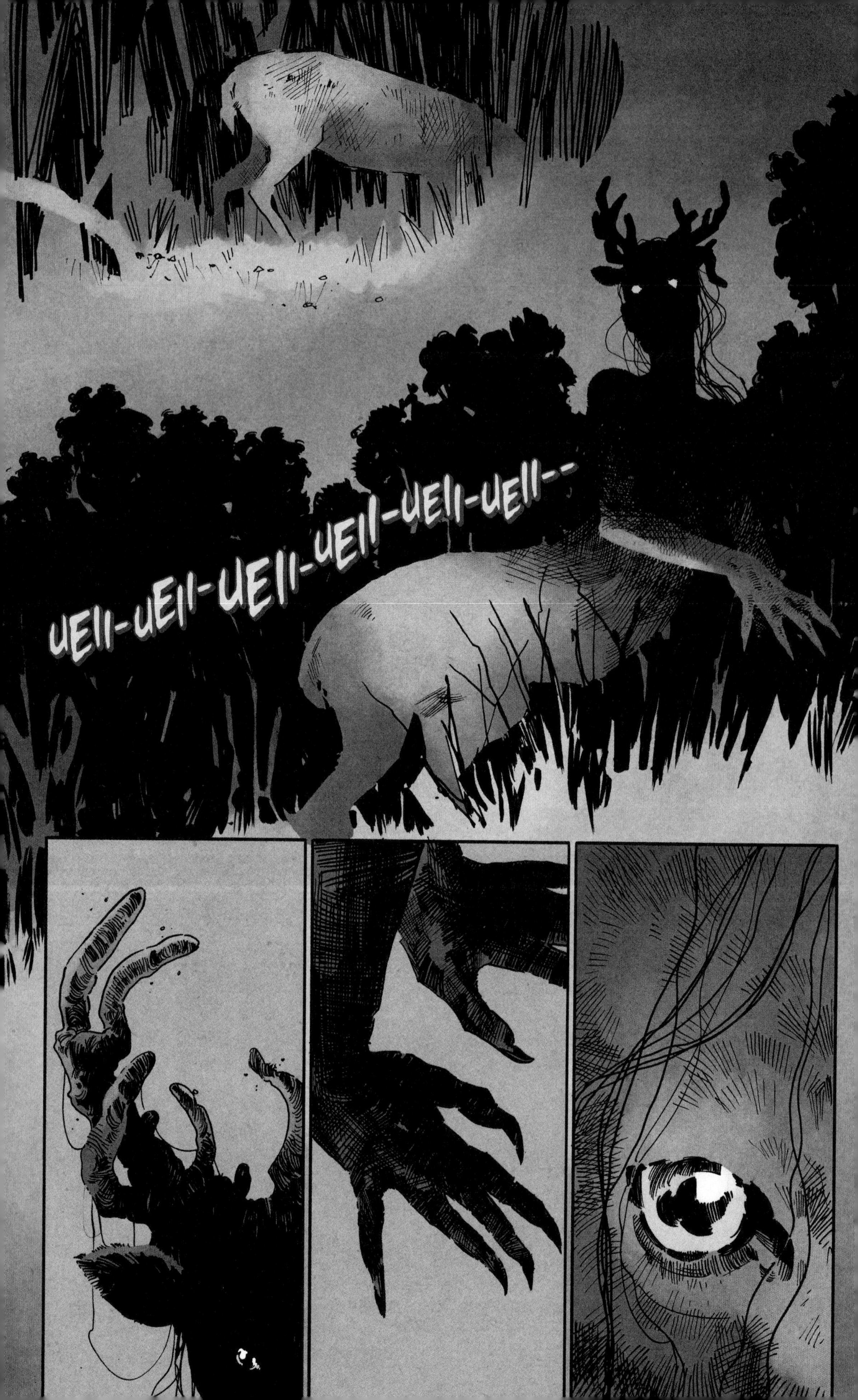
UELL-UELL-UELL-UELL-UELL-UELL-UELL--

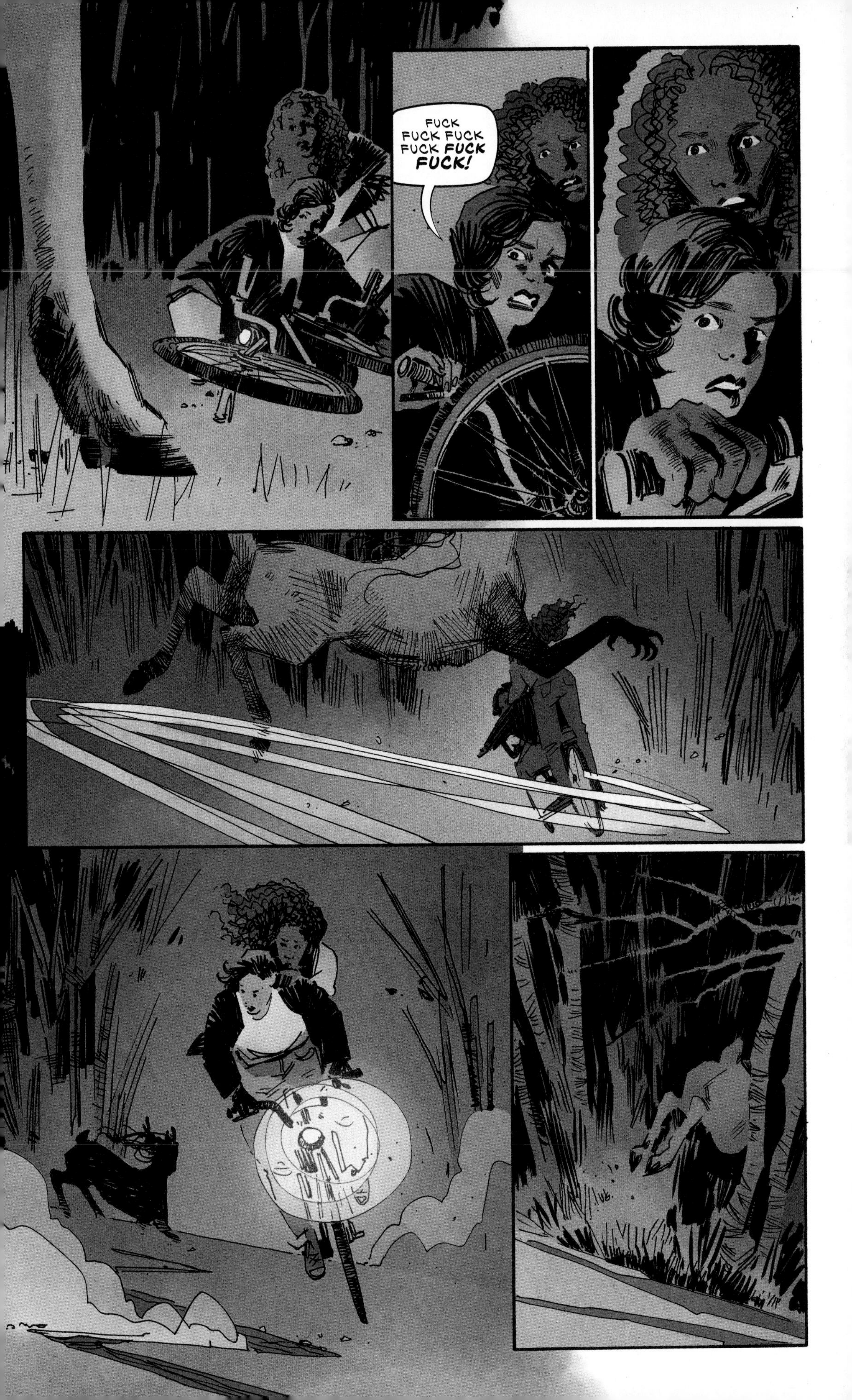
FUCK
FUCK FUCK
FUCK FUCK
FUCK!

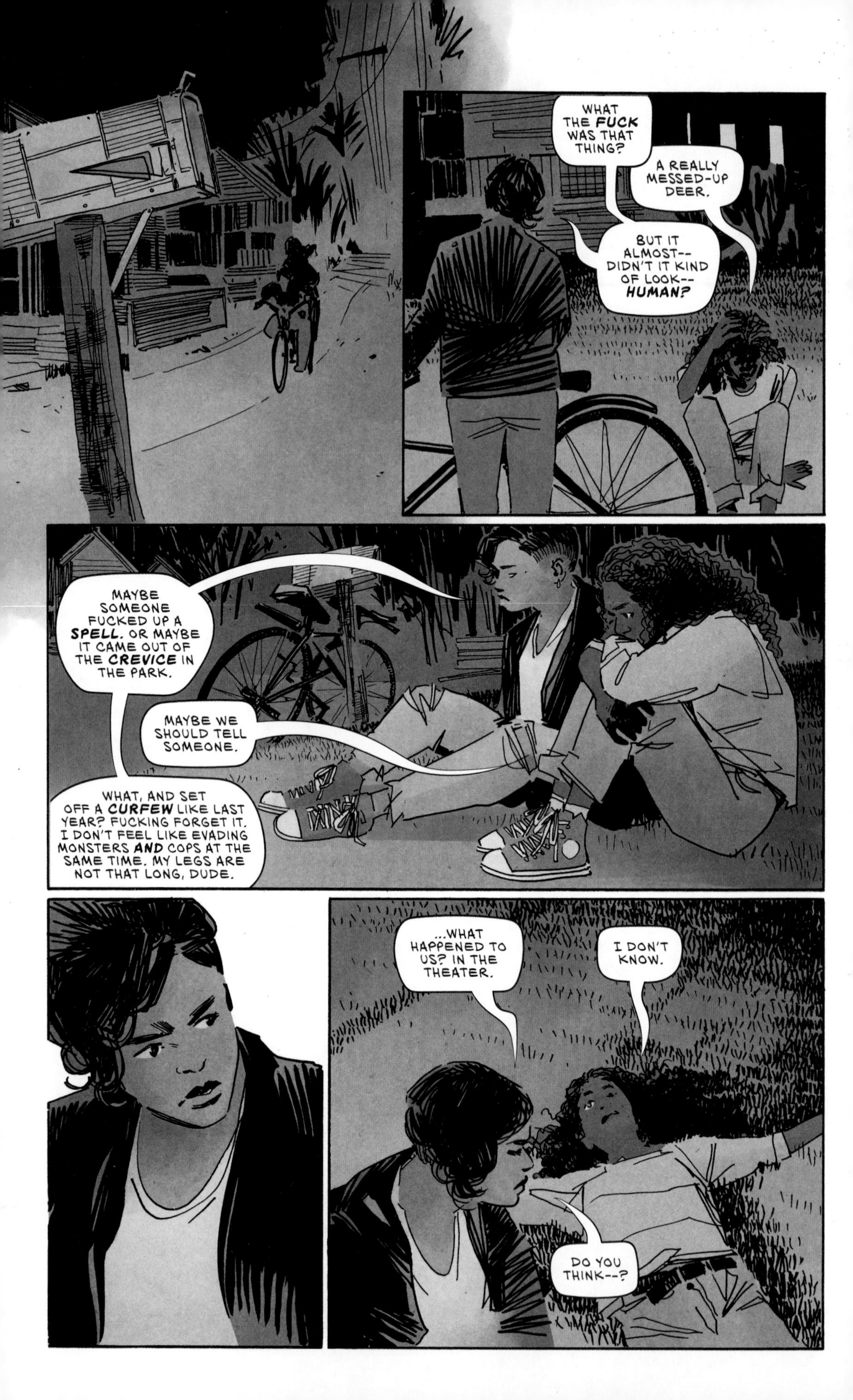
WHAT THE FUCK WAS THAT THING?
A REALLY MESSED-UP DEER.
BUT IT ALMOST-- DIDN'T IT KIND OF LOOK-- HUMAN?
MAYBE SOMEONE FUCKED UP A SPELL. OR MAYBE IT CAME OUT OF THE CREVICE IN THE PARK.
MAYBE WE SHOULD TELL SOMEONE.
WHAT, AND SET OFF A CURFEW LIKE LAST YEAR? FUCKING FORGET IT. I DON'T FEEL LIKE EVADING MONSTERS AND COPS AT THE SAME TIME. MY LEGS ARE NOT THAT LONG, DUDE.
...WHAT HAPPENED TO US? IN THE THEATER.
I DON'T KNOW.
DO YOU THINK--?

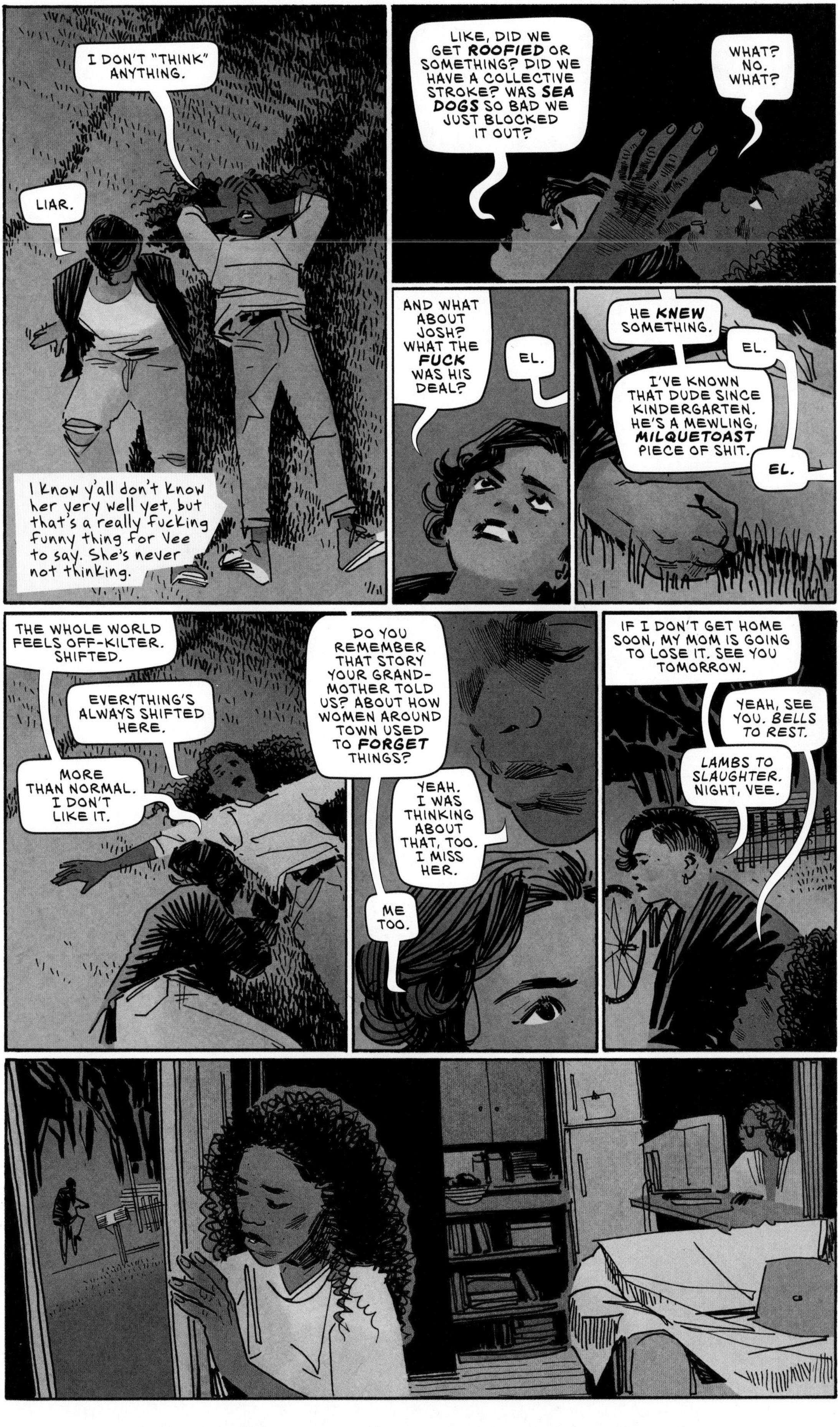
I DON'T "THINK" ANYTHING.
LIAR.
I know y'all don't know her very well yet, but that's a really fucking funny thing for Vee to say. She's never not thinking.
LIKE, DID WE GET ROOFIED OR SOMETHING? DID WE HAVE A COLLECTIVE STROKE? WAS SEA DOGS SO BAD WE JUST BLOCKED IT OUT?
WHAT? NO. WHAT?
AND WHAT ABOUT JOSH? WHAT THE FUCK WAS HIS DEAL?
EL.
HE KNEW SOMETHING.
EL.
I'VE KNOWN THAT DUDE SINCE KINDERGARTEN. HE'S A MEWLING, MILQUETOAST PIECE OF SHIT.
EL.
THE WHOLE WORLD FEELS OFF-KILTER. SHIFTED.
EVERYTHING'S ALWAYS SHIFTED HERE.
MORE THAN NORMAL. I DON'T LIKE IT.
DO YOU REMEMBER THAT STORY YOUR GRAND-MOTHER TOLD US? ABOUT HOW WOMEN AROUND TOWN USED TO FORGET THINGS?
YEAH. I WAS THINKING ABOUT THAT, TOO. I MISS HER.
ME TOO.
IF I DON'T GET HOME SOON, MY MOM IS GOING TO LOSE IT. SEE YOU TOMORROW.
YEAH, SEE YOU. BELLS TO REST.
LAMBS TO SLAUGHTER. NIGHT, VEE.

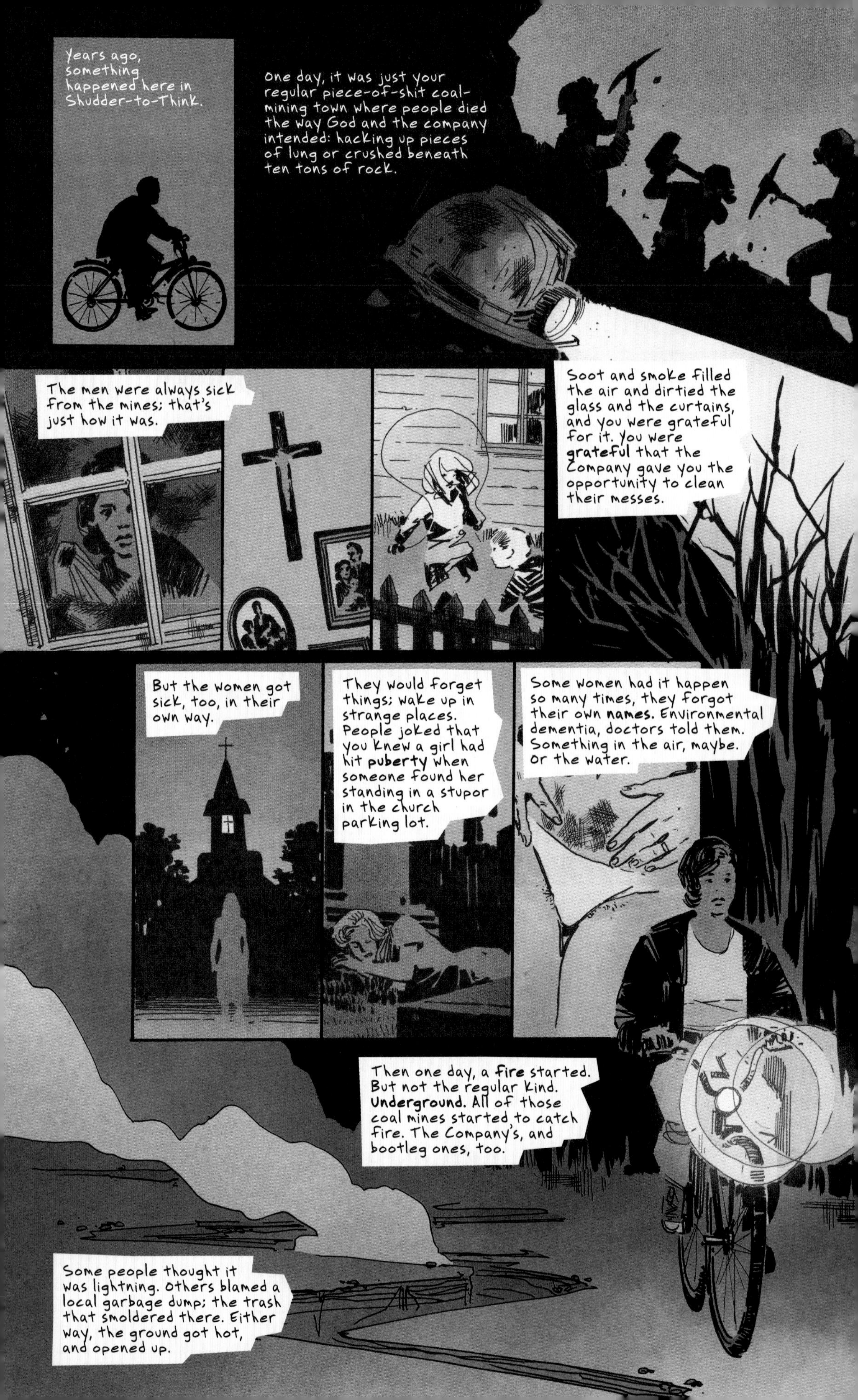
Years ago, something happened here in Shudder-to-Think.
One day, it was just your regular piece-of-shit coal-mining town where people died the way God and the company intended: hacking up pieces of lung or crushed beneath ten tons of rock.
The men were always sick from the mines; that's just how it was.
Soot and smoke filled the air and dirtied the glass and the curtains, and you were grateful for it. You were **grateful** that the Company gave you the opportunity to clean their messes.
But the women got sick, too, in their own way.
They would forget things; wake up in strange places. People joked that you knew a girl had hit **puberty** when someone found her standing in a stupor in the church parking lot.
Some women had it happen so many times, they forgot their own **names.** Environmental dementia, doctors told them. Something in the air, maybe. Or the water.
Then one day, a **fire** started. But not the regular kind. **Underground.** All of those coal mines started to catch fire. The Company's, and bootleg ones, too.
Some people thought it was lightning. Others blamed a local garbage dump; the trash that smoldered there. Either way, the ground got hot, and opened up.

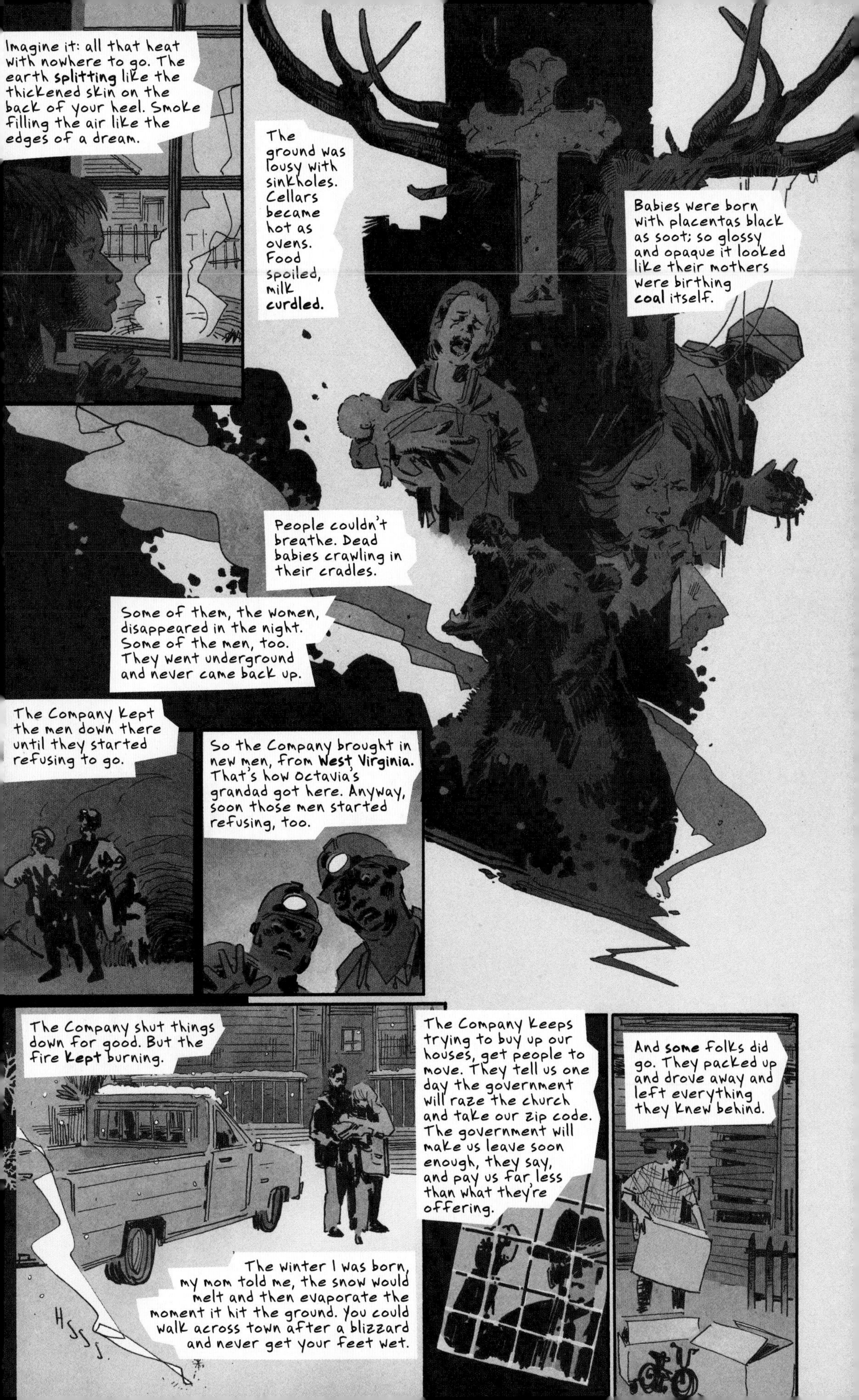
Imagine it: all that heat with nowhere to go. The earth splitting like the thickened skin on the back of your heel. Smoke filling the air like the edges of a dream.
The ground was lousy with sinkholes. Cellars became hot as ovens. Food spoiled, milk curdled.
Babies were born with placentas black as soot; so glossy and opaque it looked like their mothers were birthing coal itself.
People couldn't breathe. Dead babies crawling in their cradles.
Some of them, the women, disappeared in the night. Some of the men, too. They went underground and never came back up.
The Company kept the men down there until they started refusing to go.
So the Company brought in new men, from West Virginia. That's how Octavia's grandad got here. Anyway, soon those men started refusing, too.
The Company shut things down for good. But the fire kept burning.
The winter I was born, my mom told me, the snow would melt and then evaporate the moment it hit the ground. You could walk across town after a blizzard and never get your feet wet.
The Company keeps trying to buy up our houses, get people to move. They tell us one day the government will raze the church and take our zip code. The government will make us leave soon enough, they say, and pay us far less than what they're offering.
And some folks did go. They packed up and drove away and left everything they knew behind.

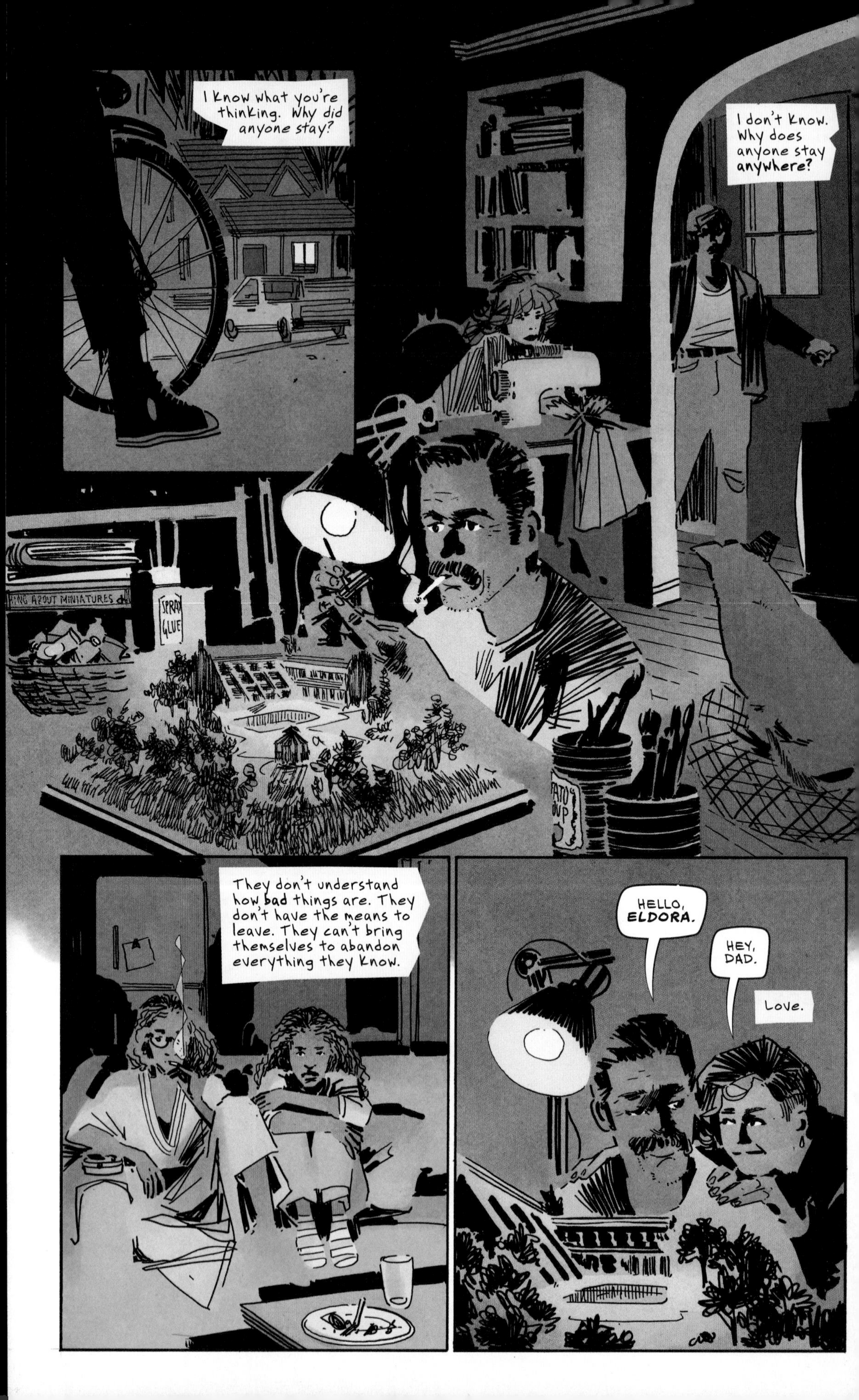
I know what you're thinking. Why did anyone stay?
I don't know. Why does anyone stay anywhere?
...ING ABOUT MINIATURES
SPRAY GLUE
They don't understand how bad things are. They don't have the means to leave. They can't bring themselves to abandon everything they know.
HELLO, ELDORA.
HEY, DAD.
Love.

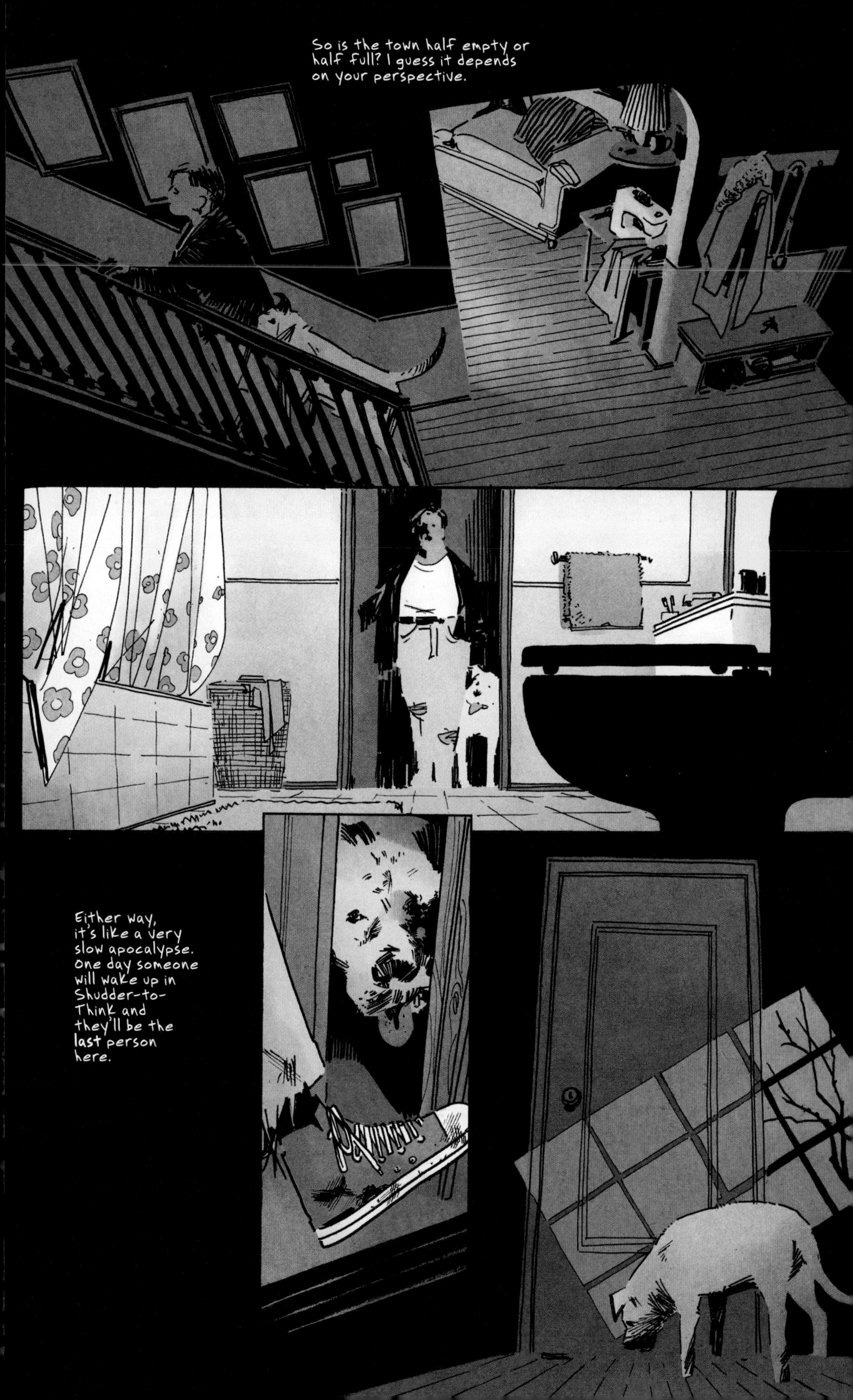

So is the town half empty or half full? I guess it depends on your perspective.
Either way, it's like a very slow apocalypse. One day someone will wake up in Shudder-to-Think and they'll be the **last** person here.

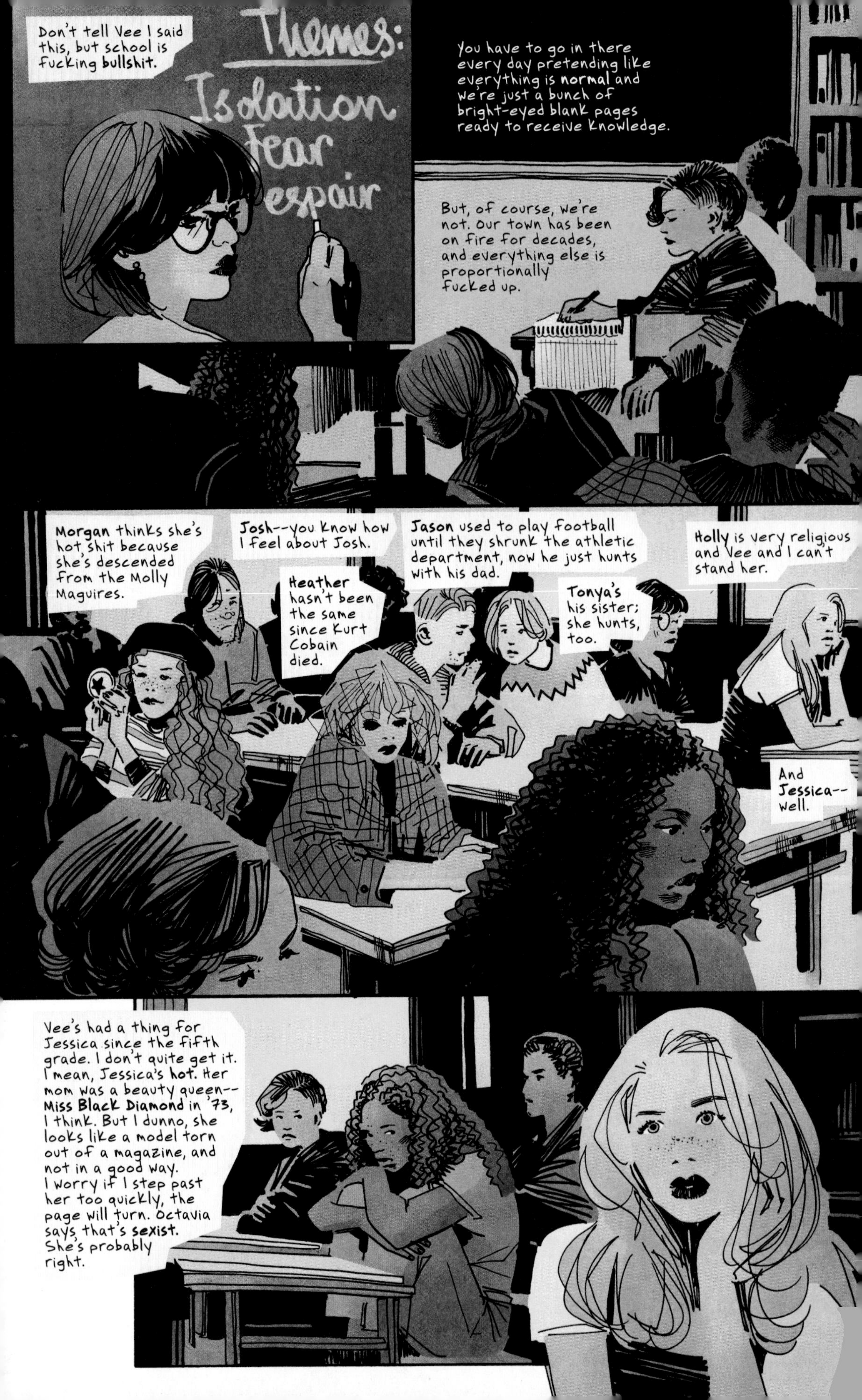
Don't tell Vee I said this, but school is fucking **bullshit.**
Themes:
Isolation
Fear
espair
You have to go in there every day pretending like everything is **normal** and we're just a bunch of bright-eyed blank pages ready to receive knowledge.
But, of course, we're not. Our town has been on fire for decades, and everything else is proportionally fucked up.
Morgan thinks she's hot shit because she's descended from the Molly Maguires.
Josh--you know how I feel about Josh.
Heather hasn't been the same since Kurt Cobain died.
Jason used to play football until they shrunk the athletic department, now he just hunts with his dad.
Tonya's his sister; she hunts, too.
Holly is very religious and Vee and I can't stand her.
And **Jessica**--well.
Vee's had a thing for Jessica since the fifth grade. I don't quite get it. I mean, Jessica's **hot.** Her mom was a beauty queen-- **Miss Black Diamond** in '73, I think. But I dunno, she looks like a model torn out of a magazine, and not in a good way. I worry if I step past her too quickly, the page will turn. Octavia says that's **sexist.** She's probably right.

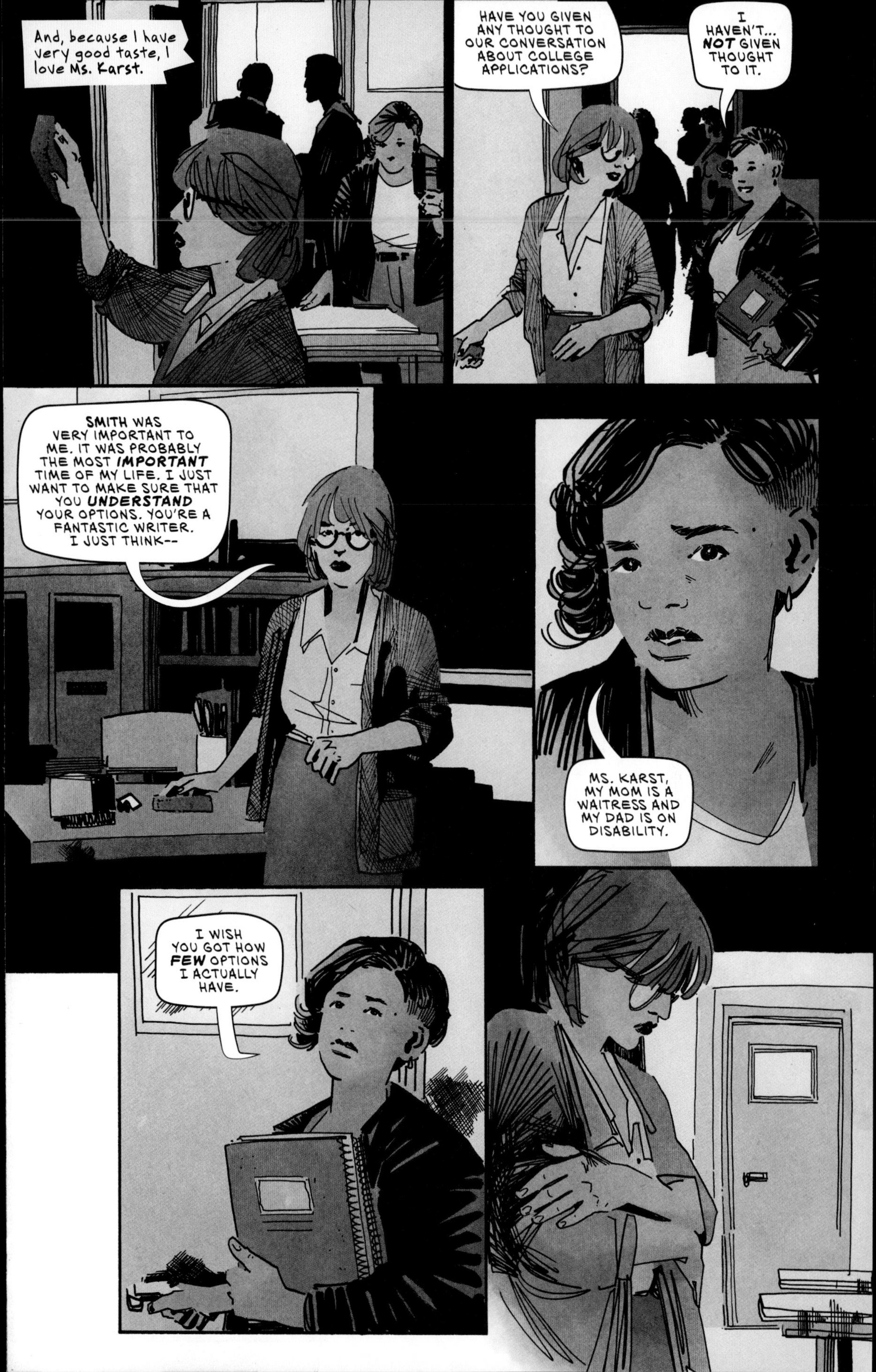
And, because I have very good taste, I love Ms. Karst.
HAVE YOU GIVEN ANY THOUGHT TO OUR CONVERSATION ABOUT COLLEGE APPLICATIONS?
I HAVEN'T... **NOT** GIVEN THOUGHT TO IT.
SMITH WAS VERY IMPORTANT TO ME. IT WAS PROBABLY THE MOST ***IMPORTANT*** TIME OF MY LIFE. I JUST WANT TO MAKE SURE THAT YOU ***UNDERSTAND*** YOUR OPTIONS. YOU'RE A FANTASTIC WRITER. I JUST THINK--
MS. KARST, MY MOM IS A WAITRESS AND MY DAD IS ON DISABILITY.
I WISH YOU GOT HOW ***FEW*** OPTIONS I ACTUALLY HAVE.

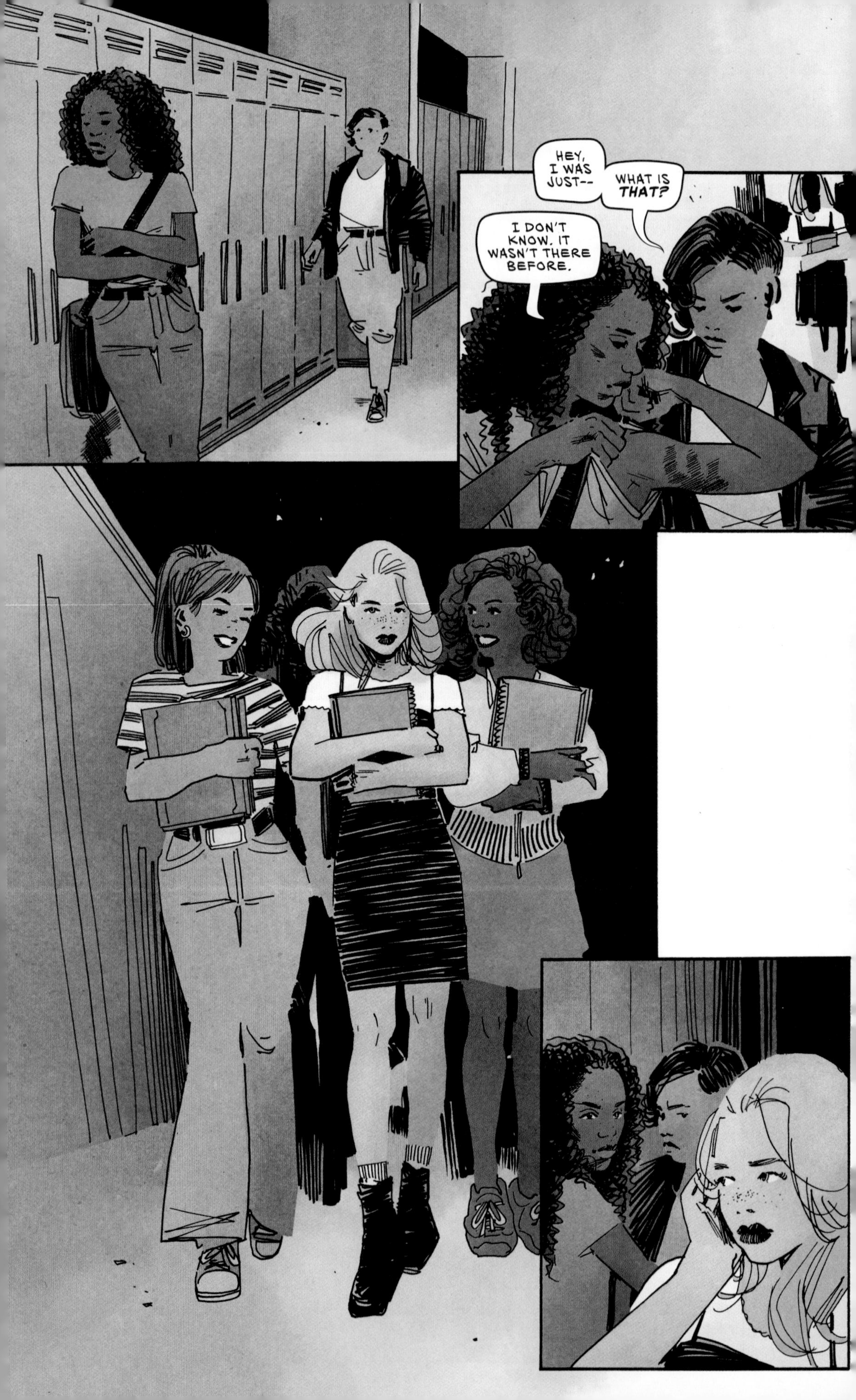
HEY, I WAS JUST--
WHAT IS THAT?
I DON'T KNOW. IT WASN'T THERE BEFORE.

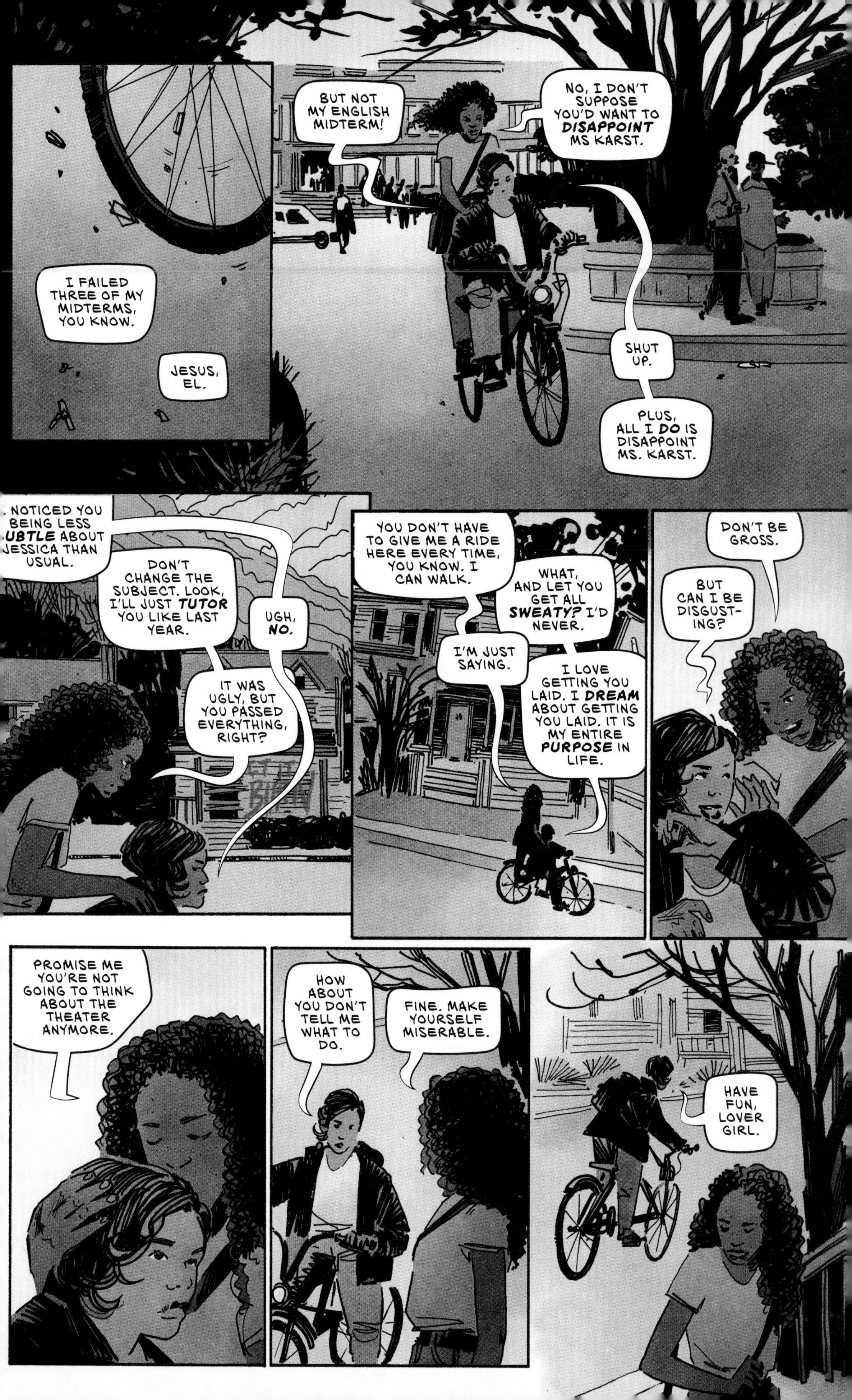
I FAILED THREE OF MY MIDTERMS, YOU KNOW.
JESUS, EL.
BUT NOT MY ENGLISH MIDTERM!
NO, I DON'T SUPPOSE YOU'D WANT TO DISAPPOINT MS KARST.
SHUT UP.
PLUS, ALL I DO IS DISAPPOINT MS. KARST.
. NOTICED YOU BEING LESS UBTLE ABOUT JESSICA THAN USUAL.
DON'T CHANGE THE SUBJECT. LOOK, I'LL JUST TUTOR YOU LIKE LAST YEAR.
UGH, NO.
IT WAS UGLY, BUT YOU PASSED EVERYTHING, RIGHT?
YOU DON'T HAVE TO GIVE ME A RIDE HERE EVERY TIME, YOU KNOW. I CAN WALK.
WHAT, AND LET YOU GET ALL SWEATY? I'D NEVER.
I'M JUST SAYING.
I LOVE GETTING YOU LAID. I DREAM ABOUT GETTING YOU LAID. IT IS MY ENTIRE PURPOSE IN LIFE.
DON'T BE GROSS.
BUT CAN I BE DISGUST-ING?
PROMISE ME YOU'RE NOT GOING TO THINK ABOUT THE THEATER ANYMORE.
HOW ABOUT YOU DON'T TELL ME WHAT TO DO.
FINE. MAKE YOURSELF MISERABLE.
HAVE FUN, LOVER GIRL.

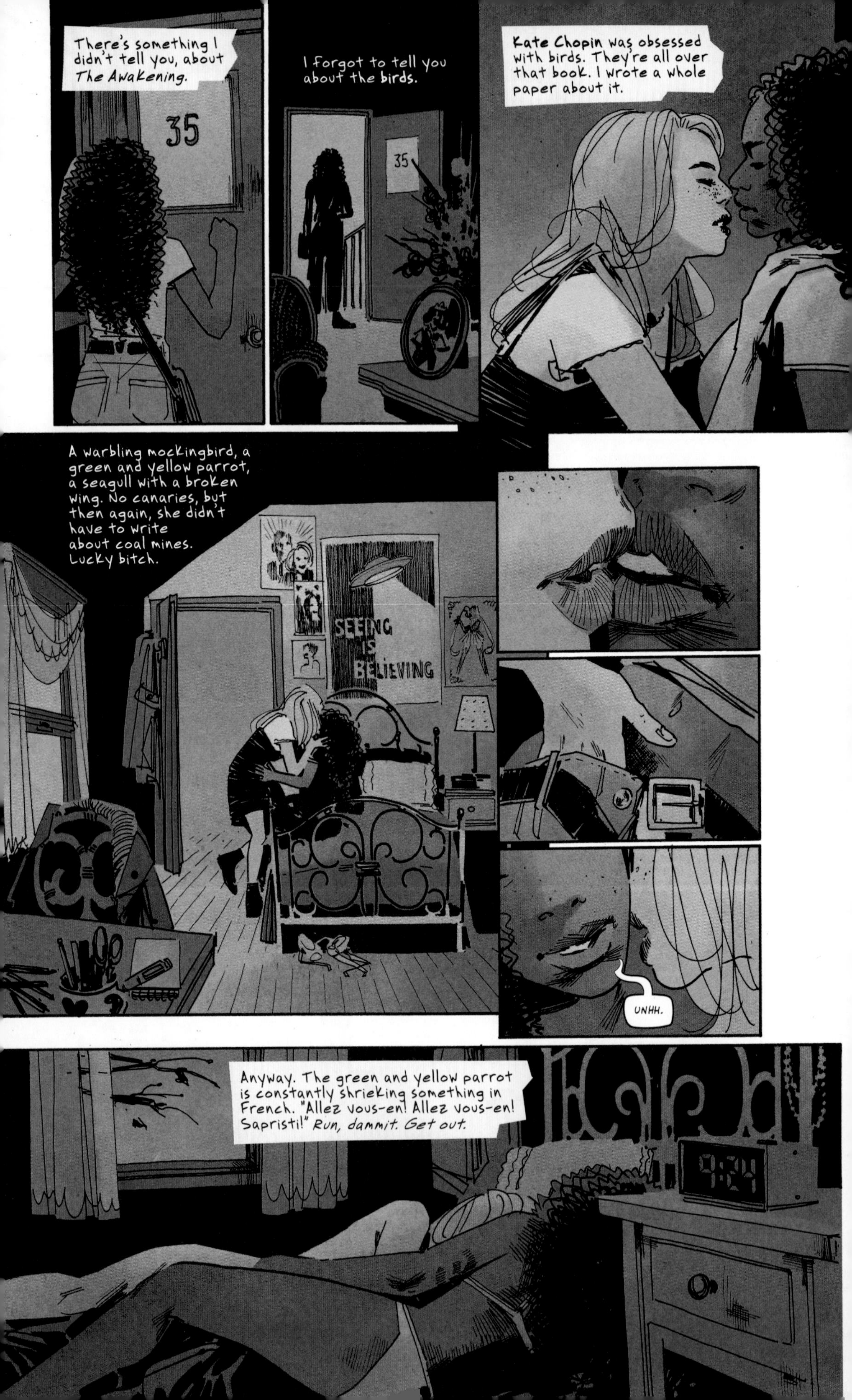
There's something I didn't tell you, about *The Awakening.*
35
I forgot to tell you about the birds.
35
Kate Chopin was obsessed with birds. They're all over that book. I wrote a whole paper about it.
A warbling mockingbird, a green and yellow parrot, a seagull with a broken wing. No canaries, but then again, she didn't have to write about coal mines. Lucky bitch.
SEEING IS BELIEVING
UNHH.
Anyway. The green and yellow parrot is constantly shrieking something in French. "Allez vous-en! Allez vous-en! Sapristi!" *Run, dammit. Get out.*

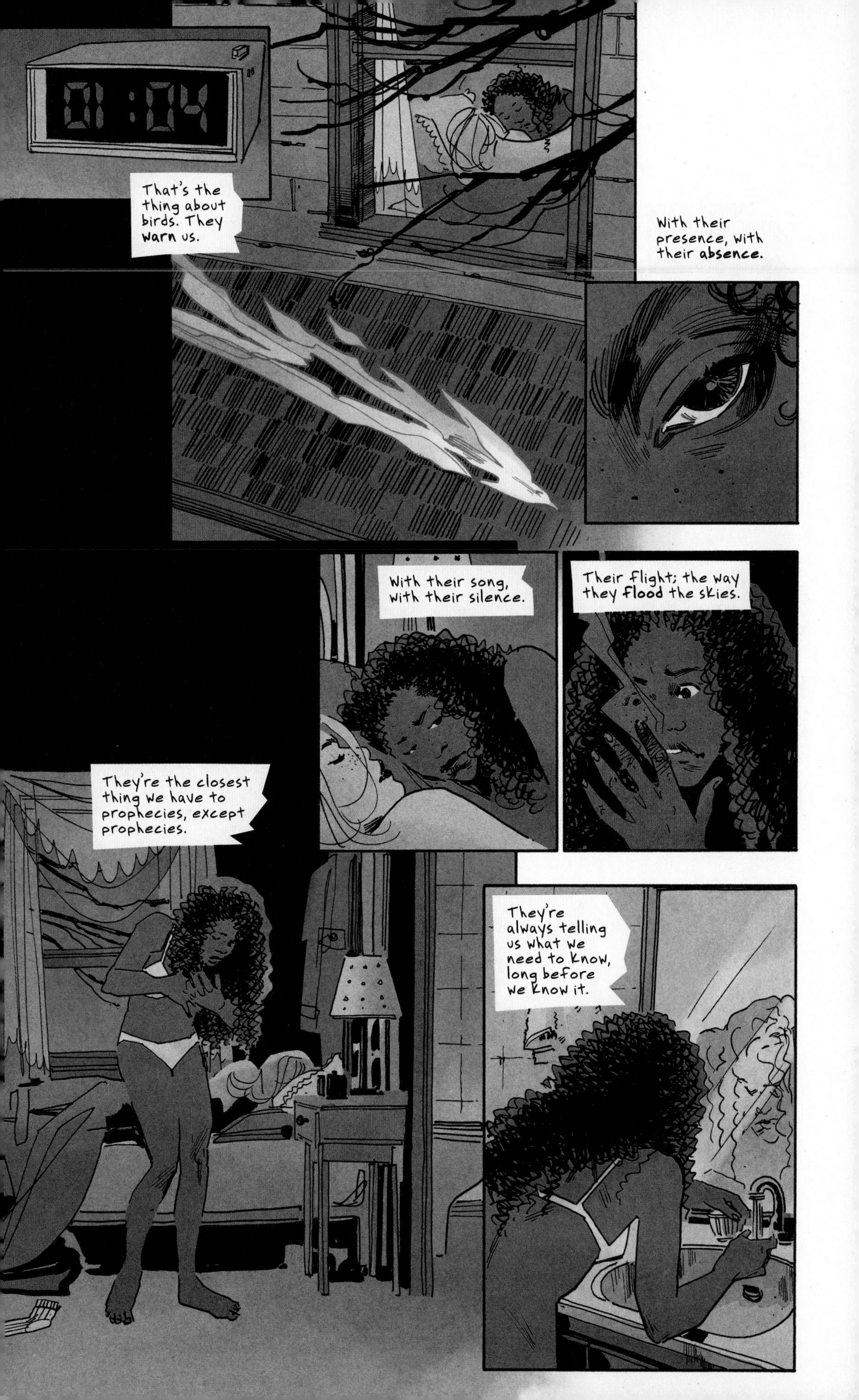
That's the thing about birds. They warn us.
With their presence, with their absence.
With their song, with their silence.
Their flight; the way they flood the skies.
They're the closest thing we have to prophecies, except prophecies.
They're always telling us what we need to know, long before we know it.

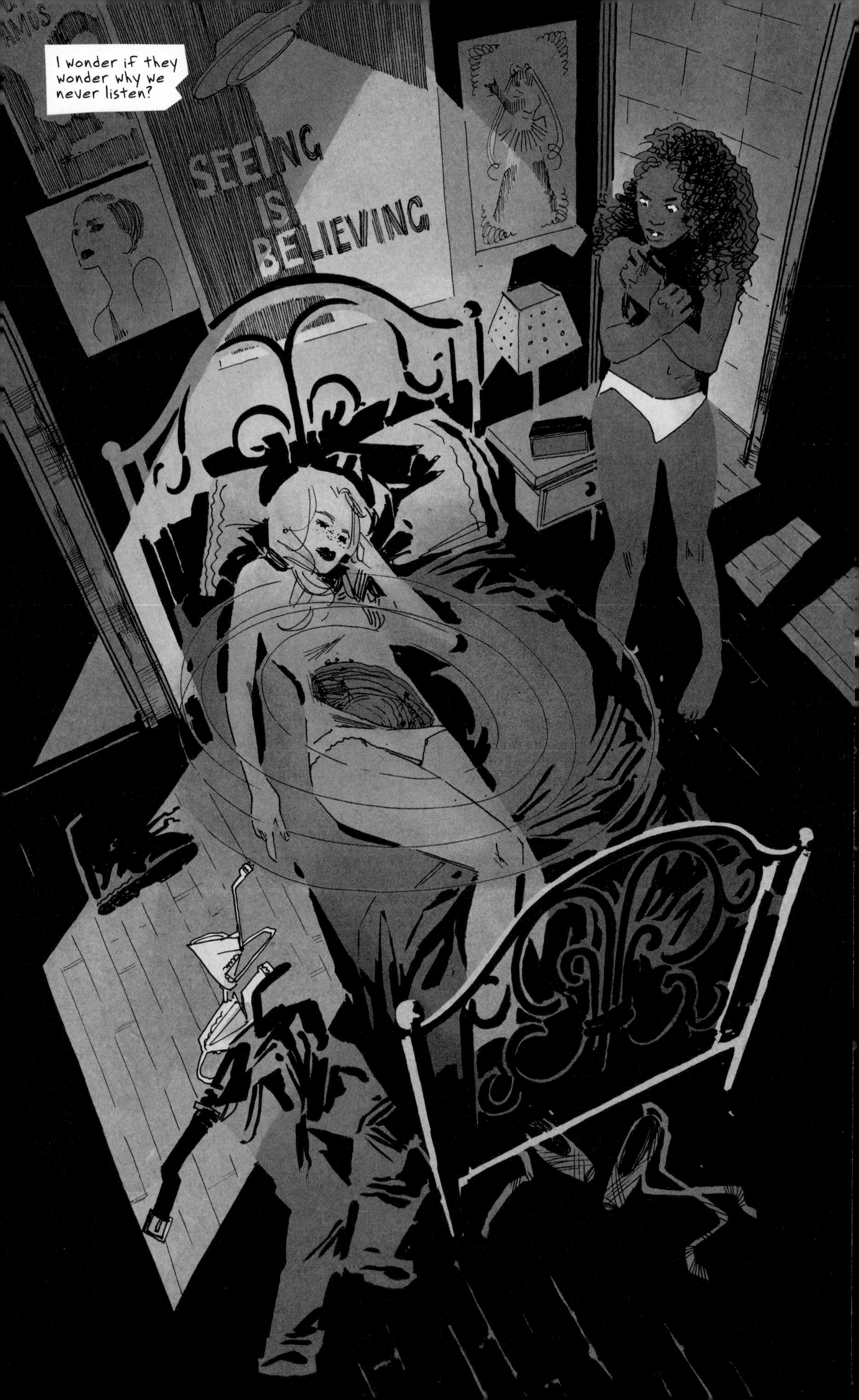
I wonder if they wonder why we never listen?
SEEING IS BELIEVING

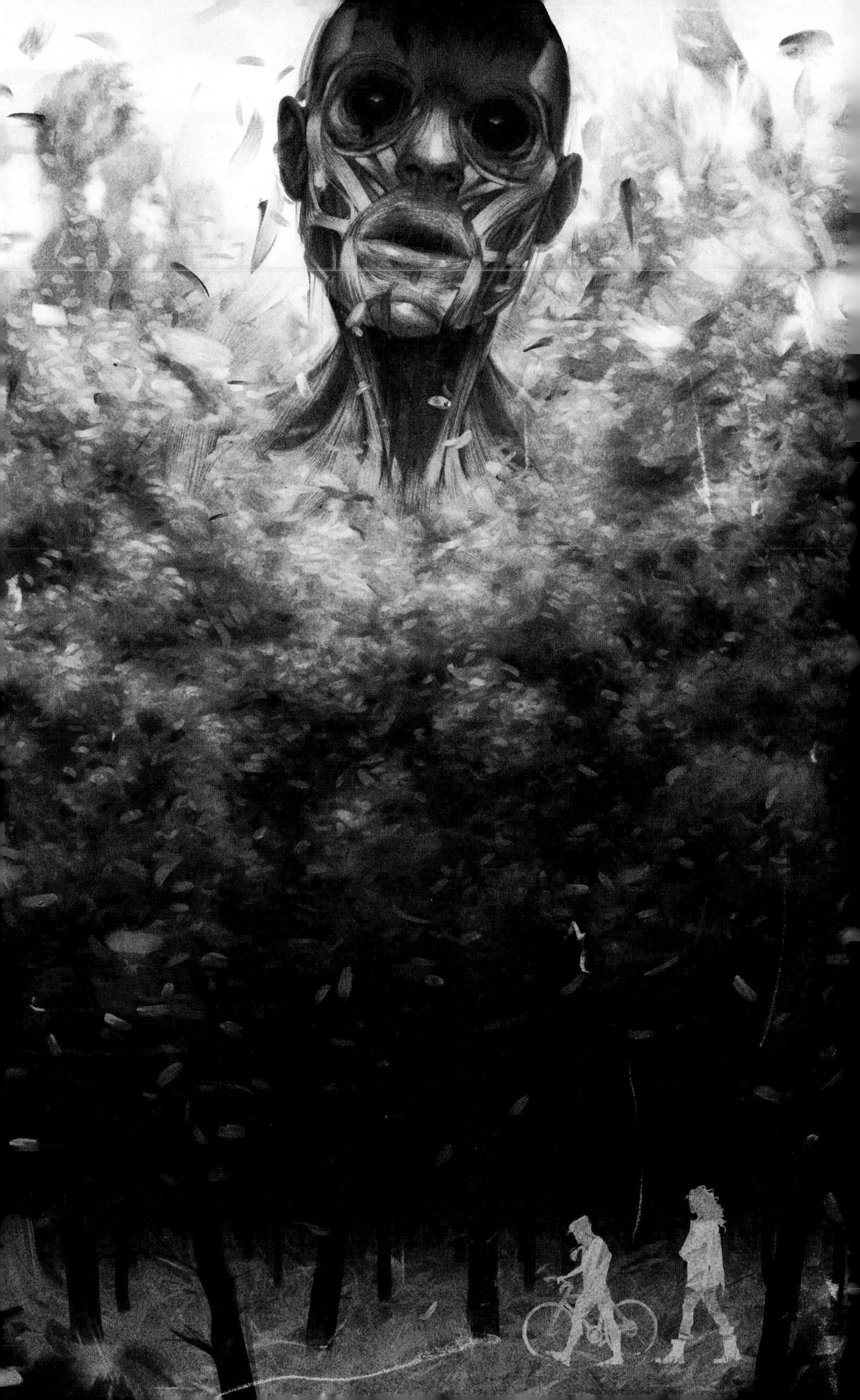

Heaven on Earth

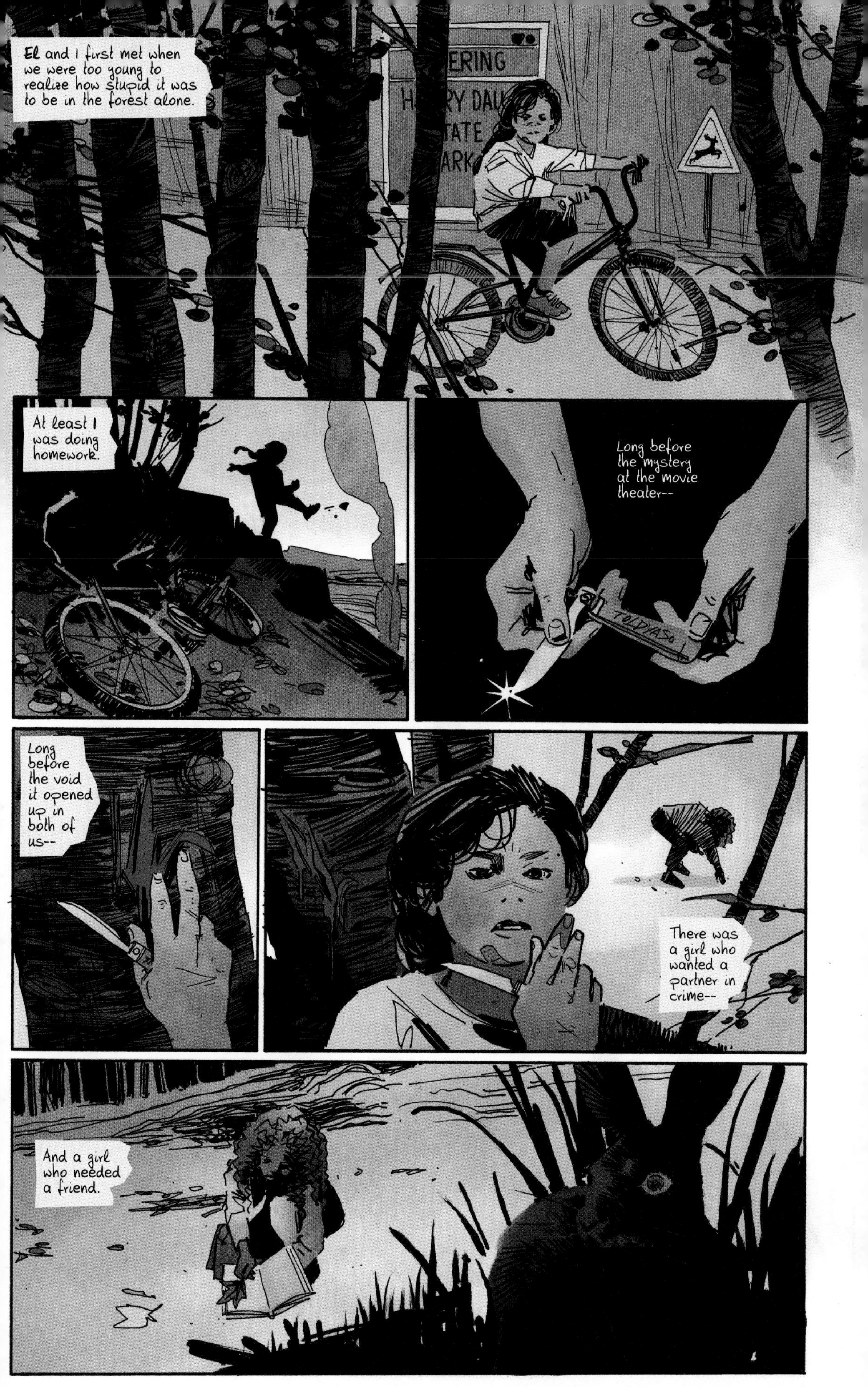
El and I first met when we were too young to realize how stupid it was to be in the forest alone.
ERING
HA RY DAU
TATE
ARK
At least I was doing homework.
Long before the mystery at the movie theater--
TOLDYASO
Long before the void it opened up in both of us--
There was a girl who wanted a partner in crime--
And a girl who needed a friend.

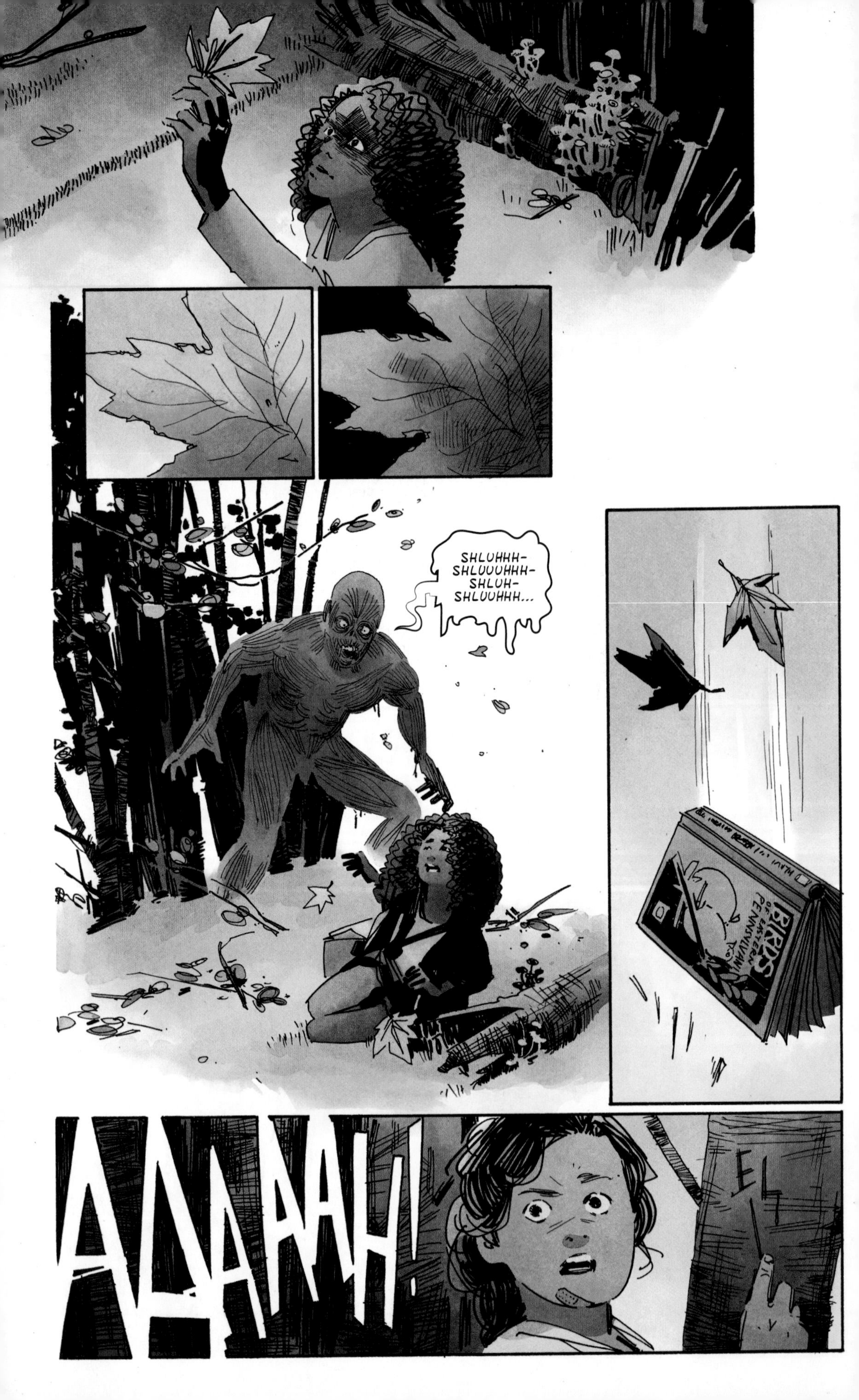
SHLUHHH-
SHLUUUHHH-
SHLUH-
SHLUUHHH...
BIRDS OF EASTERN PENNSYLVANIA
AAAAAH!

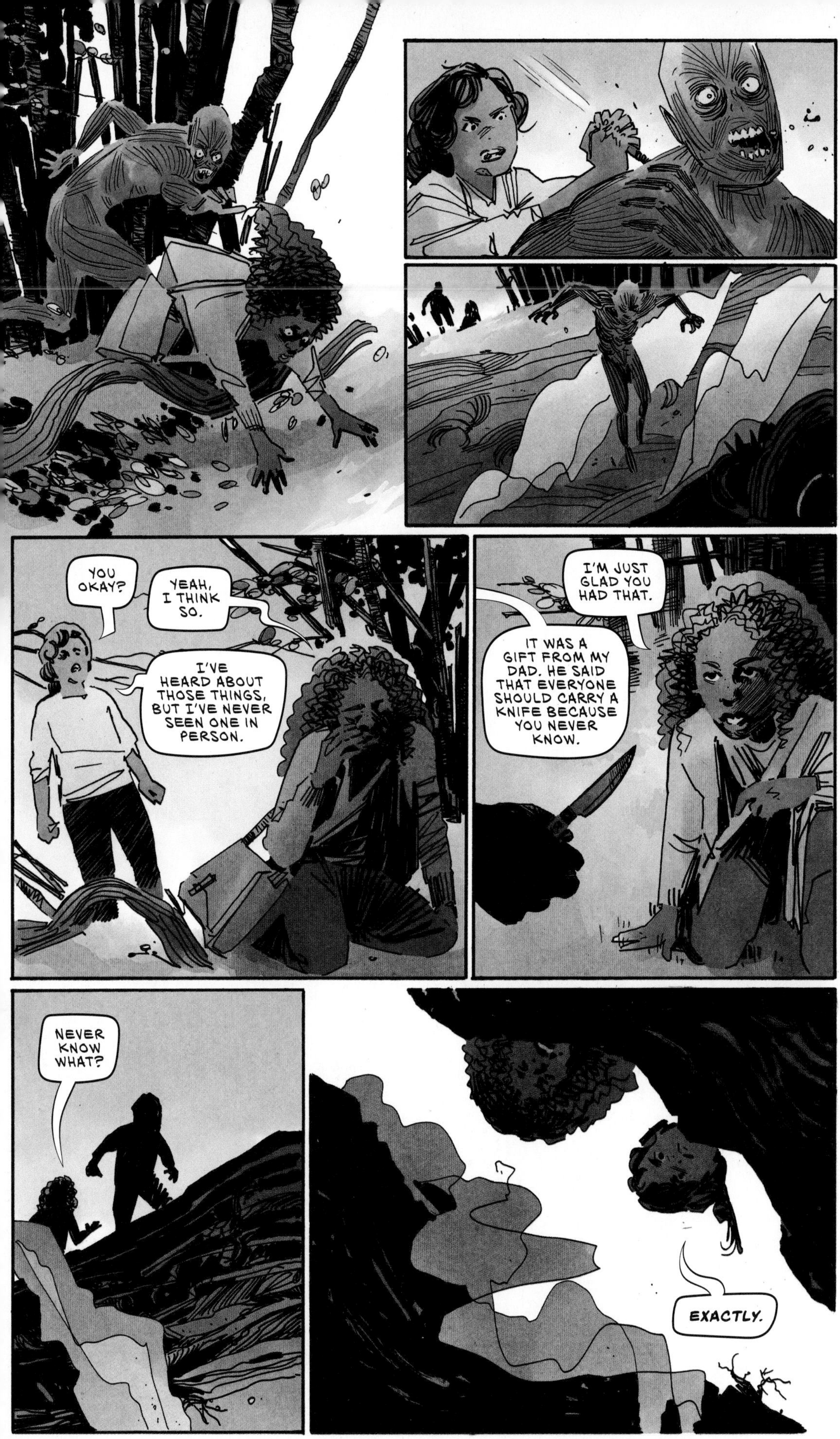
YOU OKAY?
YEAH, I THINK SO.
I'VE HEARD ABOUT THOSE THINGS, BUT I'VE NEVER SEEN ONE IN PERSON.
I'M JUST GLAD YOU HAD THAT.
IT WAS A GIFT FROM MY DAD. HE SAID THAT EVERYONE SHOULD CARRY A KNIFE BECAUSE YOU NEVER KNOW.
NEVER KNOW WHAT?
EXACTLY.

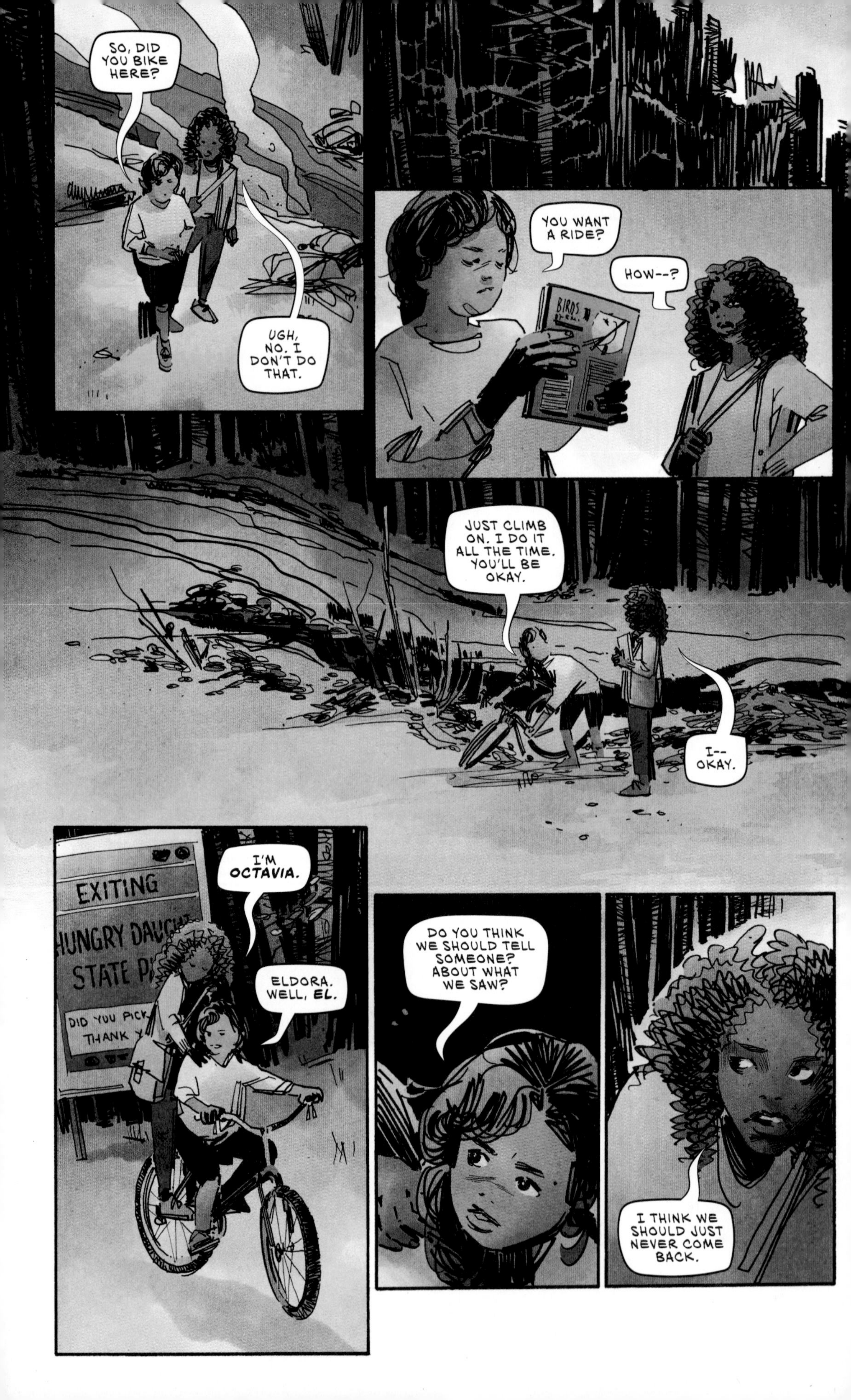
SO, DID YOU BIKE HERE?
UGH, NO. I DON'T DO THAT.
YOU WANT A RIDE?
HOW--?
BIRDS
JUST CLIMB ON. I DO IT ALL THE TIME. YOU'LL BE OKAY.
I-- OKAY.
EXITING
HUNGRY DAUGH
STATE P
DID YOU PICK
THANK Y
I'M **OCTAVIA.**
ELDORA. WELL, **EL.**
DO YOU THINK WE SHOULD TELL SOMEONE? ABOUT WHAT WE SAW?
I THINK WE SHOULD JUST NEVER COME BACK.

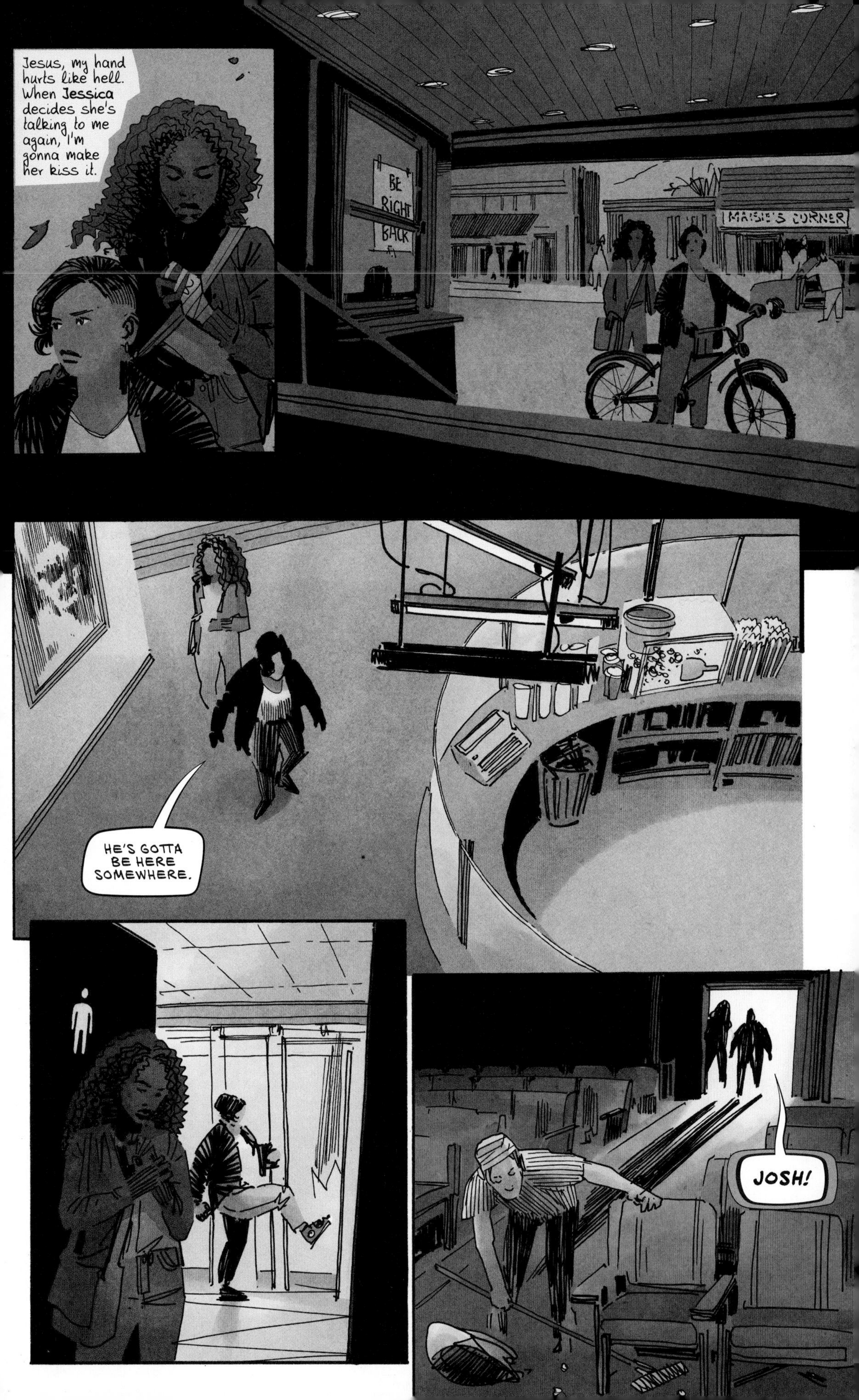

Jesus, my hand hurts like hell. When Jessica decides she's talking to me again, I'm gonna make her kiss it.
BE RIGHT BACK
MAISIE'S CORNER
HE'S GOTTA BE HERE SOMEWHERE.
JOSH!

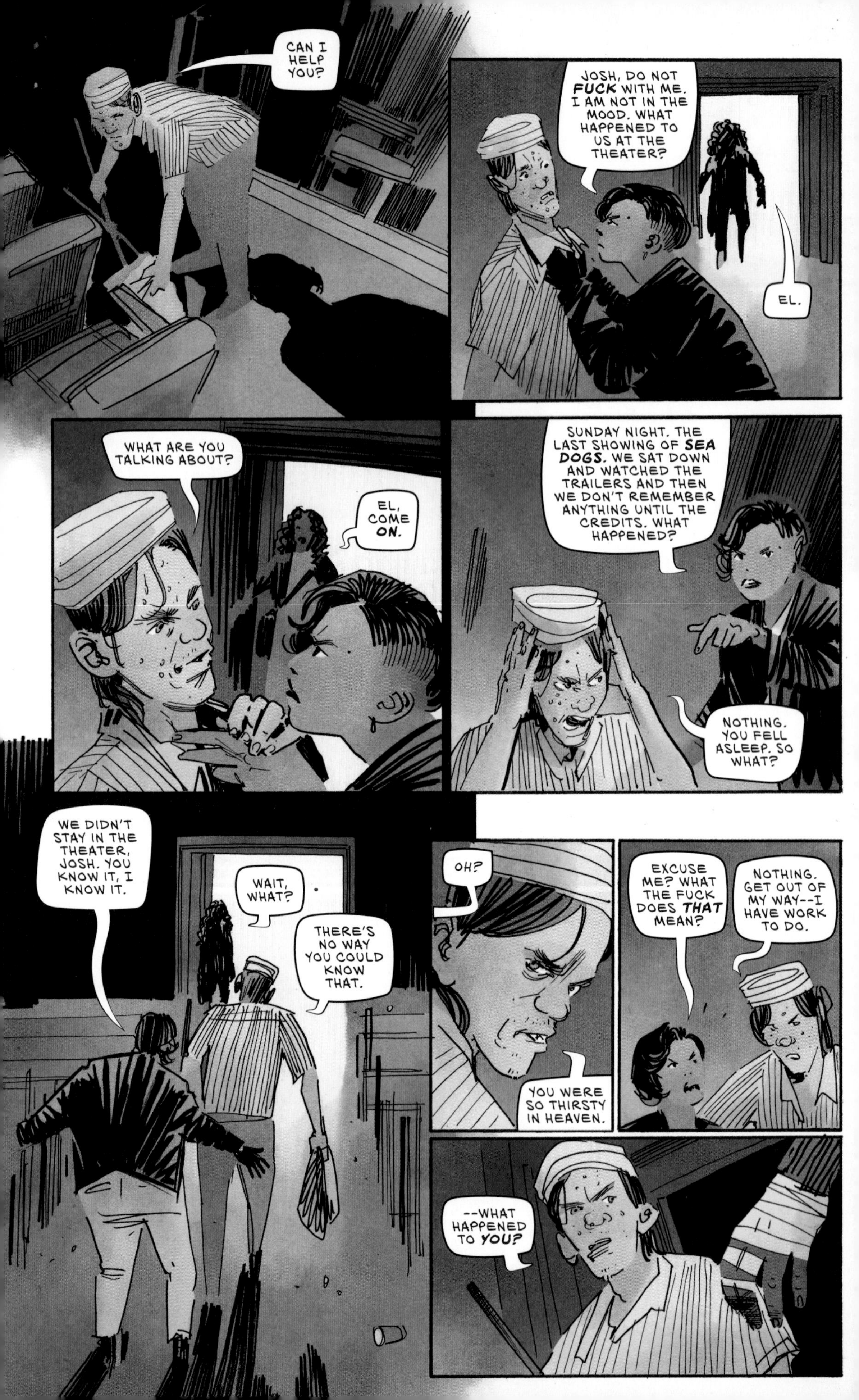
CAN I HELP YOU?
JOSH, DO NOT FUCK WITH ME. I AM NOT IN THE MOOD. WHAT HAPPENED TO US AT THE THEATER?
EL.
WHAT ARE YOU TALKING ABOUT?
EL, COME ON.
SUNDAY NIGHT. THE LAST SHOWING OF SEA DOGS. WE SAT DOWN AND WATCHED THE TRAILERS AND THEN WE DON'T REMEMBER ANYTHING UNTIL THE CREDITS. WHAT HAPPENED?
NOTHING. YOU FELL ASLEEP. SO WHAT?
WE DIDN'T STAY IN THE THEATER, JOSH. YOU KNOW IT, I KNOW IT.
WAIT, WHAT?
THERE'S NO WAY YOU COULD KNOW THAT.
OH?
YOU WERE SO THIRSTY IN HEAVEN.
EXCUSE ME? WHAT THE FUCK DOES THAT MEAN?
NOTHING. GET OUT OF MY WAY--I HAVE WORK TO DO.
--WHAT HAPPENED TO YOU?

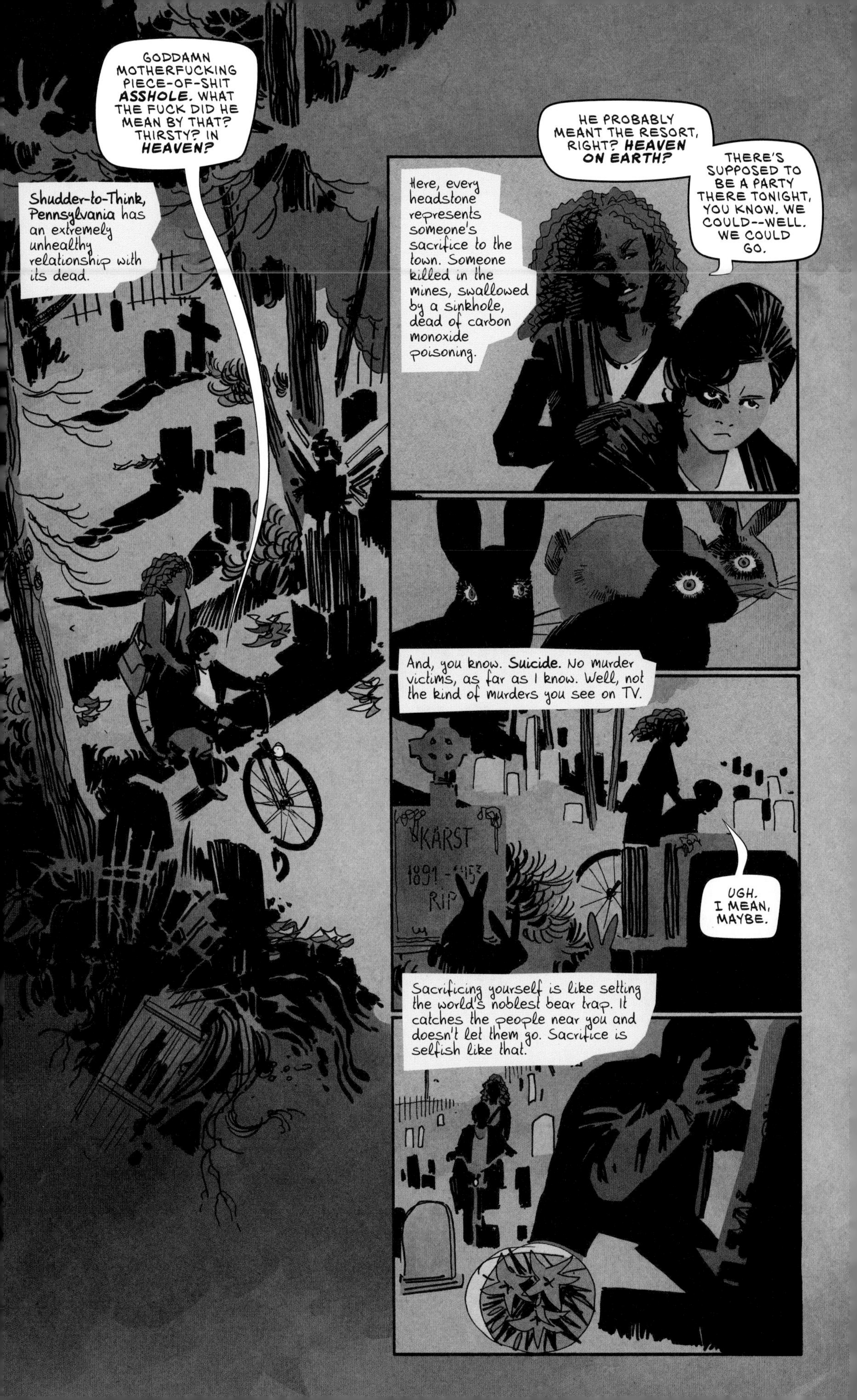
GODDAMN MOTHERFUCKING PIECE-OF-SHIT ASSHOLE. WHAT THE FUCK DID HE MEAN BY THAT? THIRSTY? IN HEAVEN?
Shudder-to-Think, Pennsylvania has an extremely unhealthy relationship with its dead.
HE PROBABLY MEANT THE RESORT, RIGHT? HEAVEN ON EARTH?
Here, every headstone represents someone's sacrifice to the town. Someone killed in the mines, swallowed by a sinkhole, dead of carbon monoxide poisoning.
THERE'S SUPPOSED TO BE A PARTY THERE TONIGHT, YOU KNOW. WE COULD--WELL. WE COULD GO.
And, you know. Suicide. No murder victims, as far as I know. Well, not the kind of murders you see on TV.
KARST
1891 - 1953
RIP
UGH. I MEAN, MAYBE.
Sacrificing yourself is like setting the world's noblest bear trap. It catches the people near you and doesn't let them go. Sacrifice is selfish like that.

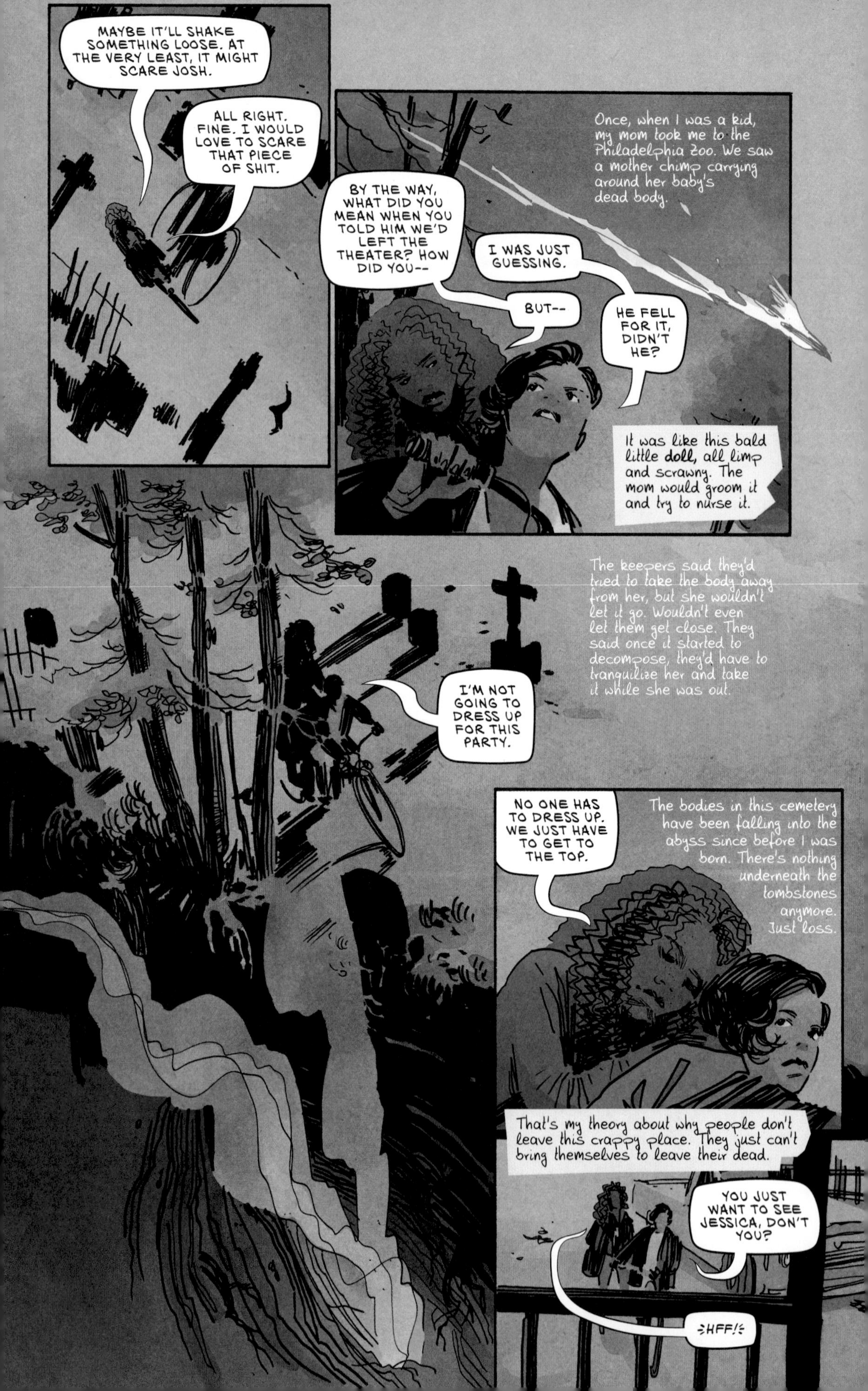
MAYBE IT'LL SHAKE SOMETHING LOOSE. AT THE VERY LEAST, IT MIGHT SCARE JOSH.
ALL RIGHT. FINE. I WOULD LOVE TO SCARE THAT PIECE OF SHIT.
Once, when I was a kid, my mom took me to the Philadelphia Zoo. We saw a mother chimp carrying around her baby's dead body.
BY THE WAY, WHAT DID YOU MEAN WHEN YOU TOLD HIM WE'D LEFT THE THEATER? HOW DID YOU--
I WAS JUST GUESSING.
BUT--
HE FELL FOR IT, DIDN'T HE?
It was like this bald little **doll**, all limp and scrawny. The mom would groom it and try to nurse it.
The keepers said they'd tried to take the body away from her, but she wouldn't let it go. Wouldn't even let them get close. They said once it started to decompose, they'd have to tranquilize her and take it while she was out.
I'M NOT GOING TO DRESS UP FOR THIS PARTY.
NO ONE HAS TO DRESS UP. WE JUST HAVE TO GET TO THE TOP.
The bodies in this cemetery have been falling into the abyss since before I was born. There's nothing underneath the tombstones anymore. Just loss.
That's my theory about why people don't leave this crappy place. They just can't bring themselves to leave their dead.
YOU JUST WANT TO SEE JESSICA, DON'T YOU?
HFF!

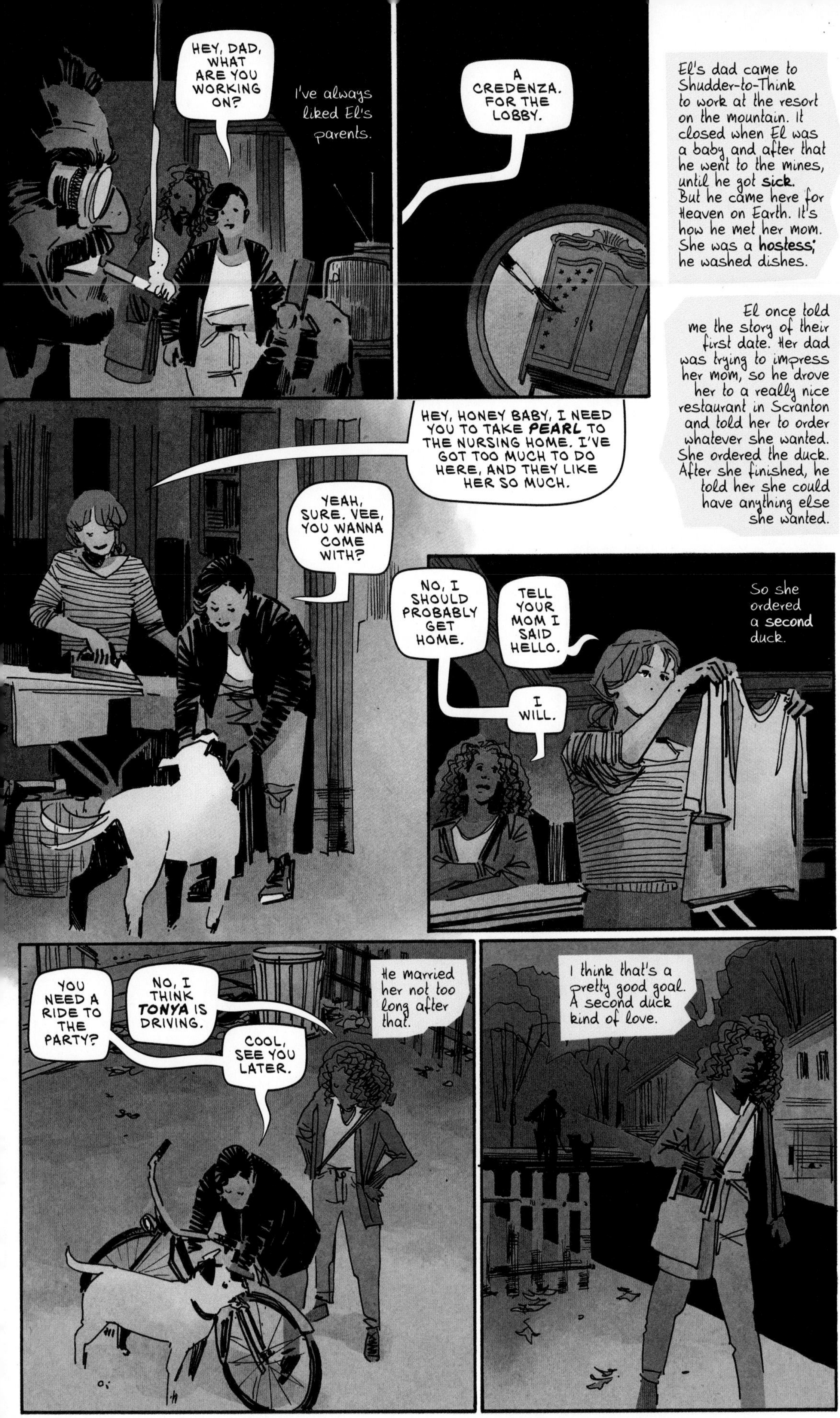
HEY, DAD, WHAT ARE YOU WORKING ON?
I've always liked El's parents.
A CREDENZA. FOR THE LOBBY.
El's dad came to Shudder-to-Think to work at the resort on the mountain. It closed when El was a baby and after that he went to the mines, until he got **sick**. But he came here for Heaven on Earth. It's how he met her mom. She was a **hostess;** he washed dishes.
El once told me the story of their first date. Her dad was trying to impress her mom, so he drove her to a really nice restaurant in Scranton and told her to order whatever she wanted. She ordered the duck. After she finished, he told her she could have anything else she wanted.
HEY, HONEY BABY, I NEED YOU TO TAKE **PEARL** TO THE NURSING HOME. I'VE GOT TOO MUCH TO DO HERE, AND THEY LIKE HER SO MUCH.
YEAH, SURE. VEE, YOU WANNA COME WITH?
NO, I SHOULD PROBABLY GET HOME.
TELL YOUR MOM I SAID HELLO.
I WILL.
So she ordered a **second** duck.
YOU NEED A RIDE TO THE PARTY?
NO, I THINK **TONYA** IS DRIVING.
COOL, SEE YOU LATER.
He married her not too long after that.
I think that's a pretty good goal. A second duck kind of love.

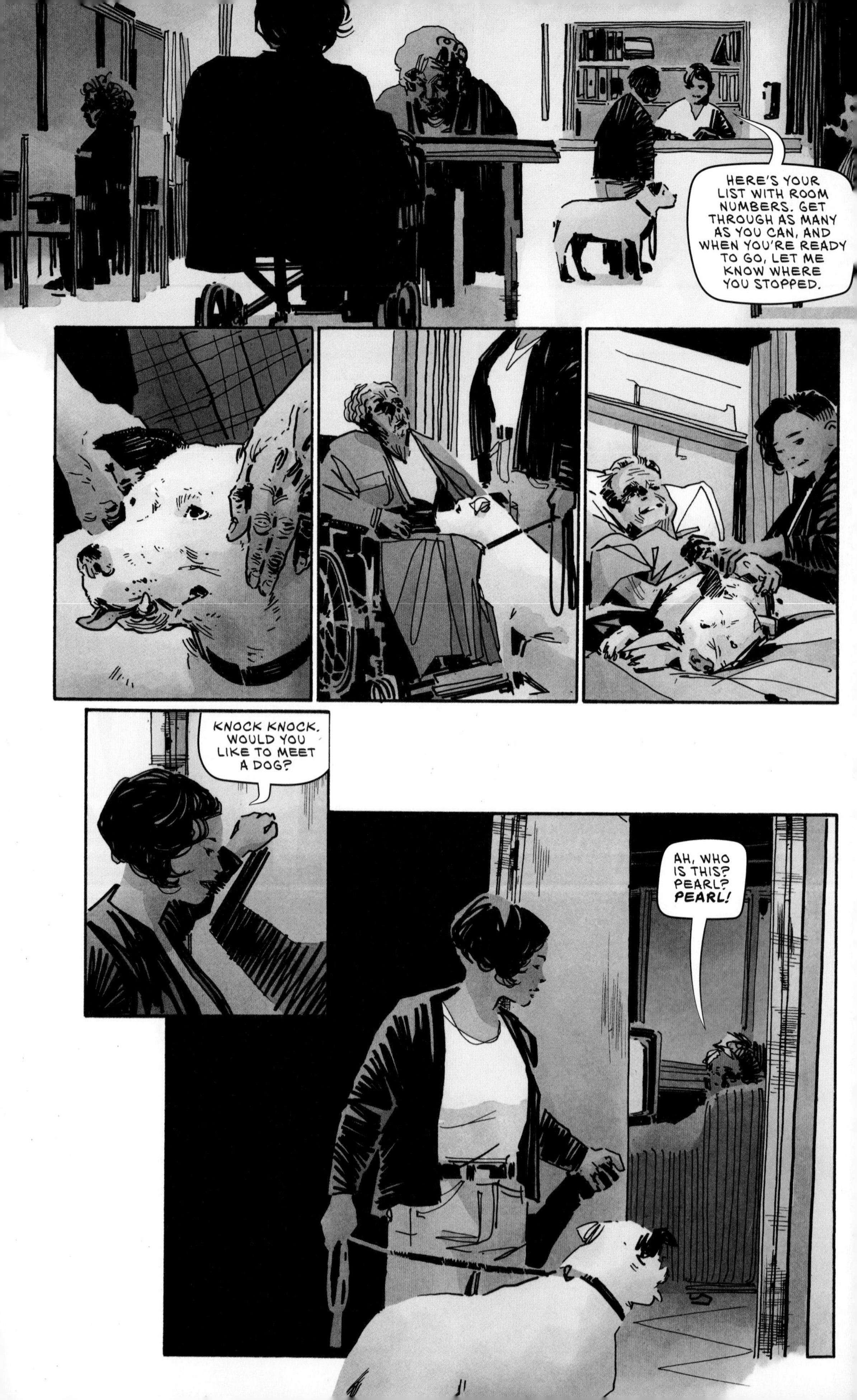
HERE'S YOUR LIST WITH ROOM NUMBERS. GET THROUGH AS MANY AS YOU CAN, AND WHEN YOU'RE READY TO GO, LET ME KNOW WHERE YOU STOPPED.
KNOCK KNOCK. WOULD YOU LIKE TO MEET A DOG?
AH, WHO IS THIS? PEARL? **PEARL!**

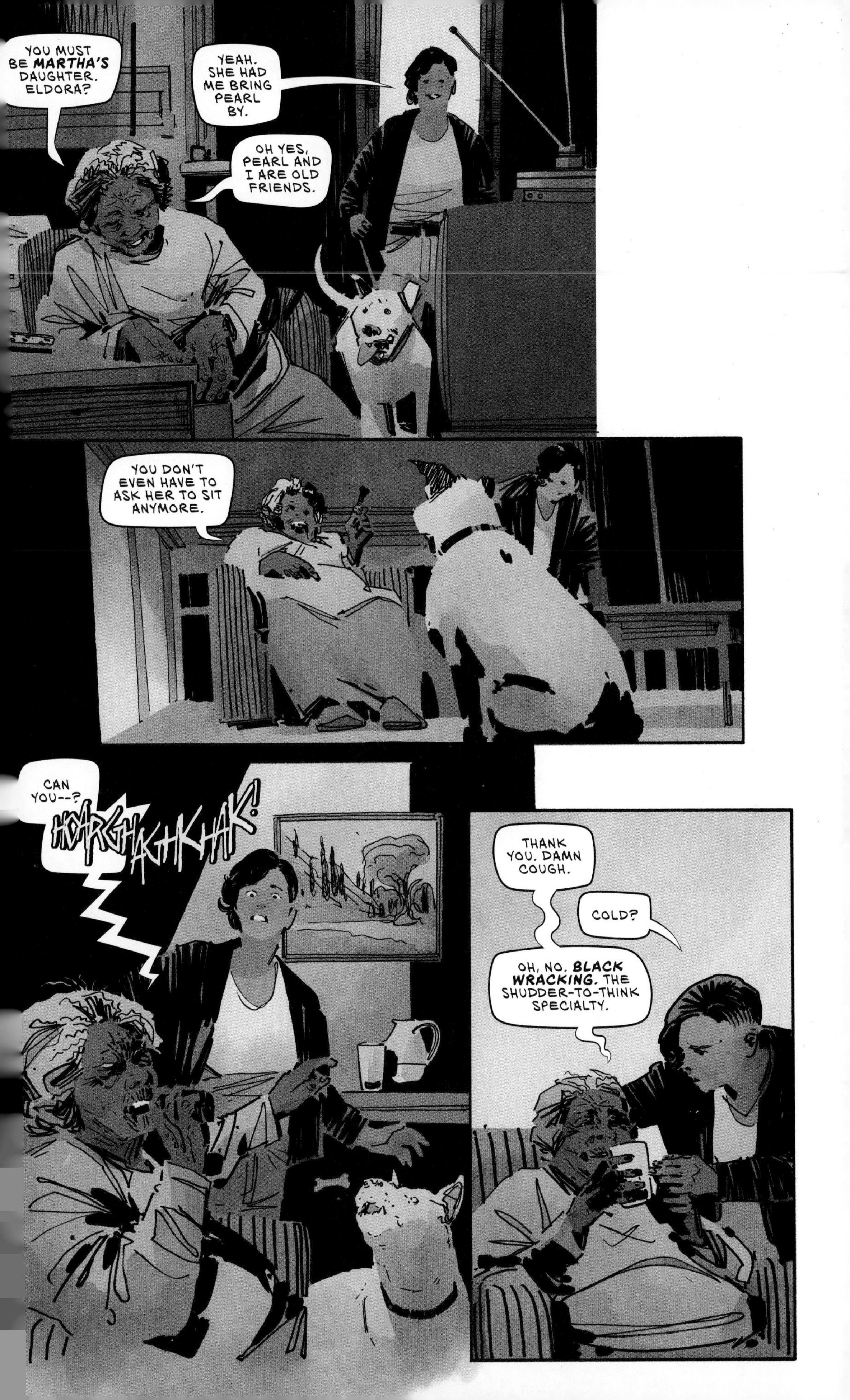

YOU MUST BE **MARTHA'S** DAUGHTER. ELDORA?
YEAH. SHE HAD ME BRING PEARL BY.
OH YES, PEARL AND I ARE OLD FRIENDS.
YOU DON'T EVEN HAVE TO ASK HER TO SIT ANYMORE.
CAN YOU--?
HOARGHAGHKHAK!
THANK YOU. DAMN COUGH.
COLD?
OH, NO. **BLACK WRACKING.** THE SHUDDER-TO-THINK SPECIALTY.

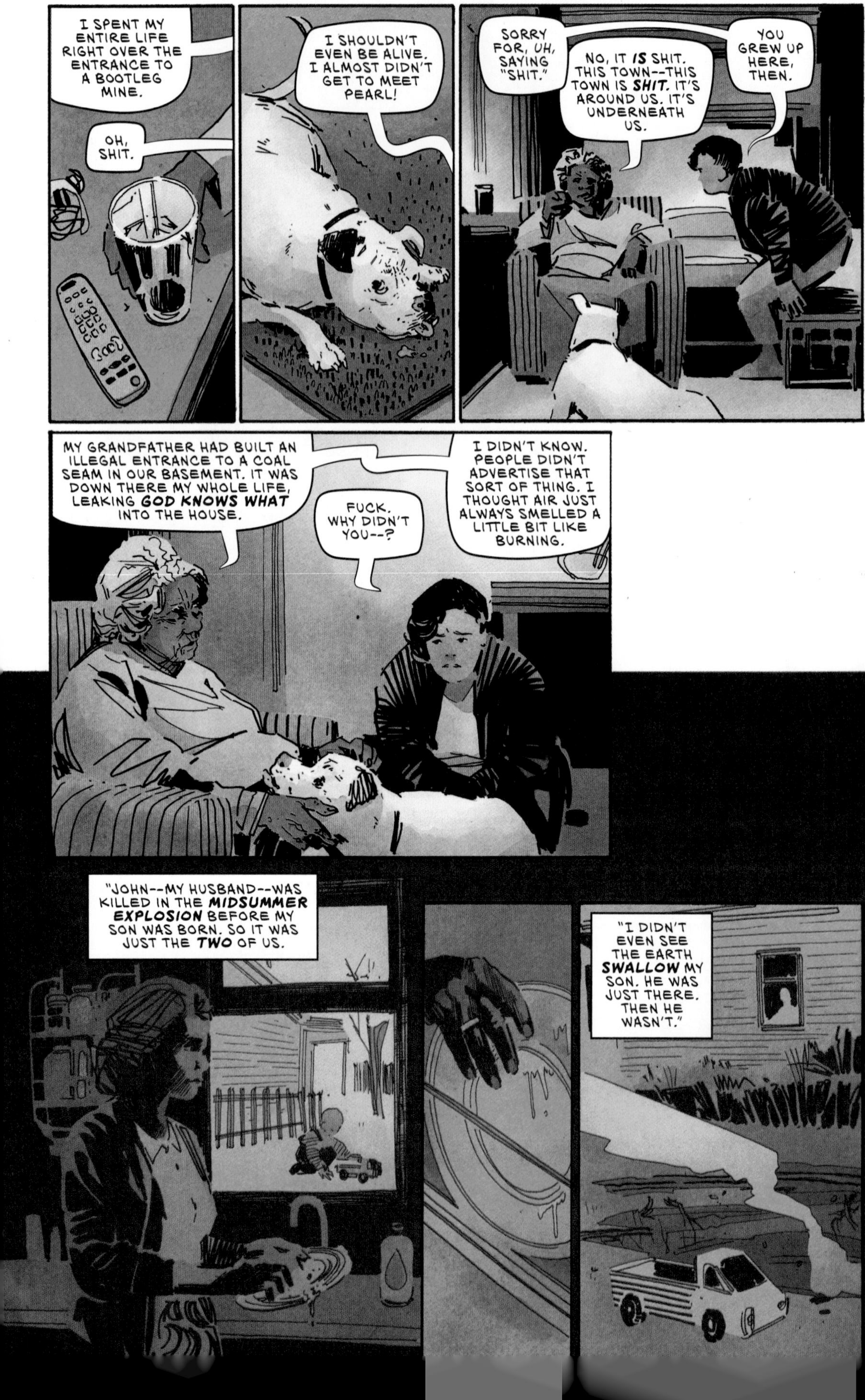
I SPENT MY ENTIRE LIFE RIGHT OVER THE ENTRANCE TO A BOOTLEG MINE.
OH, SHIT.
I SHOULDN'T EVEN BE ALIVE. I ALMOST DIDN'T GET TO MEET PEARL!
SORRY FOR, UH, SAYING "SHIT."
NO, IT IS SHIT. THIS TOWN--THIS TOWN IS SHIT. IT'S AROUND US. IT'S UNDERNEATH US.
YOU GREW UP HERE, THEN.
MY GRANDFATHER HAD BUILT AN ILLEGAL ENTRANCE TO A COAL SEAM IN OUR BASEMENT. IT WAS DOWN THERE MY WHOLE LIFE, LEAKING GOD KNOWS WHAT INTO THE HOUSE.
FUCK. WHY DIDN'T YOU--?
I DIDN'T KNOW. PEOPLE DIDN'T ADVERTISE THAT SORT OF THING. I THOUGHT AIR JUST ALWAYS SMELLED A LITTLE BIT LIKE BURNING.
"JOHN--MY HUSBAND--WAS KILLED IN THE MIDSUMMER EXPLOSION BEFORE MY SON WAS BORN. SO IT WAS JUST THE TWO OF US.
"I DIDN'T EVEN SEE THE EARTH SWALLOW MY SON. HE WAS JUST THERE. THEN HE WASN'T."

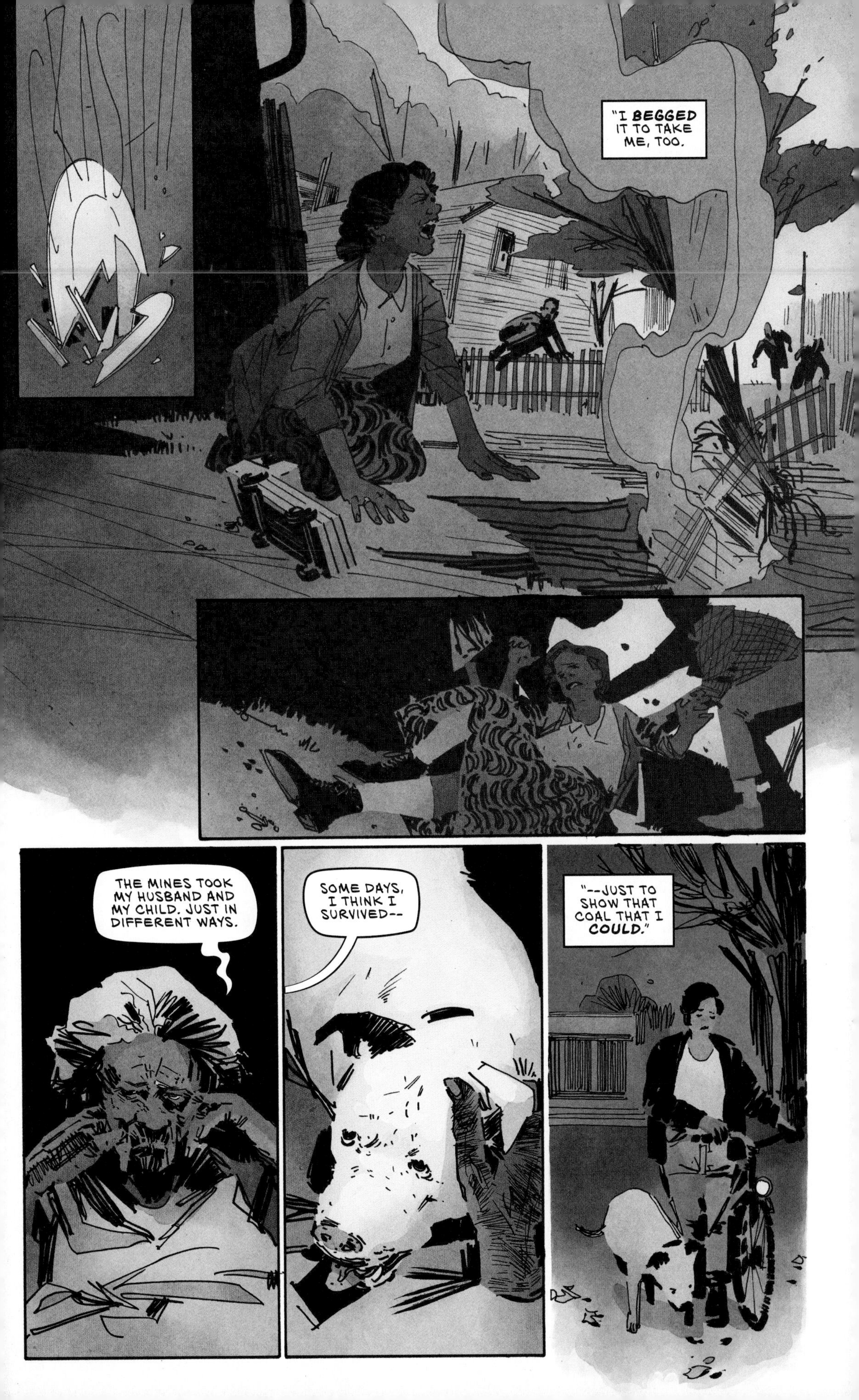
CRASH!
"I BEGGED IT TO TAKE ME, TOO.
THE MINES TOOK MY HUSBAND AND MY CHILD. JUST IN DIFFERENT WAYS.
SOME DAYS, I THINK I SURVIVED--
"--JUST TO SHOW THAT COAL THAT I COULD."

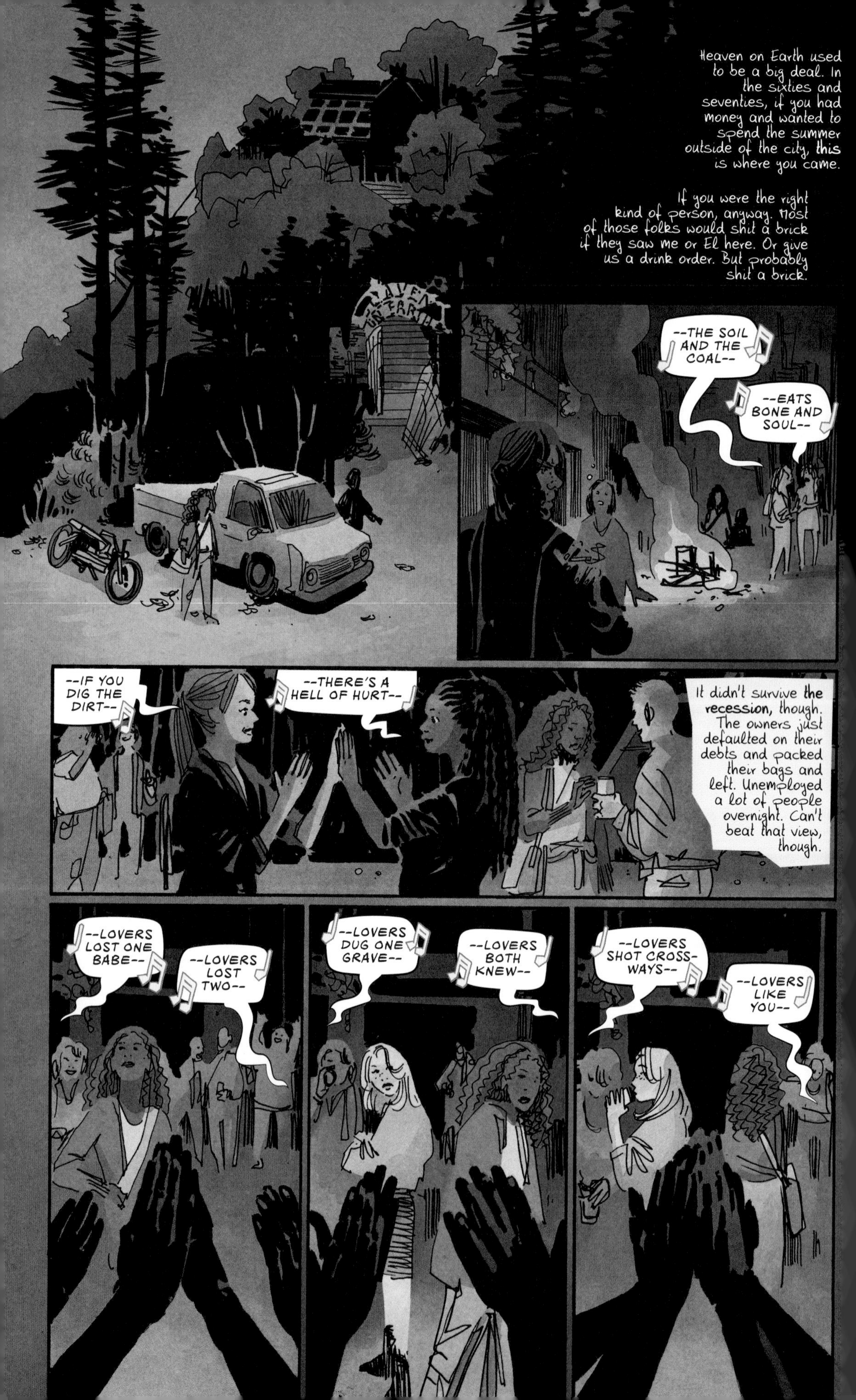
Heaven on Earth used to be a big deal. In the sixties and seventies, if you had money and wanted to spend the summer outside of the city, this is where you came.
If you were the right kind of person, anyway. Most of those folks would shit a brick if they saw me or El here. Or give us a drink order. But probably shit a brick.
--THE SOIL AND THE COAL--
--EATS BONE AND SOUL--
--IF YOU DIG THE DIRT--
--THERE'S A HELL OF HURT--
It didn't survive the recession, though. The owners just defaulted on their debts and packed their bags and left. Unemployed a lot of people overnight. Can't beat that view, though.
--LOVERS LOST ONE BABE--
--LOVERS LOST TWO--
--LOVERS DUG ONE GRAVE--
--LOVERS BOTH KNEW--
--LOVERS SHOT CROSS-WAYS--
--LOVERS LIKE YOU--

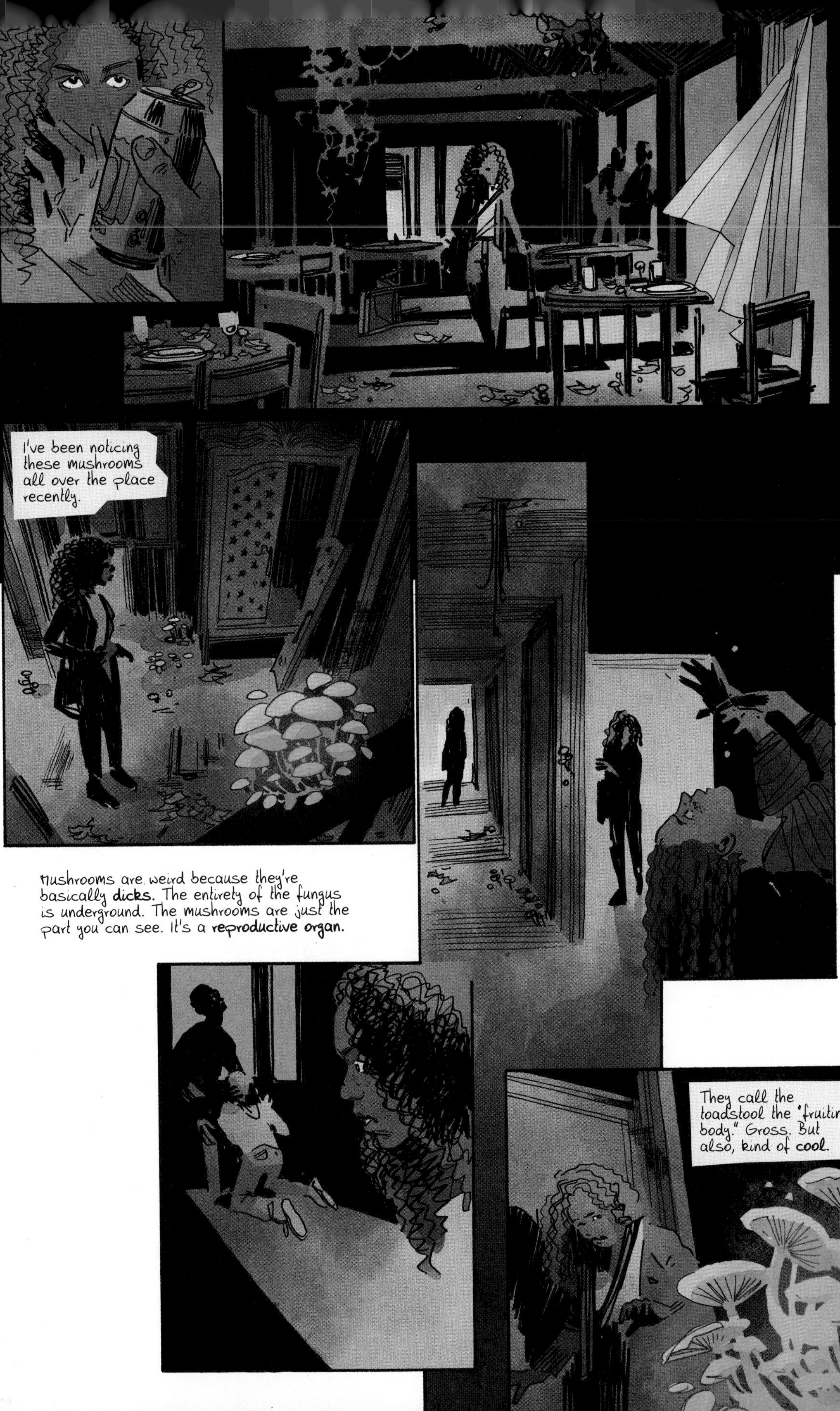
I've been noticing these mushrooms all over the place recently.
Mushrooms are weird because they're basically **dicks.** The entirety of the fungus is underground. The mushrooms are just the part you can see. It's a **reproductive organ.**
They call the toadstool the "fruiting body." Gross. But also, kind of **cool.**

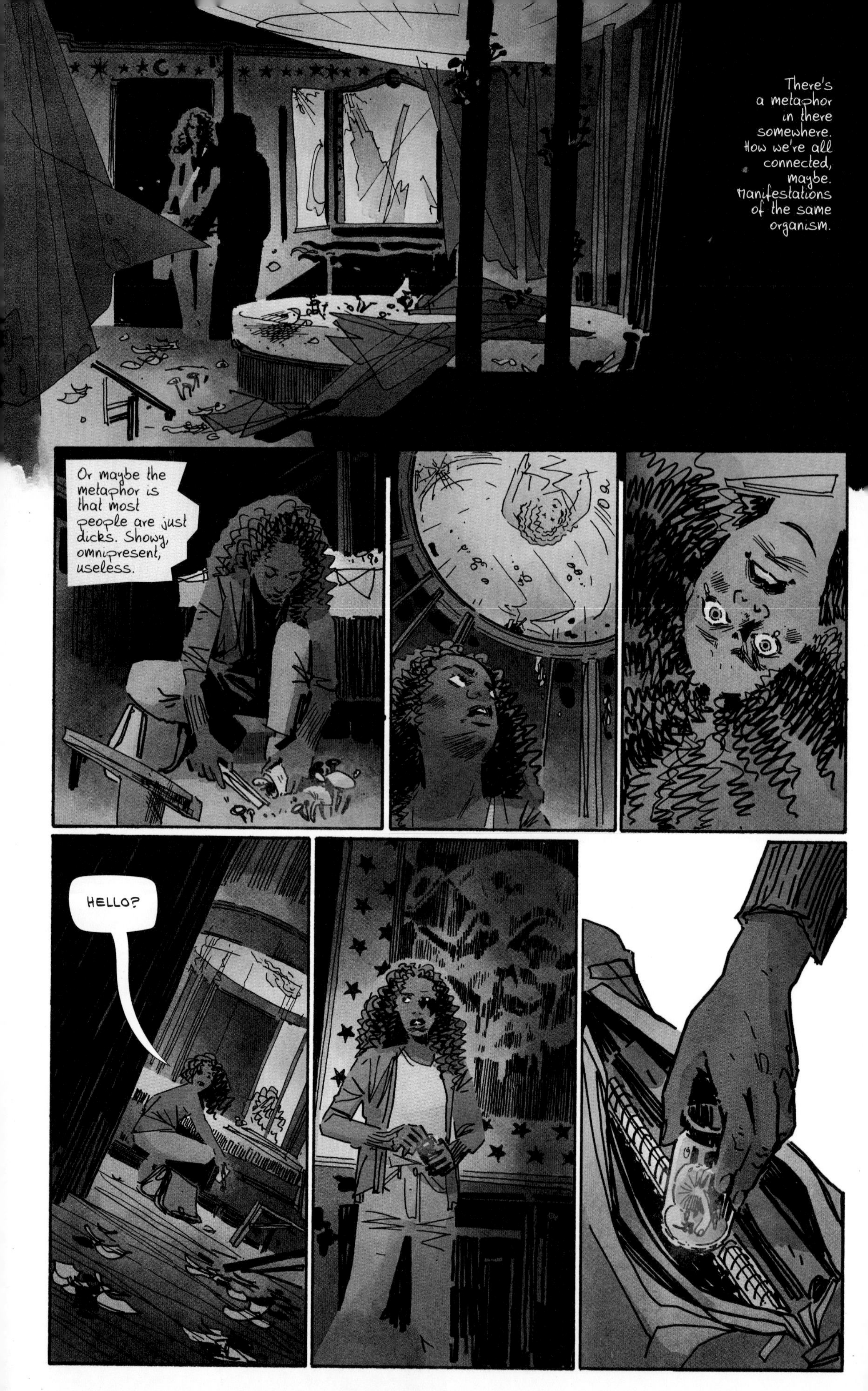
There's a metaphor in there somewhere. How we're all connected, maybe. Manifestations of the same organism.
Or maybe the metaphor is that most people are just dicks. Showy, omnipresent, useless.
HELLO?

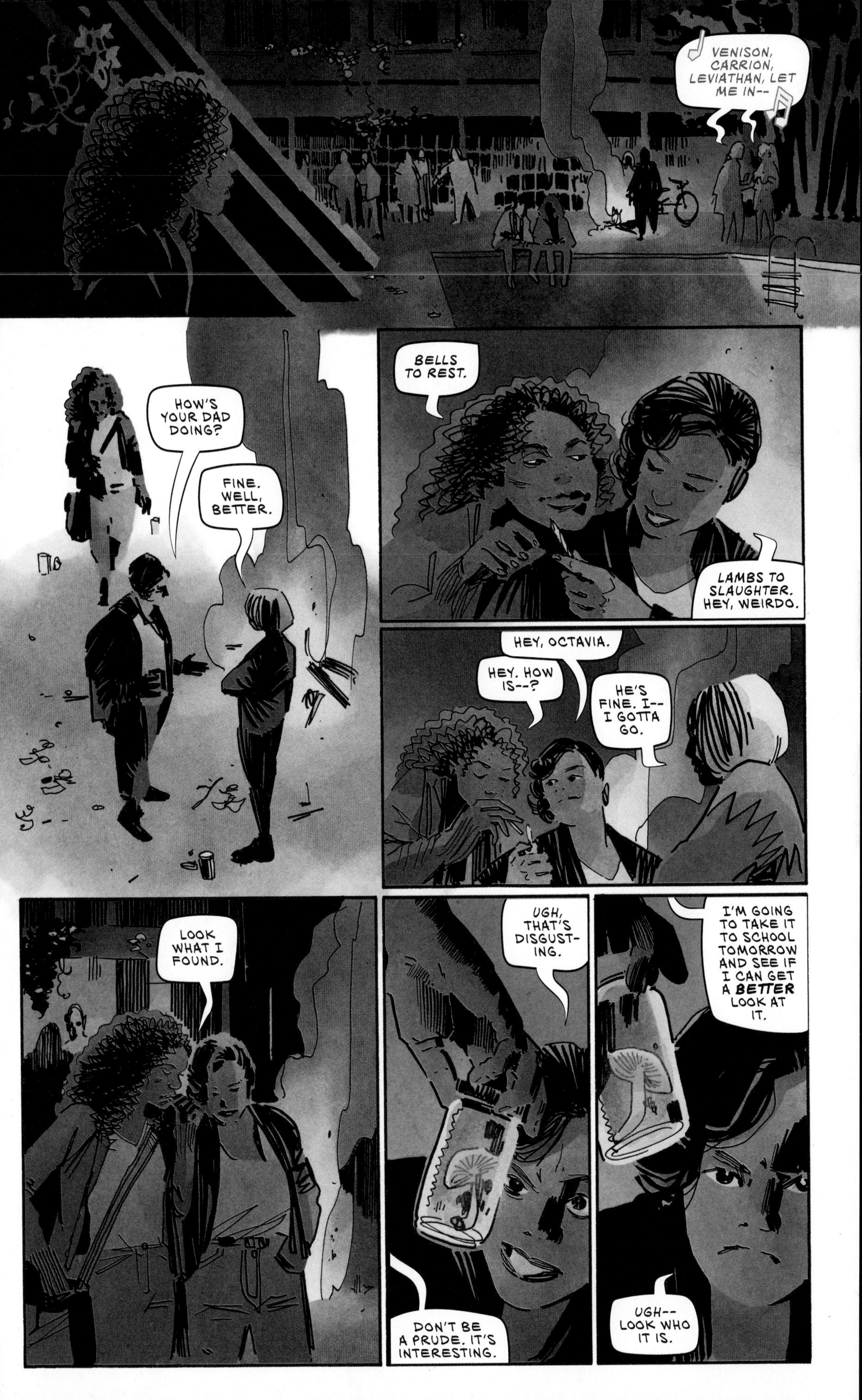
VENISON, CARRION, LEVIATHAN, LET ME IN--
HOW'S YOUR DAD DOING?
FINE. WELL, BETTER.
BELLS TO REST.
LAMBS TO SLAUGHTER. HEY, WEIRDO.
HEY, OCTAVIA.
HEY. HOW IS--?
HE'S FINE. I-- I GOTTA GO.
LOOK WHAT I FOUND.
UGH, THAT'S DISGUST-ING.
DON'T BE A PRUDE. IT'S INTERESTING.
I'M GOING TO TAKE IT TO SCHOOL TOMORROW AND SEE IF I CAN GET A BETTER LOOK AT IT.
UGH-- LOOK WHO IT IS.

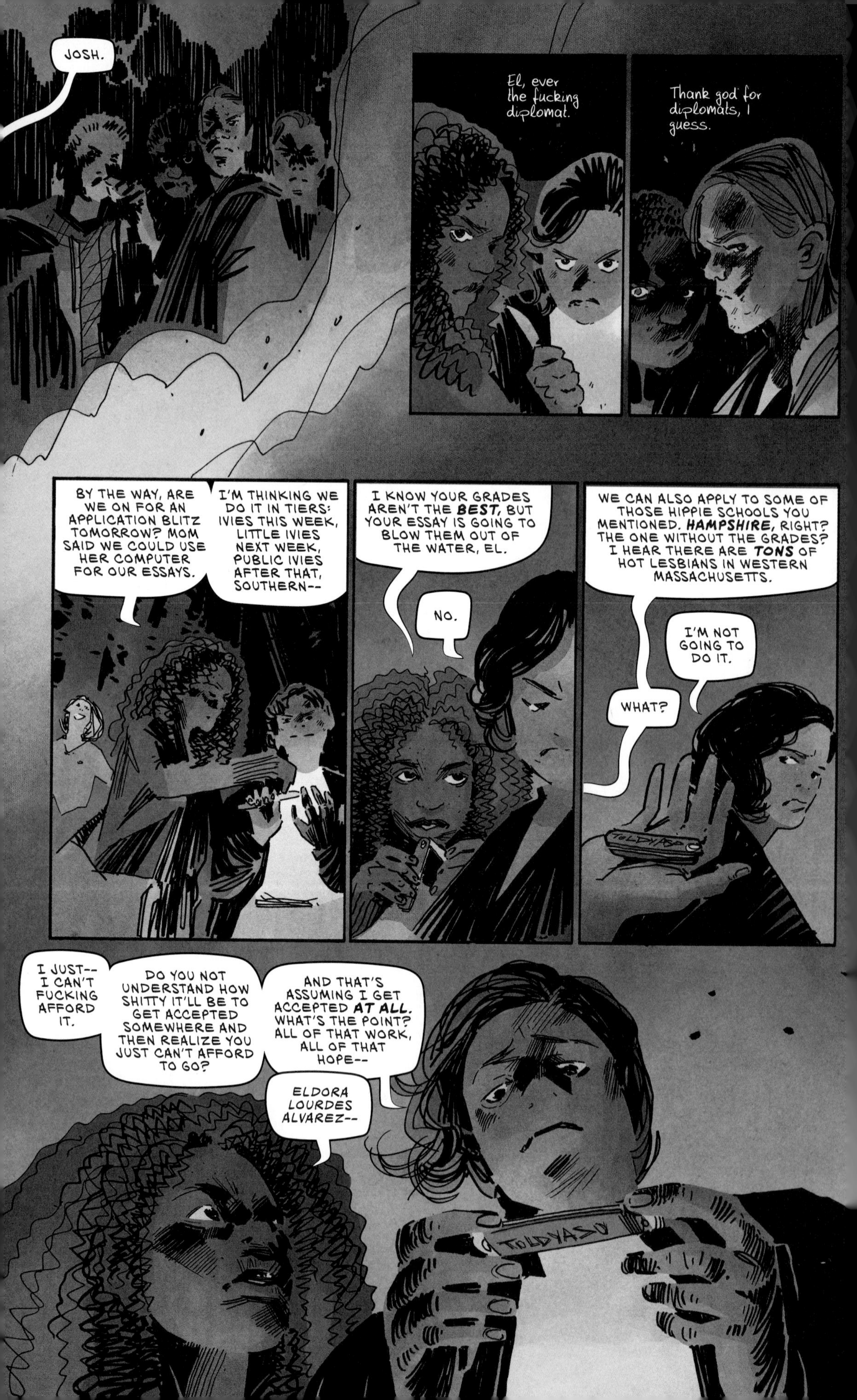
JOSH.
El, ever the fucking diplomat.
Thank god for diplomats, I guess.
BY THE WAY, ARE WE ON FOR AN APPLICATION BLITZ TOMORROW? MOM SAID WE COULD USE HER COMPUTER FOR OUR ESSAYS.
I'M THINKING WE DO IT IN TIERS: IVIES THIS WEEK, LITTLE IVIES NEXT WEEK, PUBLIC IVIES AFTER THAT, SOUTHERN--
I KNOW YOUR GRADES AREN'T THE **BEST,** BUT YOUR ESSAY IS GOING TO BLOW THEM OUT OF THE WATER, EL.
NO.
WE CAN ALSO APPLY TO SOME OF THOSE HIPPIE SCHOOLS YOU MENTIONED. **HAMPSHIRE,** RIGHT? THE ONE WITHOUT THE GRADES? I HEAR THERE ARE **TONS** OF HOT LESBIANS IN WESTERN MASSACHUSETTS.
I'M NOT GOING TO DO IT.
WHAT?
TOLDYASO
I JUST-- I CAN'T FUCKING AFFORD IT.
DO YOU NOT UNDERSTAND HOW SHITTY IT'LL BE TO GET ACCEPTED SOMEWHERE AND THEN REALIZE YOU JUST CAN'T AFFORD TO GO?
AND THAT'S ASSUMING I GET ACCEPTED **AT ALL.** WHAT'S THE POINT? ALL OF THAT WORK, ALL OF THAT HOPE--
ELDORA LOURDES ALVAREZ--
TOLDYASO

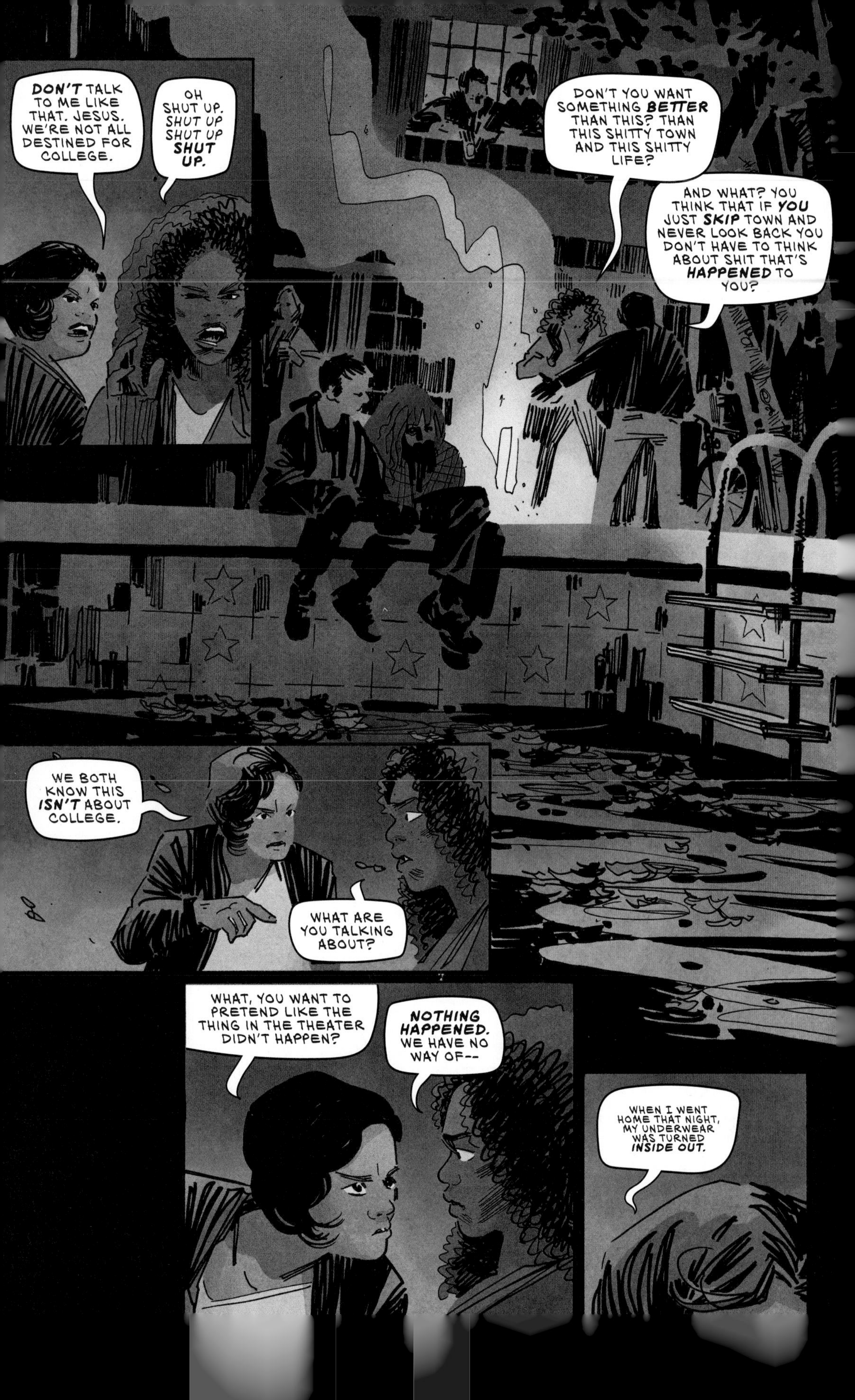
DON'T TALK TO ME LIKE THAT. JESUS. WE'RE NOT ALL DESTINED FOR COLLEGE.
OH SHUT UP. SHUT UP SHUT UP SHUT UP.
DON'T YOU WANT SOMETHING BETTER THAN THIS? THAN THIS SHITTY TOWN AND THIS SHITTY LIFE?
AND WHAT? YOU THINK THAT IF YOU JUST SKIP TOWN AND NEVER LOOK BACK YOU DON'T HAVE TO THINK ABOUT SHIT THAT'S HAPPENED TO YOU?
WE BOTH KNOW THIS ISN'T ABOUT COLLEGE.
WHAT ARE YOU TALKING ABOUT?
WHAT, YOU WANT TO PRETEND LIKE THE THING IN THE THEATER DIDN'T HAPPEN?
NOTHING HAPPENED. WE HAVE NO WAY OF--
WHEN I WENT HOME THAT NIGHT, MY UNDERWEAR WAS TURNED INSIDE OUT.

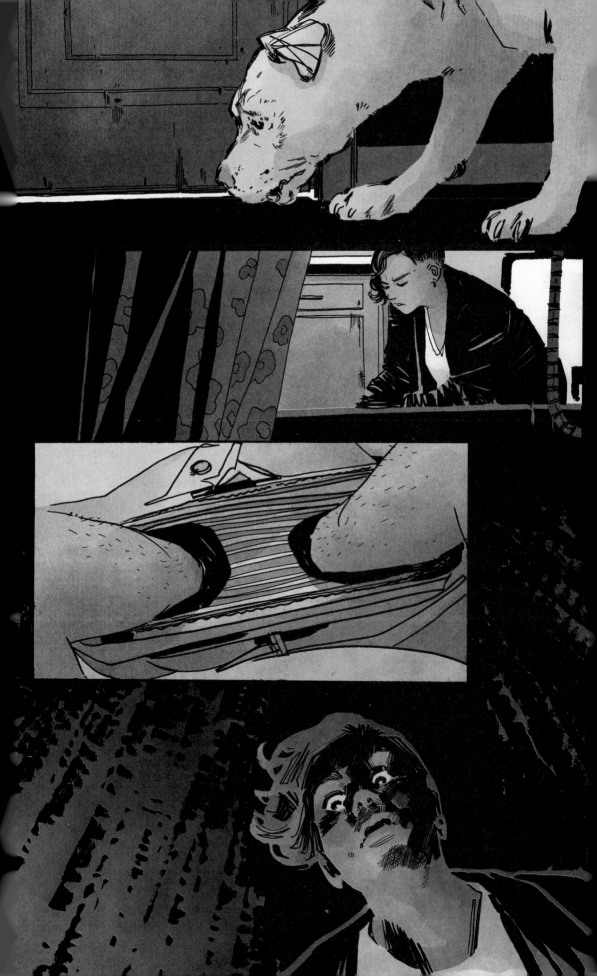

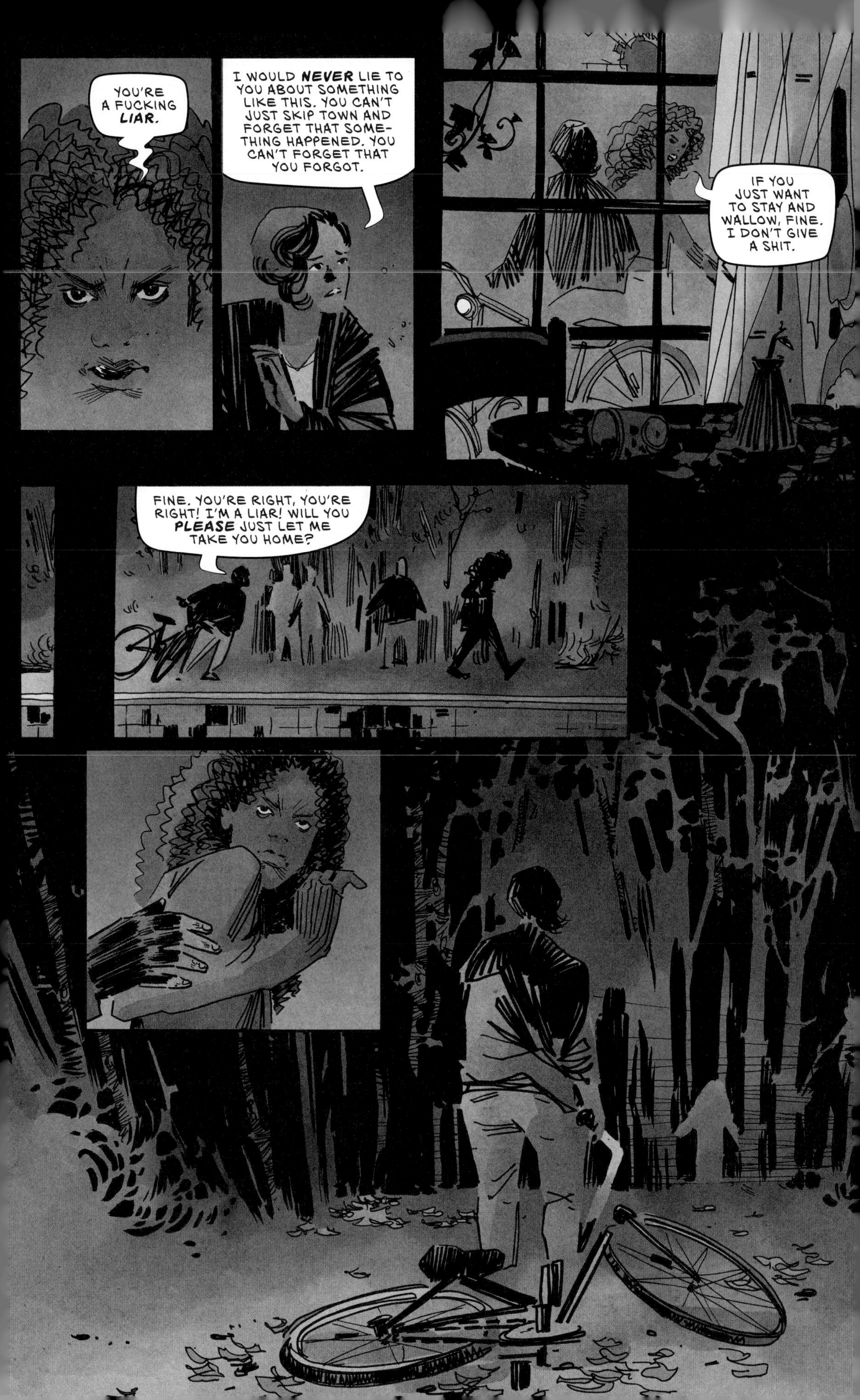
YOU'RE A FUCKING **LIAR.**
I WOULD **NEVER** LIE TO YOU ABOUT SOMETHING LIKE THIS. YOU CAN'T JUST SKIP TOWN AND FORGET THAT SOMETHING HAPPENED. YOU CAN'T FORGET THAT YOU FORGOT.
IF YOU JUST WANT TO STAY AND WALLOW, FINE. I DON'T GIVE A SHIT.
FINE. YOU'RE RIGHT, YOU'RE RIGHT! I'M A LIAR! WILL YOU **PLEASE** JUST LET ME TAKE YOU HOME?

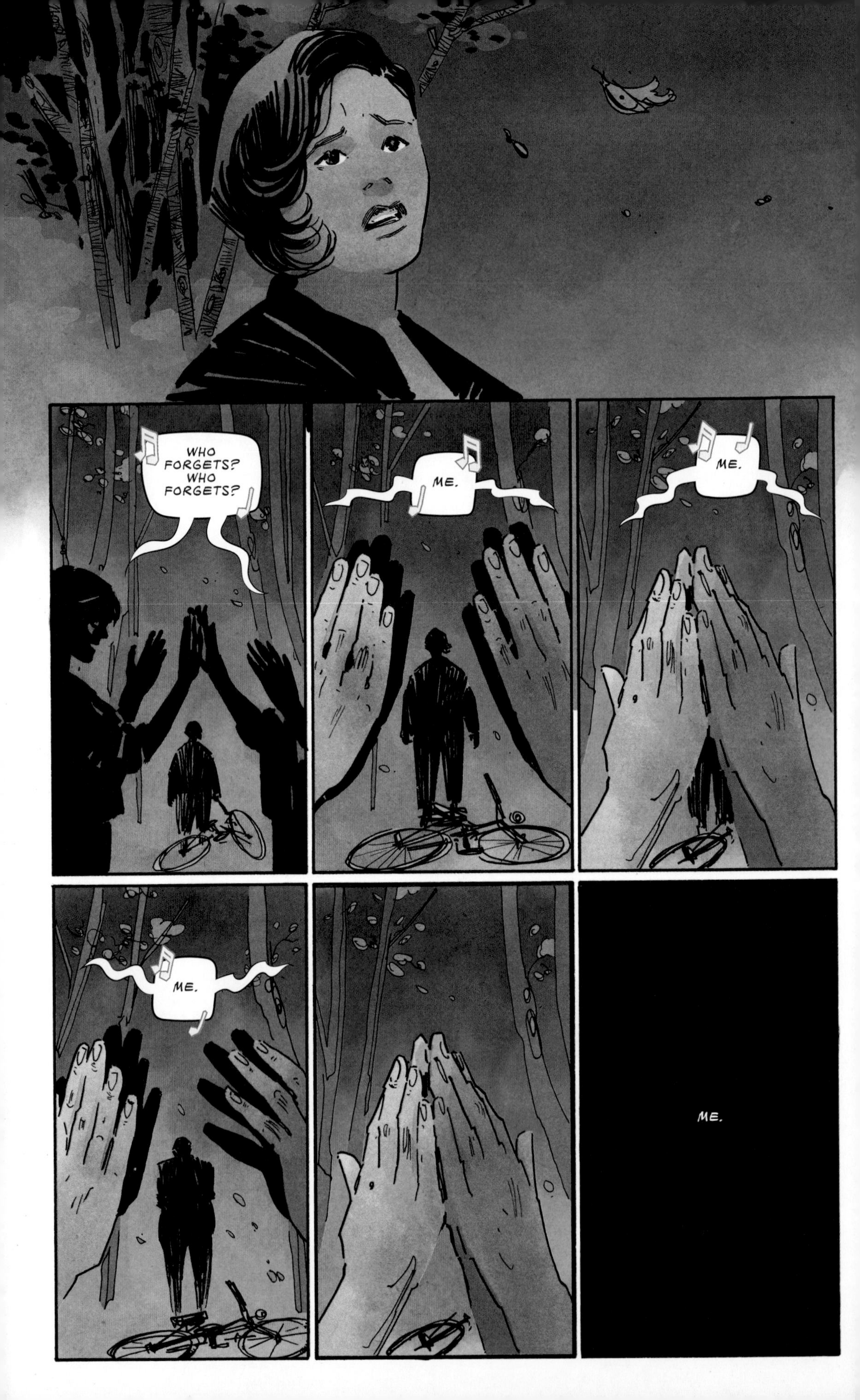
WHO FORGETS? WHO FORGETS?
ME.
ME.
ME.
ME.

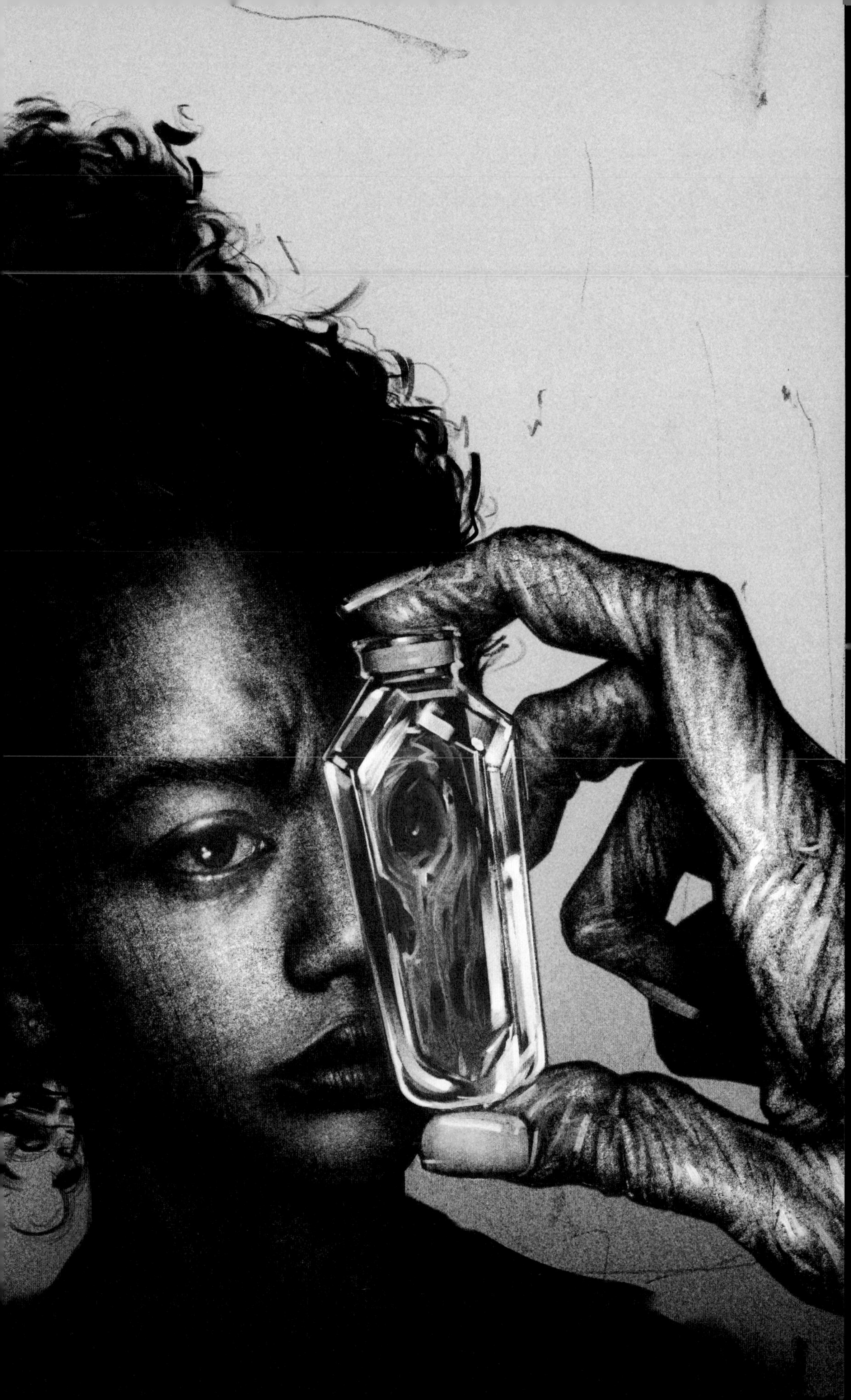

The Fruiting Body

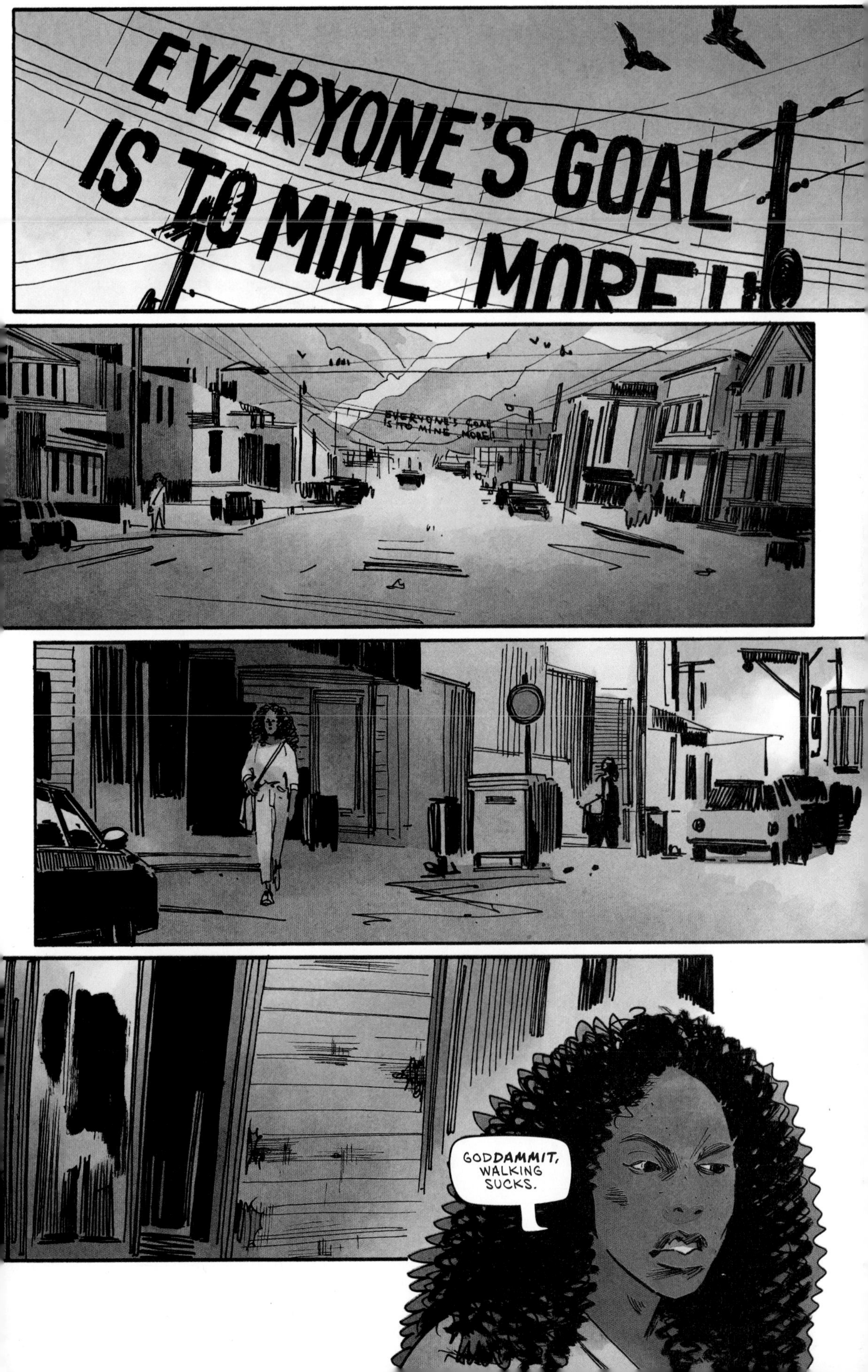
EVERYONE'S GOAL IS TO MINE MORE!!
GODDAMMIT, WALKING SUCKS.

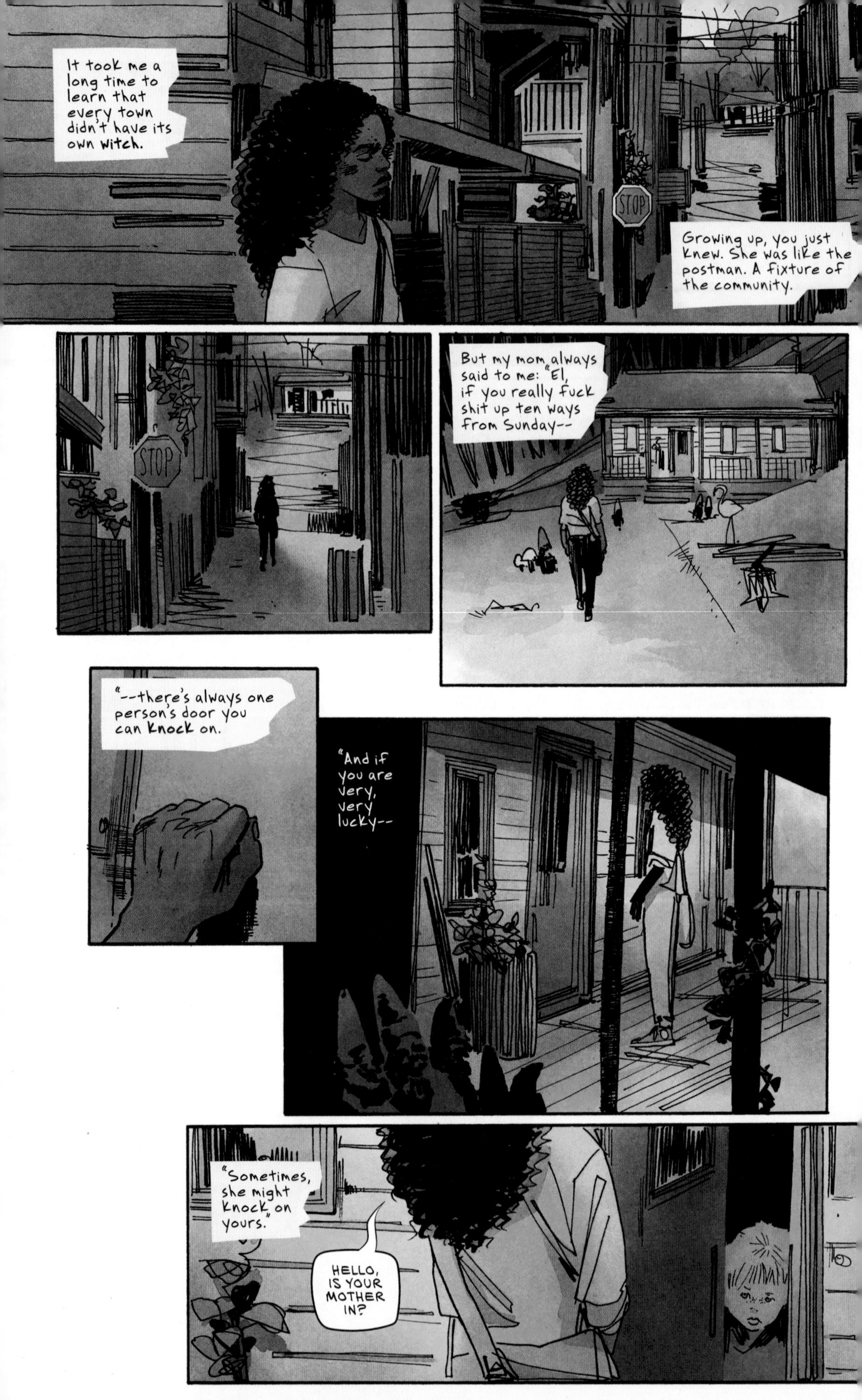
It took me a long time to learn that every town didn't have its own witch.
Growing up, you just knew. She was like the postman. A fixture of the community.
STOP
STOP
But my mom always said to me: "El, if you really fuck shit up ten ways from Sunday--
"--there's always one person's door you can knock on.
"And if you are very, very lucky--
"Sometimes, she might knock on yours."
HELLO, IS YOUR MOTHER IN?

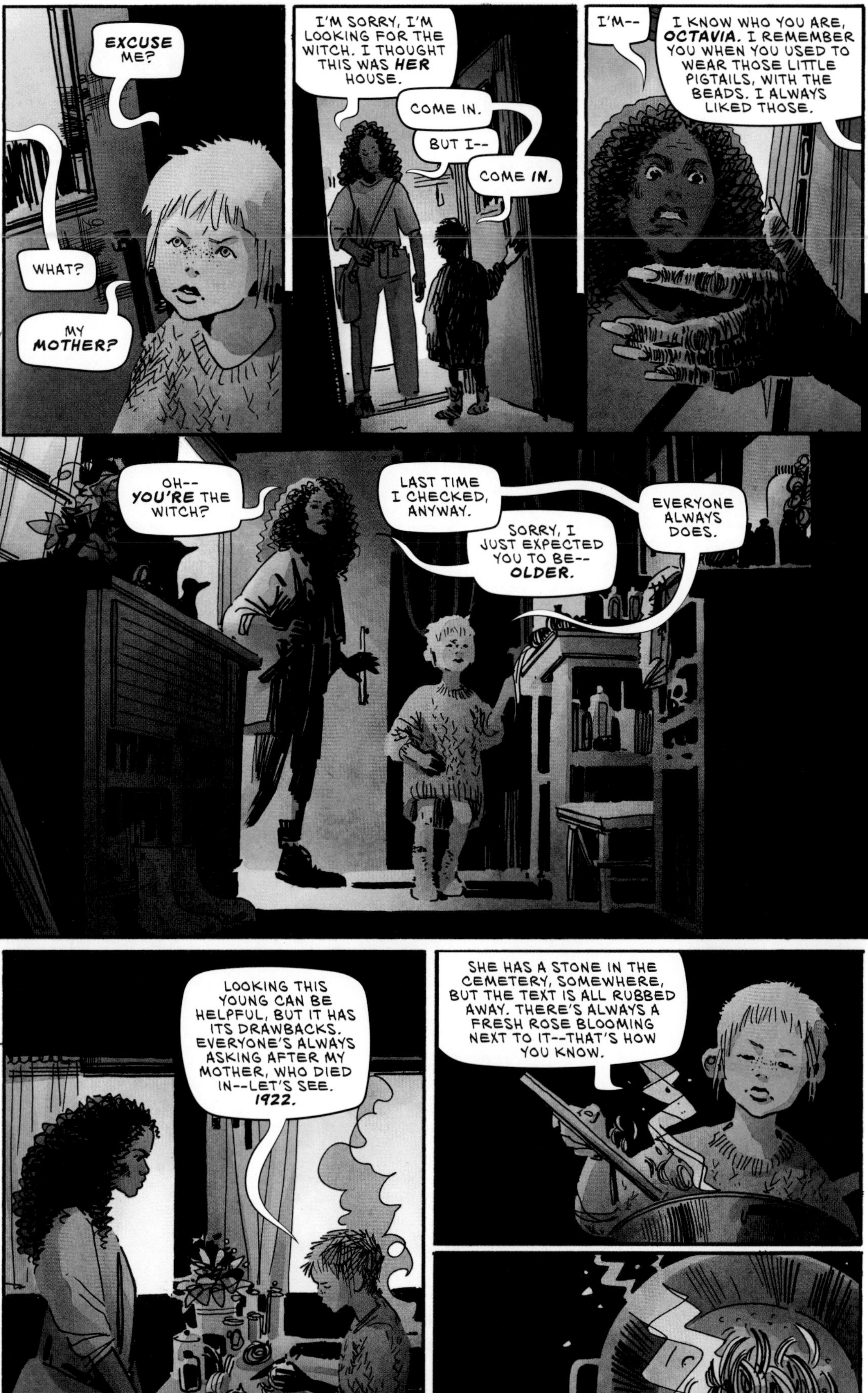

EXCUSE ME?
WHAT?
MY MOTHER?
I'M SORRY, I'M LOOKING FOR THE WITCH. I THOUGHT THIS WAS HER HOUSE.
COME IN.
BUT I--
COME IN.
I'M--
I KNOW WHO YOU ARE, OCTAVIA. I REMEMBER YOU WHEN YOU USED TO WEAR THOSE LITTLE PIGTAILS, WITH THE BEADS. I ALWAYS LIKED THOSE.
OH-- YOU'RE THE WITCH?
LAST TIME I CHECKED, ANYWAY.
SORRY, I JUST EXPECTED YOU TO BE-- OLDER.
EVERYONE ALWAYS DOES.
LOOKING THIS YOUNG CAN BE HELPFUL, BUT IT HAS ITS DRAWBACKS. EVERYONE'S ALWAYS ASKING AFTER MY MOTHER, WHO DIED IN--LET'S SEE. 1922.
SHE HAS A STONE IN THE CEMETERY, SOMEWHERE, BUT THE TEXT IS ALL RUBBED AWAY. THERE'S ALWAYS A FRESH ROSE BLOOMING NEXT TO IT--THAT'S HOW YOU KNOW.

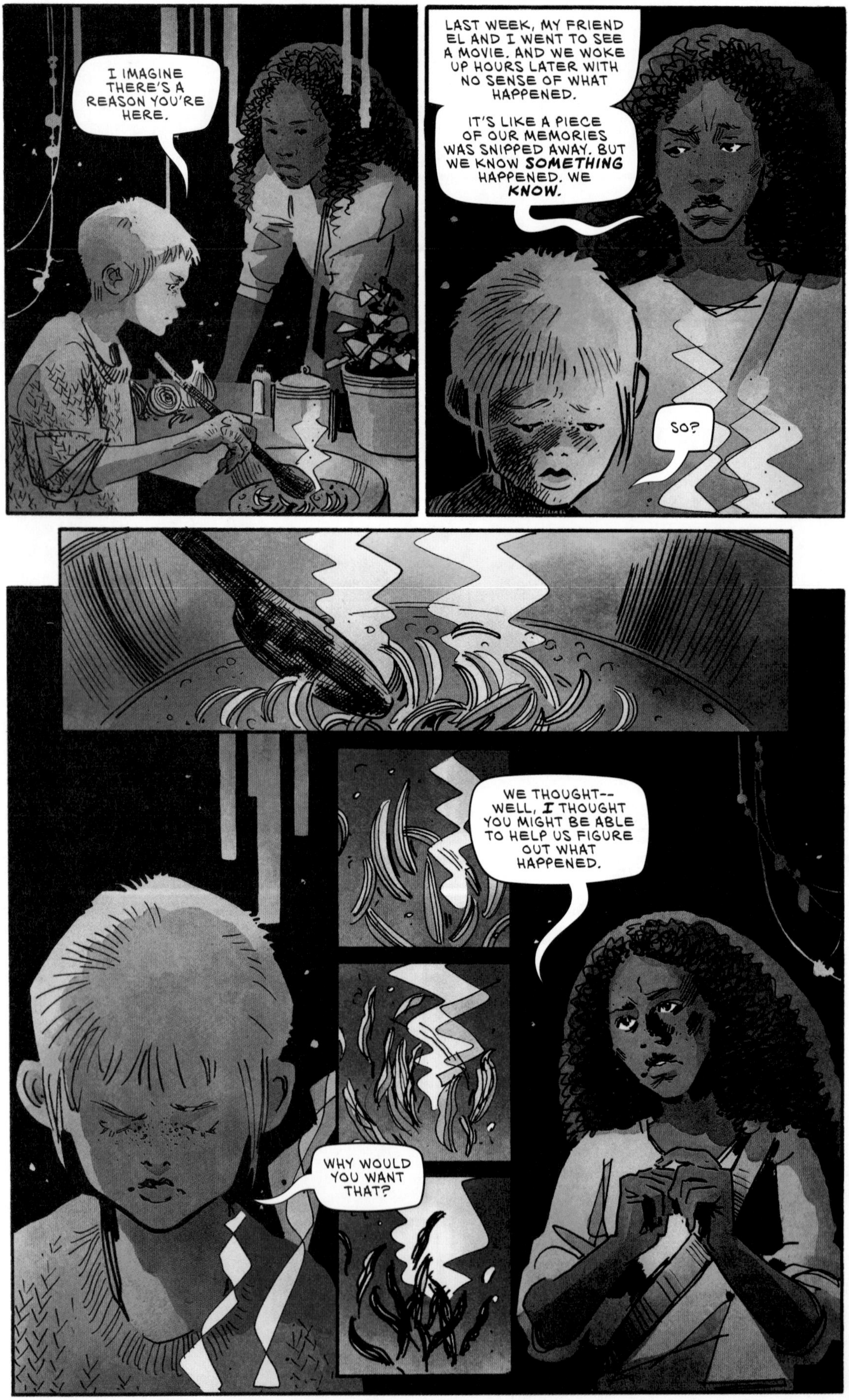
I IMAGINE THERE'S A REASON YOU'RE HERE.
LAST WEEK, MY FRIEND EL AND I WENT TO SEE A MOVIE. AND WE WOKE UP HOURS LATER WITH NO SENSE OF WHAT HAPPENED.
IT'S LIKE A PIECE OF OUR MEMORIES WAS SNIPPED AWAY. BUT WE KNOW SOMETHING HAPPENED. WE KNOW.
SO?
WE THOUGHT-- WELL, I THOUGHT YOU MIGHT BE ABLE TO HELP US FIGURE OUT WHAT HAPPENED.
WHY WOULD YOU WANT THAT?

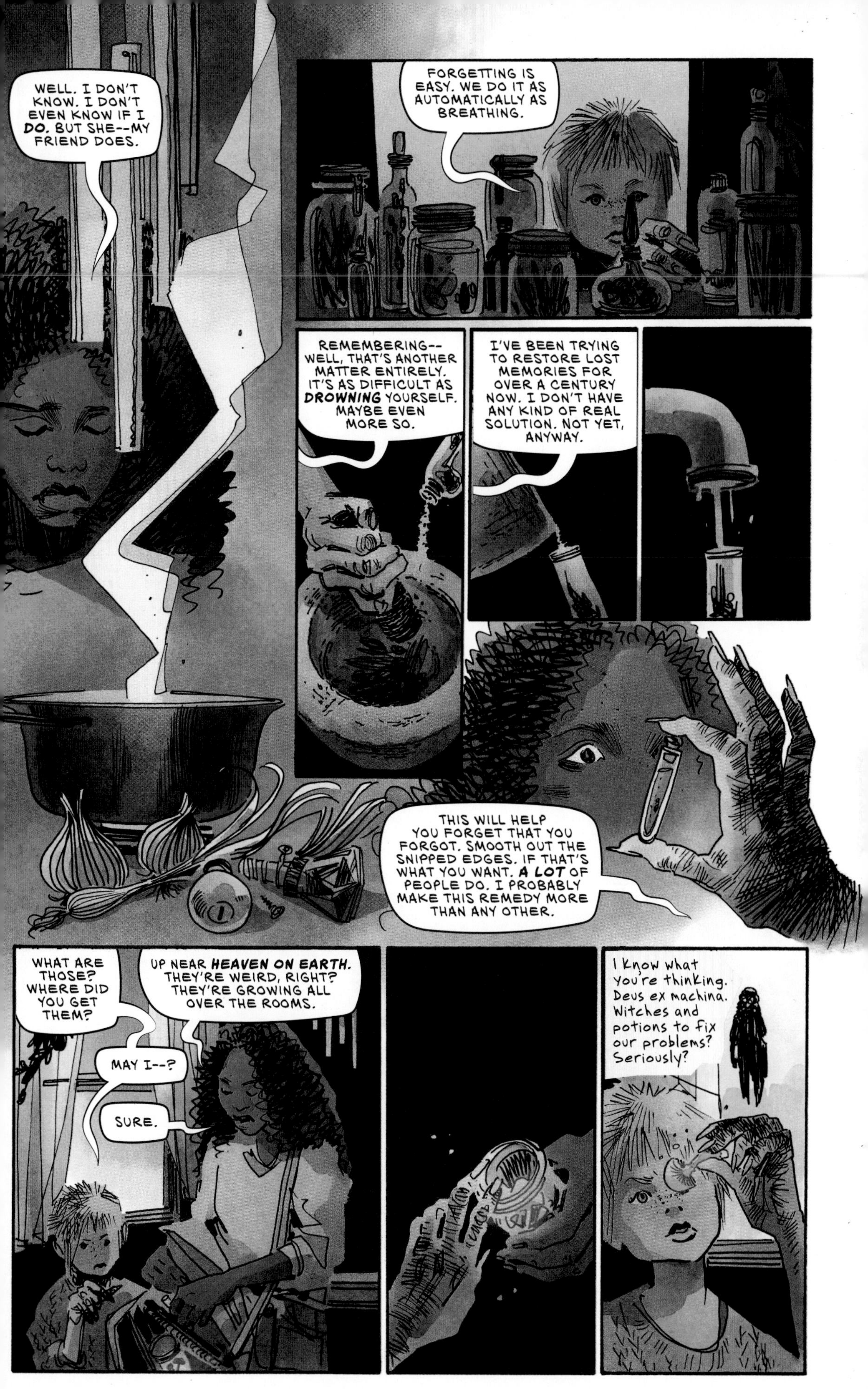
WELL. I DON'T KNOW. I DON'T EVEN KNOW IF I **DO.** BUT SHE--MY FRIEND DOES.
FORGETTING IS EASY. WE DO IT AS AUTOMATICALLY AS BREATHING.
REMEMBERING--WELL, THAT'S ANOTHER MATTER ENTIRELY. IT'S AS DIFFICULT AS **DROWNING** YOURSELF. MAYBE EVEN MORE SO.
I'VE BEEN TRYING TO RESTORE LOST MEMORIES FOR OVER A CENTURY NOW. I DON'T HAVE ANY KIND OF REAL SOLUTION. NOT YET, ANYWAY.
THIS WILL HELP YOU FORGET THAT YOU FORGOT. SMOOTH OUT THE SNIPPED EDGES. IF THAT'S WHAT YOU WANT. **A LOT** OF PEOPLE DO. I PROBABLY MAKE THIS REMEDY MORE THAN ANY OTHER.
WHAT ARE THOSE? WHERE DID YOU GET THEM?
UP NEAR **HEAVEN ON EARTH.** THEY'RE WEIRD, RIGHT? THEY'RE GROWING ALL OVER THE ROOMS.
MAY I--?
SURE.
I know what you're thinking. Deus ex machina. Witches and potions to fix our problems? Seriously?

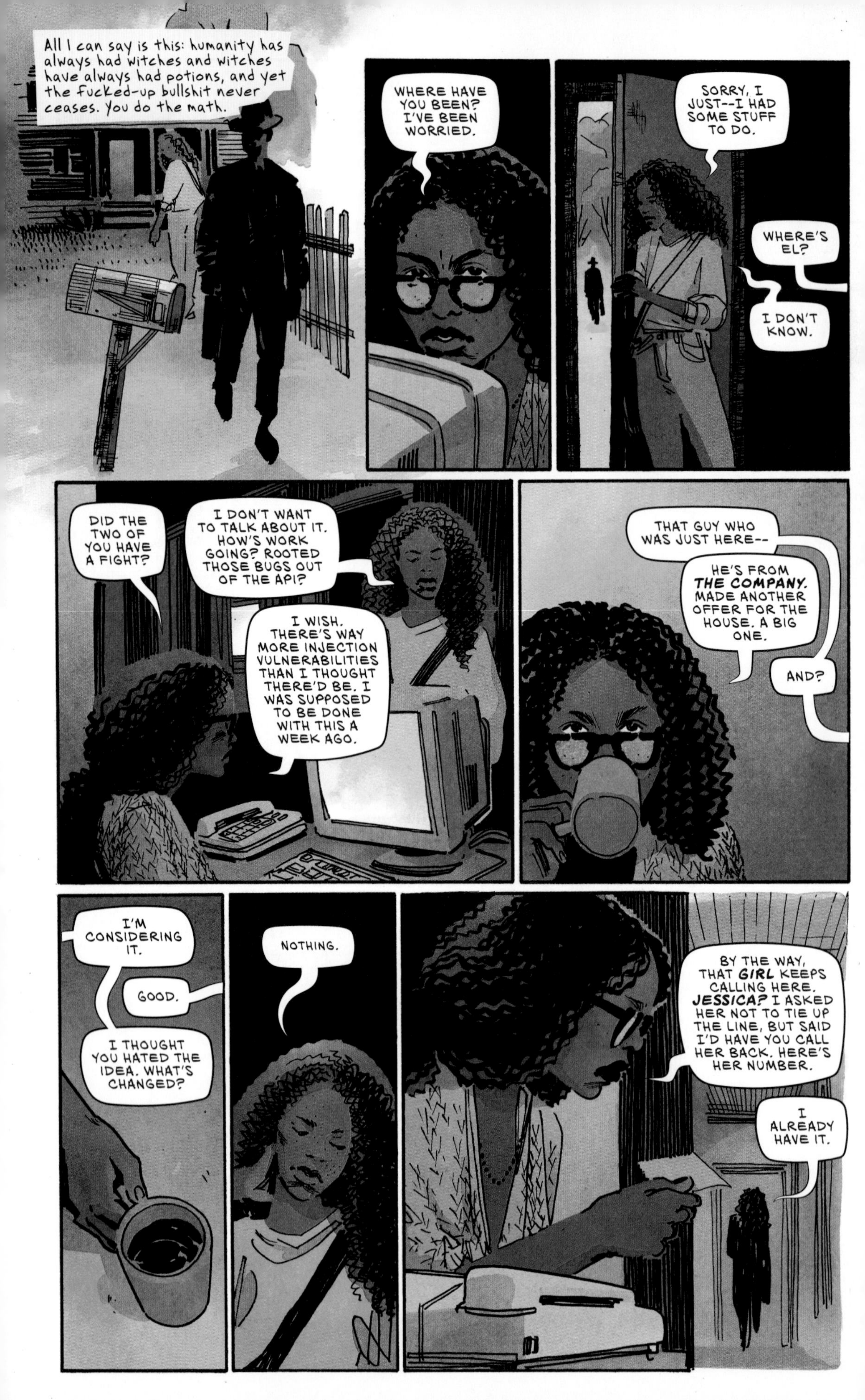
All I can say is this: humanity has always had witches and witches have always had potions, and yet the fucked-up bullshit never ceases. You do the math.
WHERE HAVE YOU BEEN? I'VE BEEN WORRIED.
SORRY, I JUST--I HAD SOME STUFF TO DO.
WHERE'S EL?
I DON'T KNOW.
DID THE TWO OF YOU HAVE A FIGHT?
I DON'T WANT TO TALK ABOUT IT. HOW'S WORK GOING? ROOTED THOSE BUGS OUT OF THE API?
I WISH. THERE'S WAY MORE INJECTION VULNERABILITIES THAN I THOUGHT THERE'D BE. I WAS SUPPOSED TO BE DONE WITH THIS A WEEK AGO.
THAT GUY WHO WAS JUST HERE--
HE'S FROM **THE COMPANY.** MADE ANOTHER OFFER FOR THE HOUSE. A BIG ONE.
AND?
I'M CONSIDERING IT.
GOOD.
I THOUGHT YOU HATED THE IDEA. WHAT'S CHANGED?
NOTHING.
BY THE WAY, THAT **GIRL** KEEPS CALLING HERE. **JESSICA?** I ASKED HER NOT TO TIE UP THE LINE, BUT SAID I'D HAVE YOU CALL HER BACK. HERE'S HER NUMBER.
I ALREADY HAVE IT.

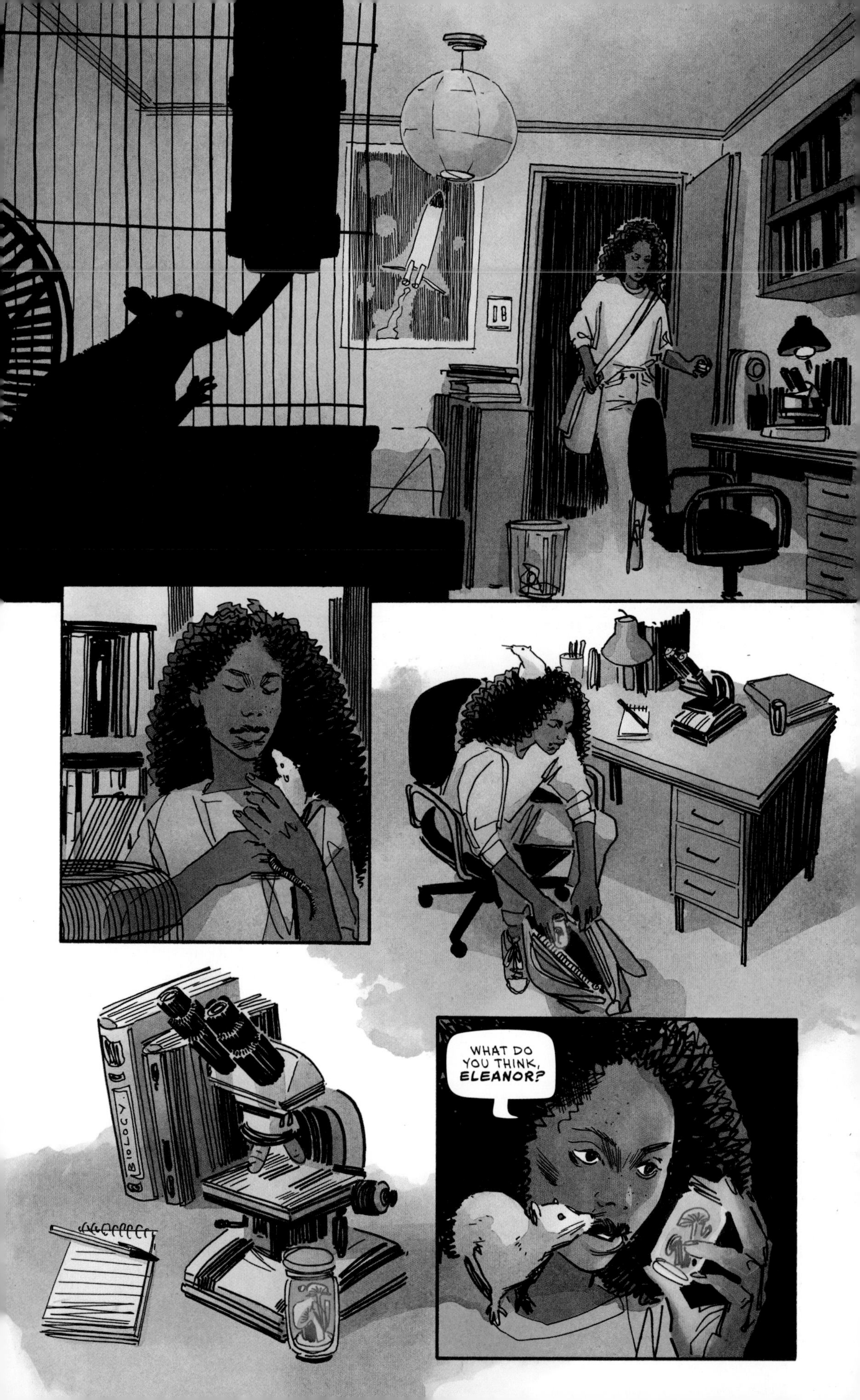
BIOLOGY
WHAT DO YOU THINK, ELEANOR?

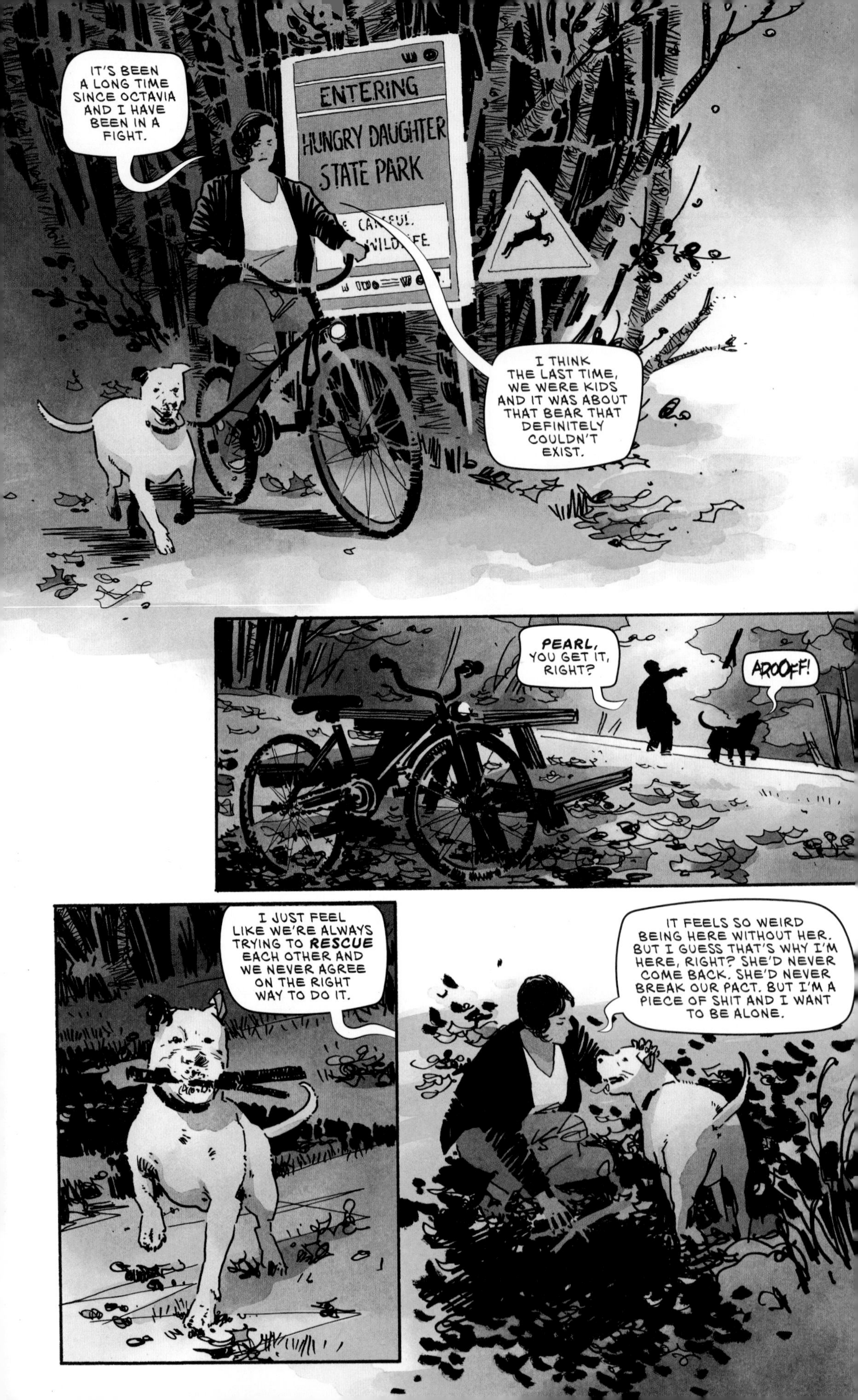
IT'S BEEN A LONG TIME SINCE OCTAVIA AND I HAVE BEEN IN A FIGHT.
ENTERING
HUNGRY DAUGHTER STATE PARK
I THINK THE LAST TIME, WE WERE KIDS AND IT WAS ABOUT THAT BEAR THAT DEFINITELY COULDN'T EXIST.
PEARL, YOU GET IT, RIGHT?
AROOFF!
I JUST FEEL LIKE WE'RE ALWAYS TRYING TO **RESCUE** EACH OTHER AND WE NEVER AGREE ON THE RIGHT WAY TO DO IT.
IT FEELS SO WEIRD BEING HERE WITHOUT HER. BUT I GUESS THAT'S WHY I'M HERE, RIGHT? SHE'D NEVER COME BACK. SHE'D NEVER BREAK OUR PACT. BUT I'M A PIECE OF SHIT AND I WANT TO BE ALONE.

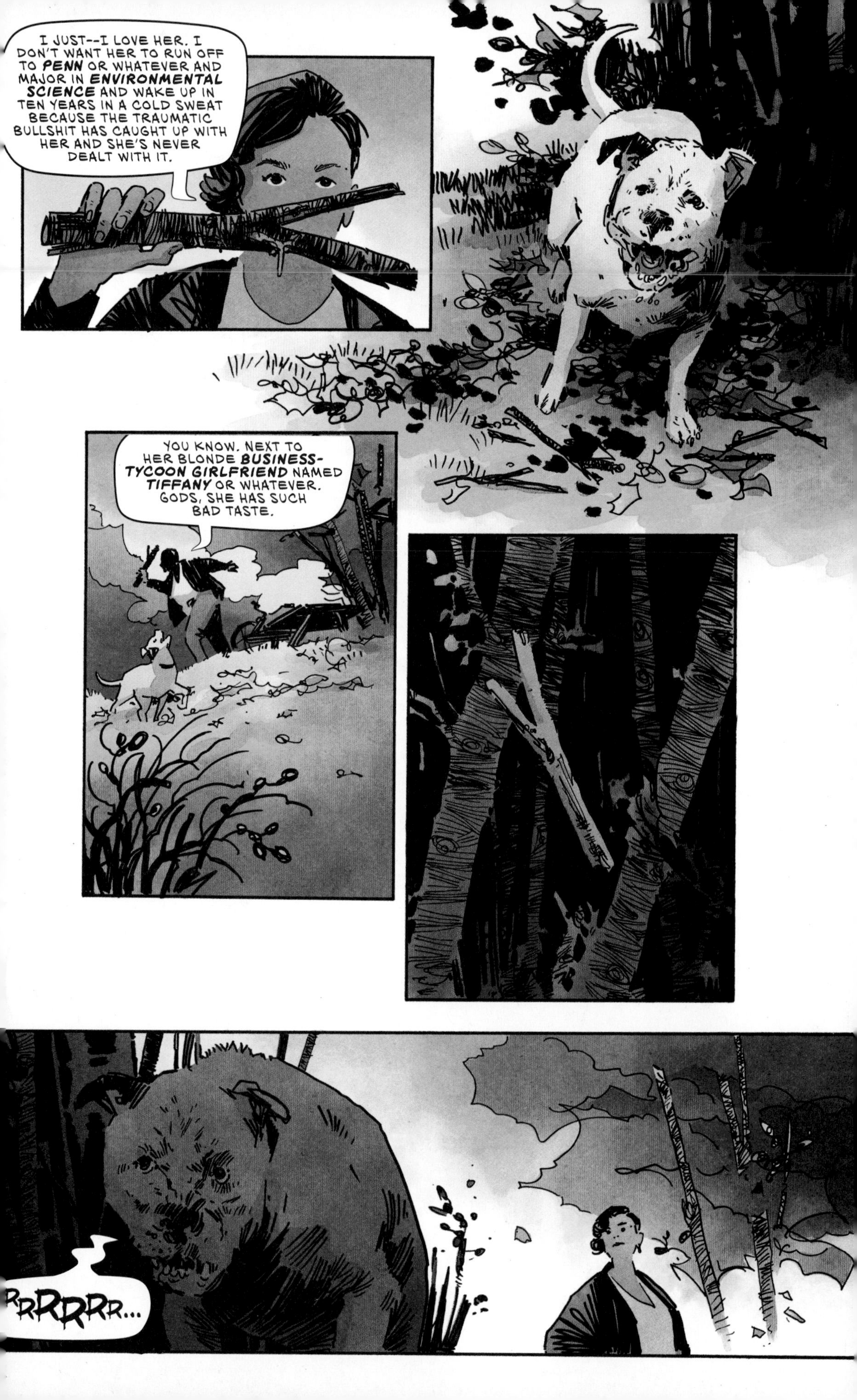
I JUST--I LOVE HER. I DON'T WANT HER TO RUN OFF TO **PENN** OR WHATEVER AND MAJOR IN **ENVIRONMENTAL SCIENCE** AND WAKE UP IN TEN YEARS IN A COLD SWEAT BECAUSE THE TRAUMATIC BULLSHIT HAS CAUGHT UP WITH HER AND SHE'S NEVER DEALT WITH IT.
YOU KNOW. NEXT TO HER BLONDE ***BUSINESS-TYCOON GIRLFRIEND*** NAMED ***TIFFANY*** OR WHATEVER. GODS, SHE HAS SUCH BAD TASTE.
RRRRRR...

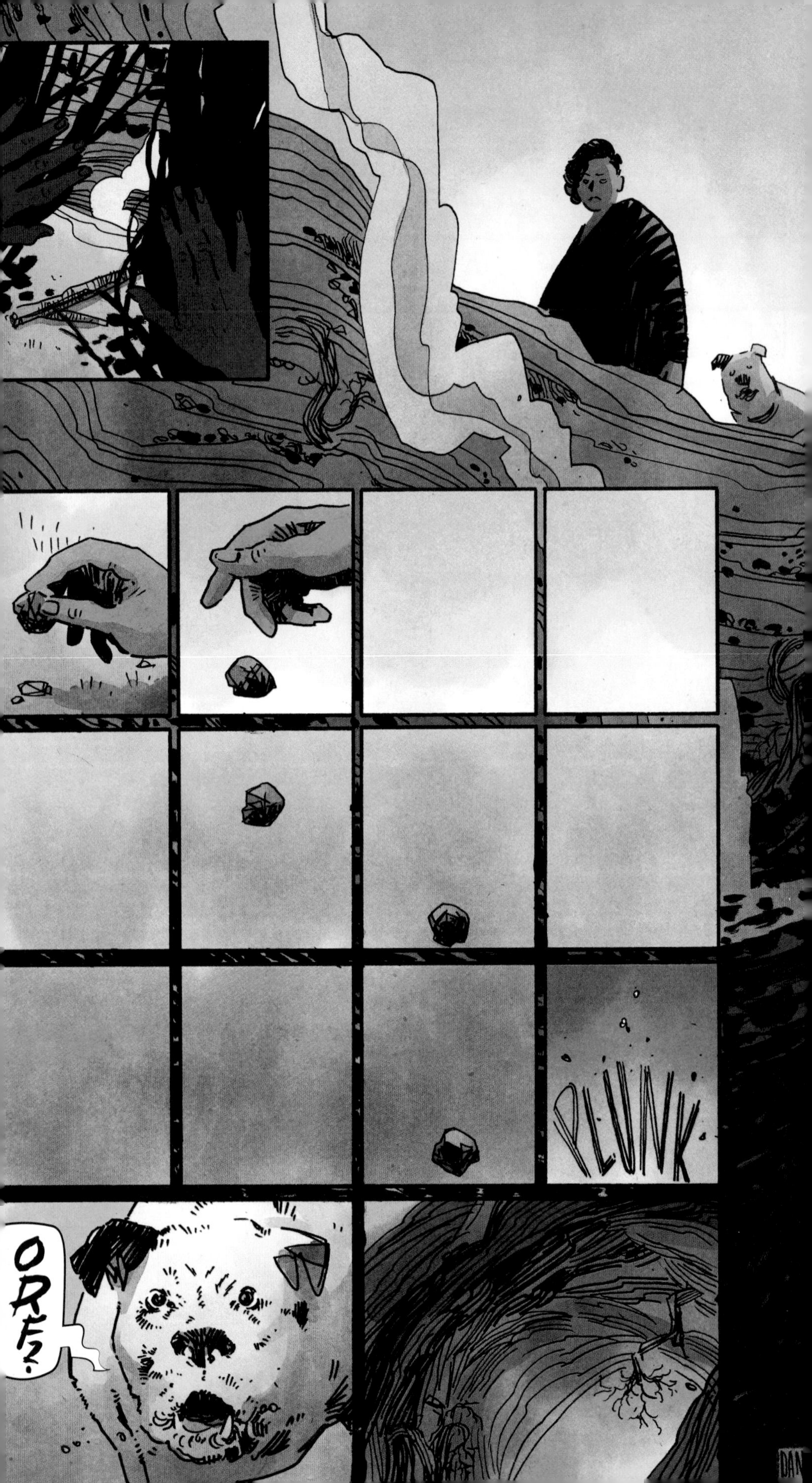
PLUNK
ORF?

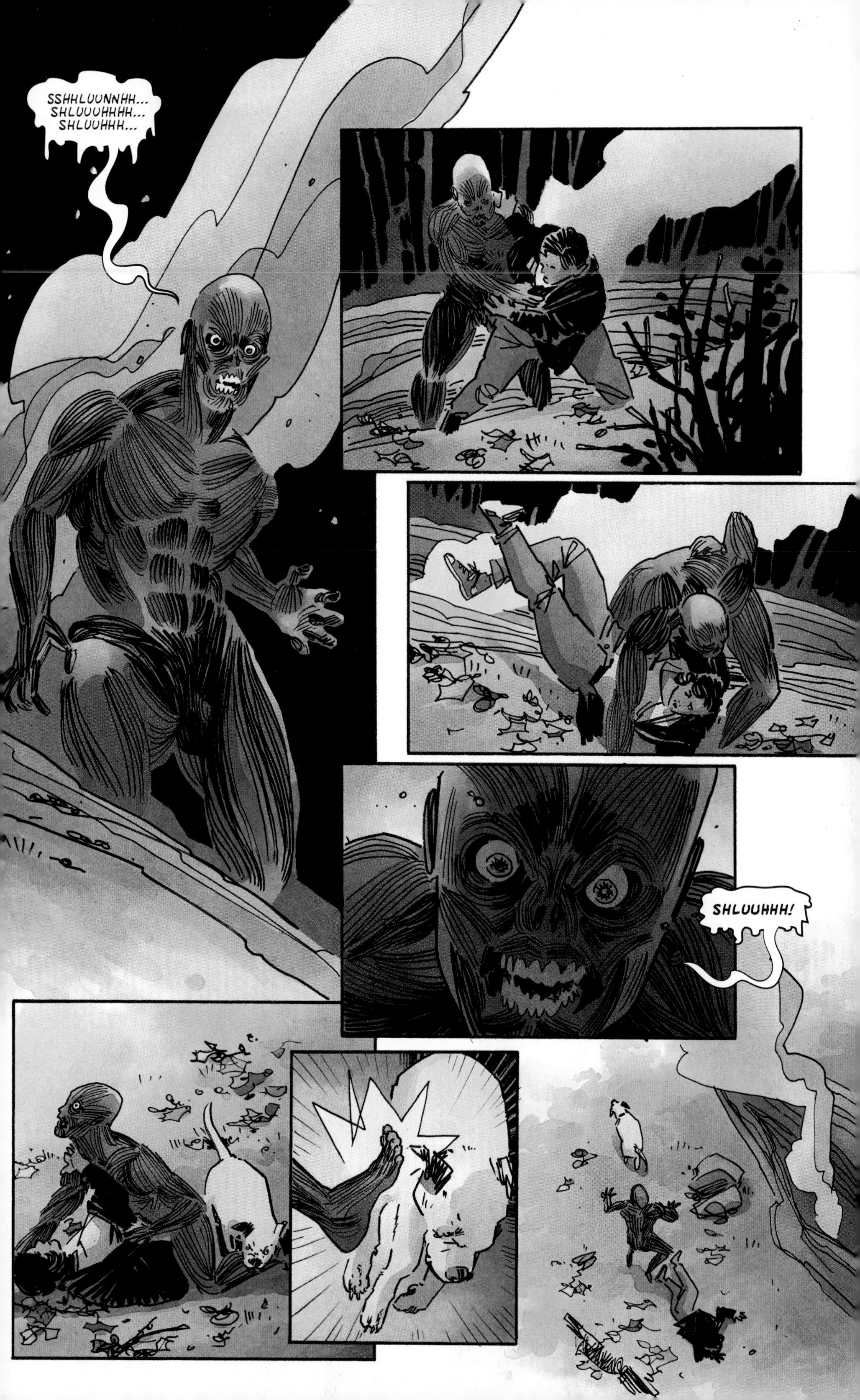
SSHHLUUNNHH...
SHLUUUHHHH...
SHLUUHHH...
SHLUUHHH!

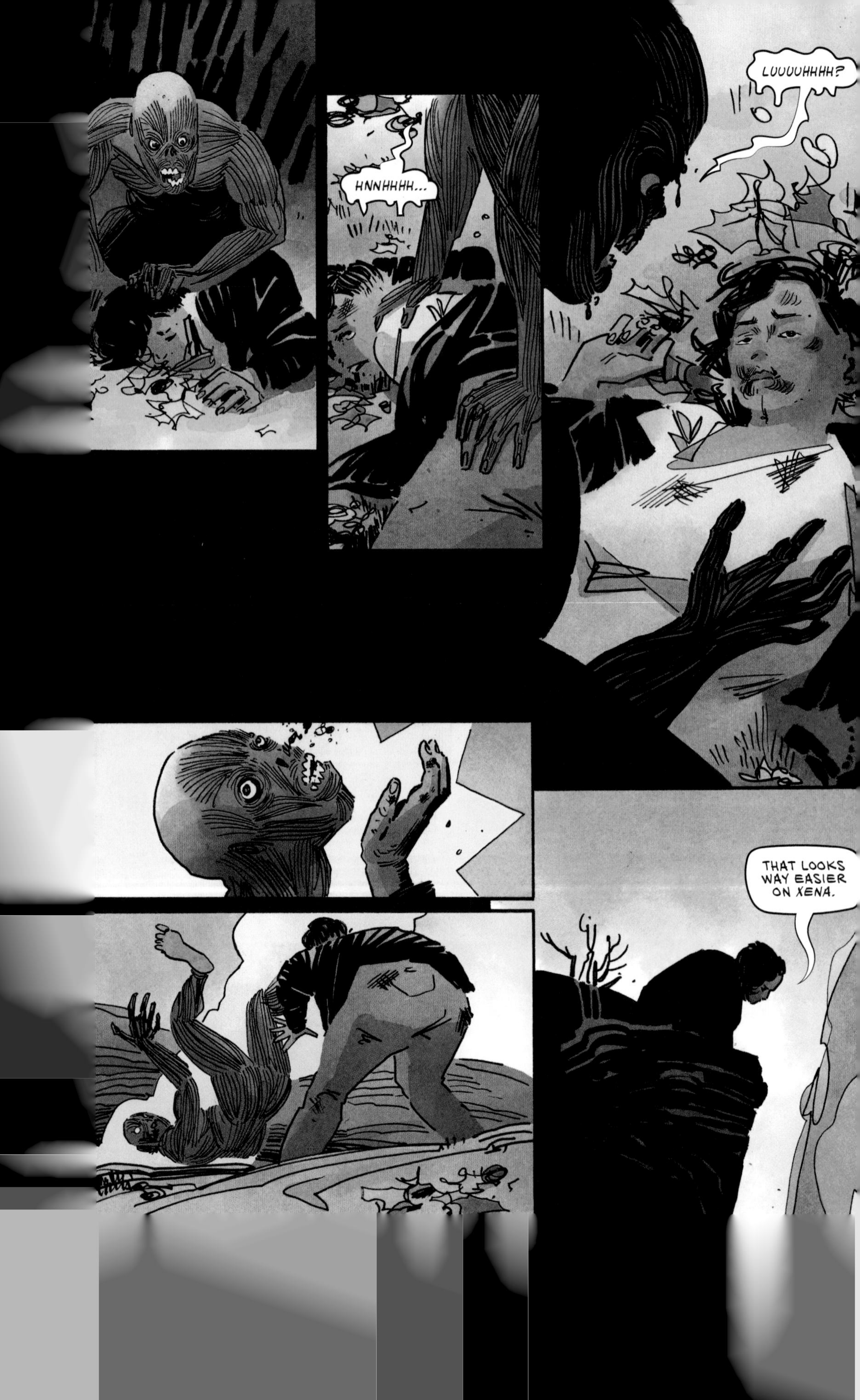
HNNHHHH...
LUUUUHHHH?
THAT LOOKS WAY EASIER ON XENA.

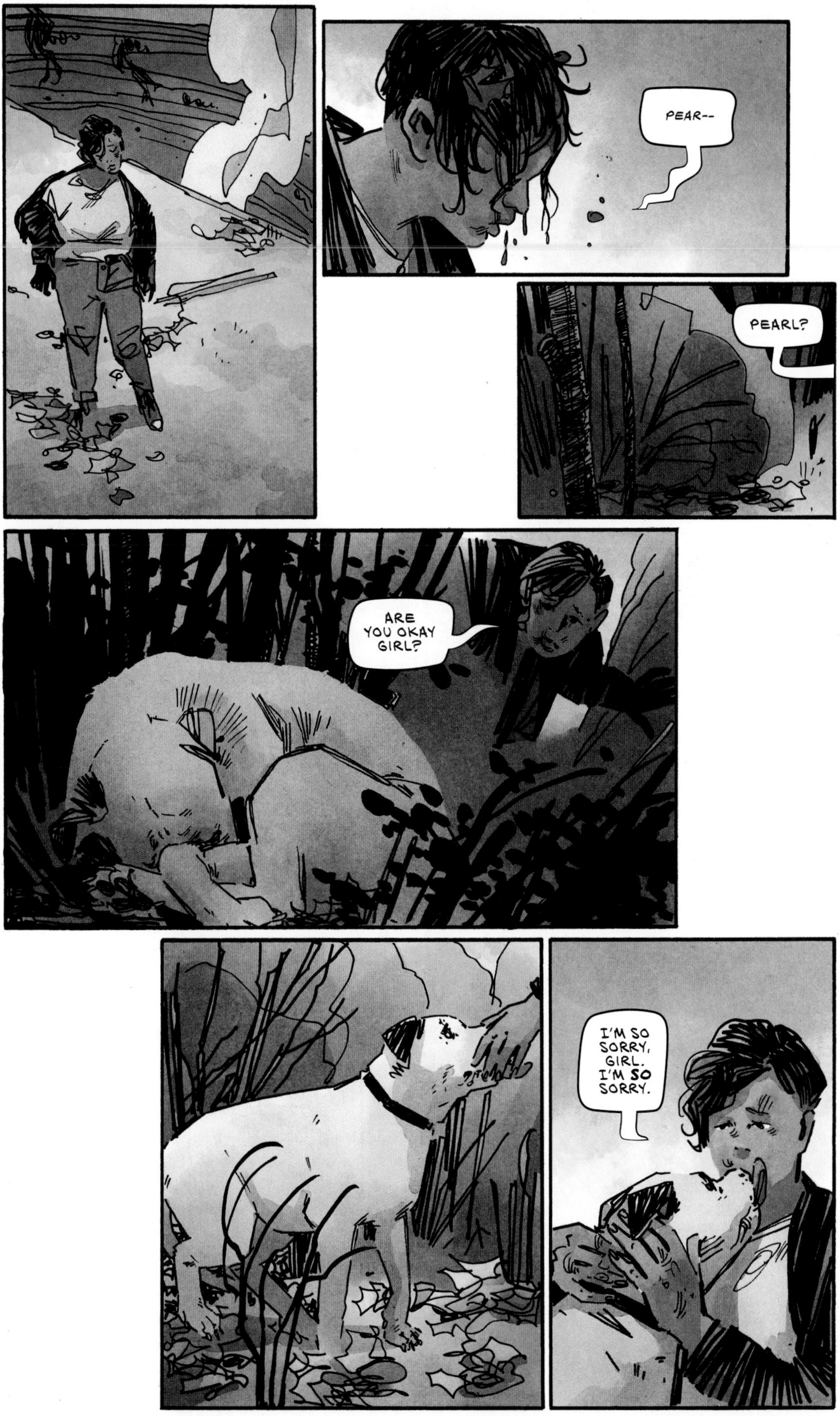
PEAR--
PEARL?
ARE YOU OKAY GIRL?
I'M SO SORRY, GIRL. I'M SO SORRY.

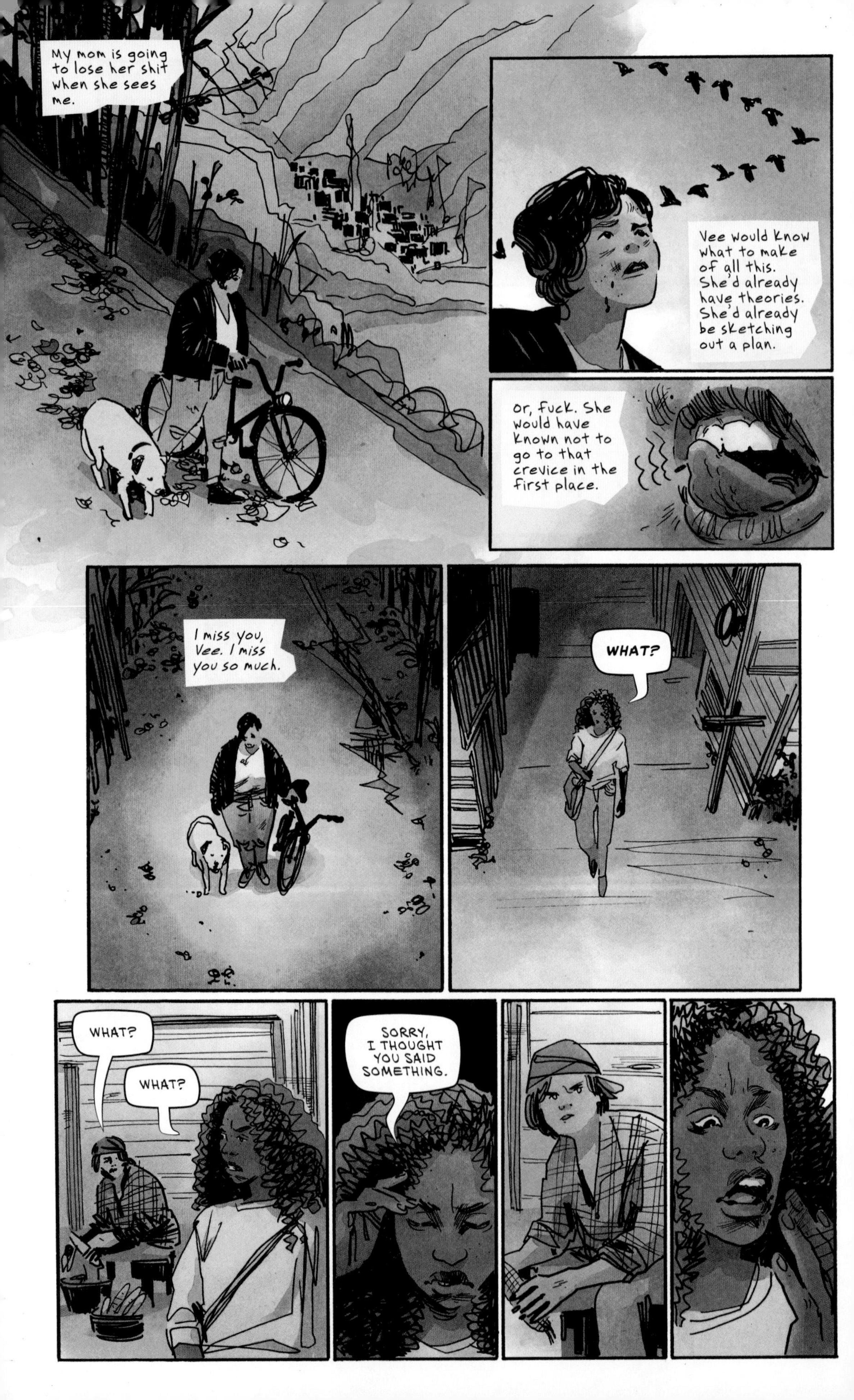
My mom is going to lose her shit when she sees me.
Vee would know what to make of all this. She'd already have theories. She'd already be sketching out a plan.
Or, fuck. She would have known not to go to that crevice in the first place.
I miss you, Vee. I miss you so much.
WHAT?
WHAT?
WHAT?
SORRY, I THOUGHT YOU SAID SOMETHING.

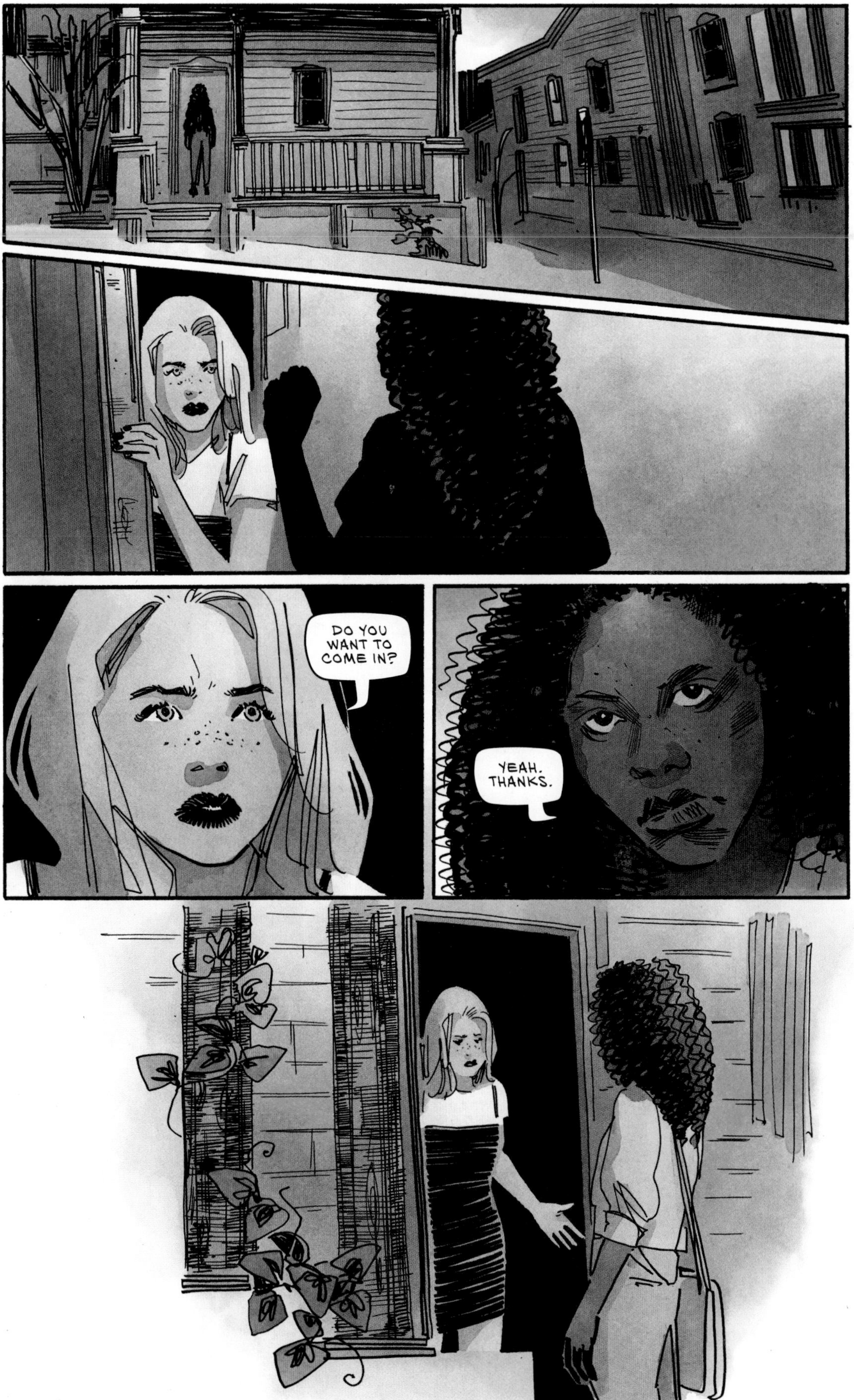
DO YOU WANT TO COME IN?
YEAH. THANKS.

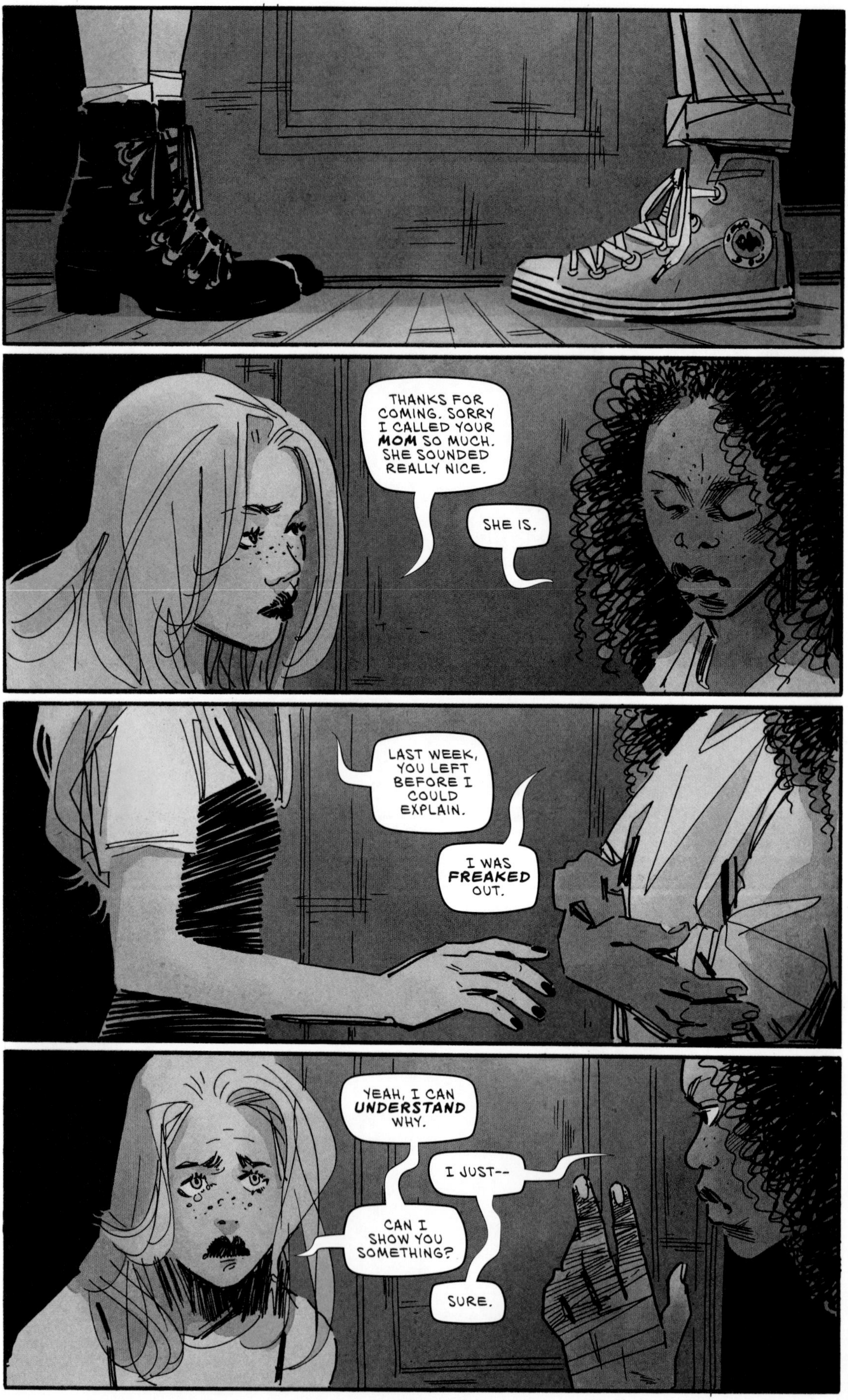
THANKS FOR COMING. SORRY I CALLED YOUR **MOM** SO MUCH. SHE SOUNDED REALLY NICE.
SHE IS.
LAST WEEK, YOU LEFT BEFORE I COULD EXPLAIN.
I WAS **FREAKED** OUT.
YEAH, I CAN **UNDERSTAND** WHY.
I JUST--
CAN I SHOW YOU SOMETHING?
SURE.

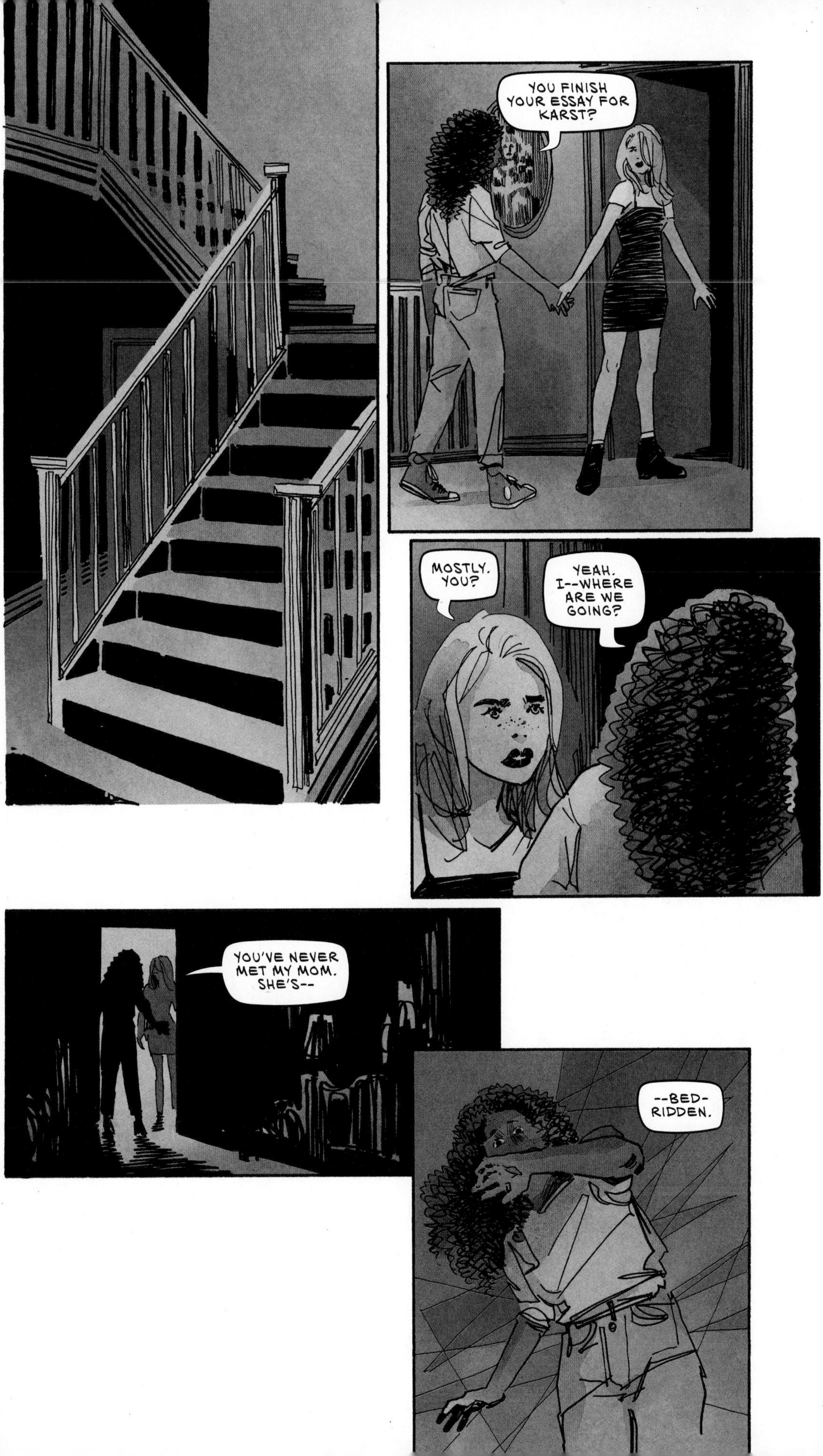
YOU FINISH YOUR ESSAY FOR KARST?
MOSTLY. YOU?
YEAH. I--WHERE ARE WE GOING?
YOU'VE NEVER MET MY MOM. SHE'S--
--BED-RIDDEN.

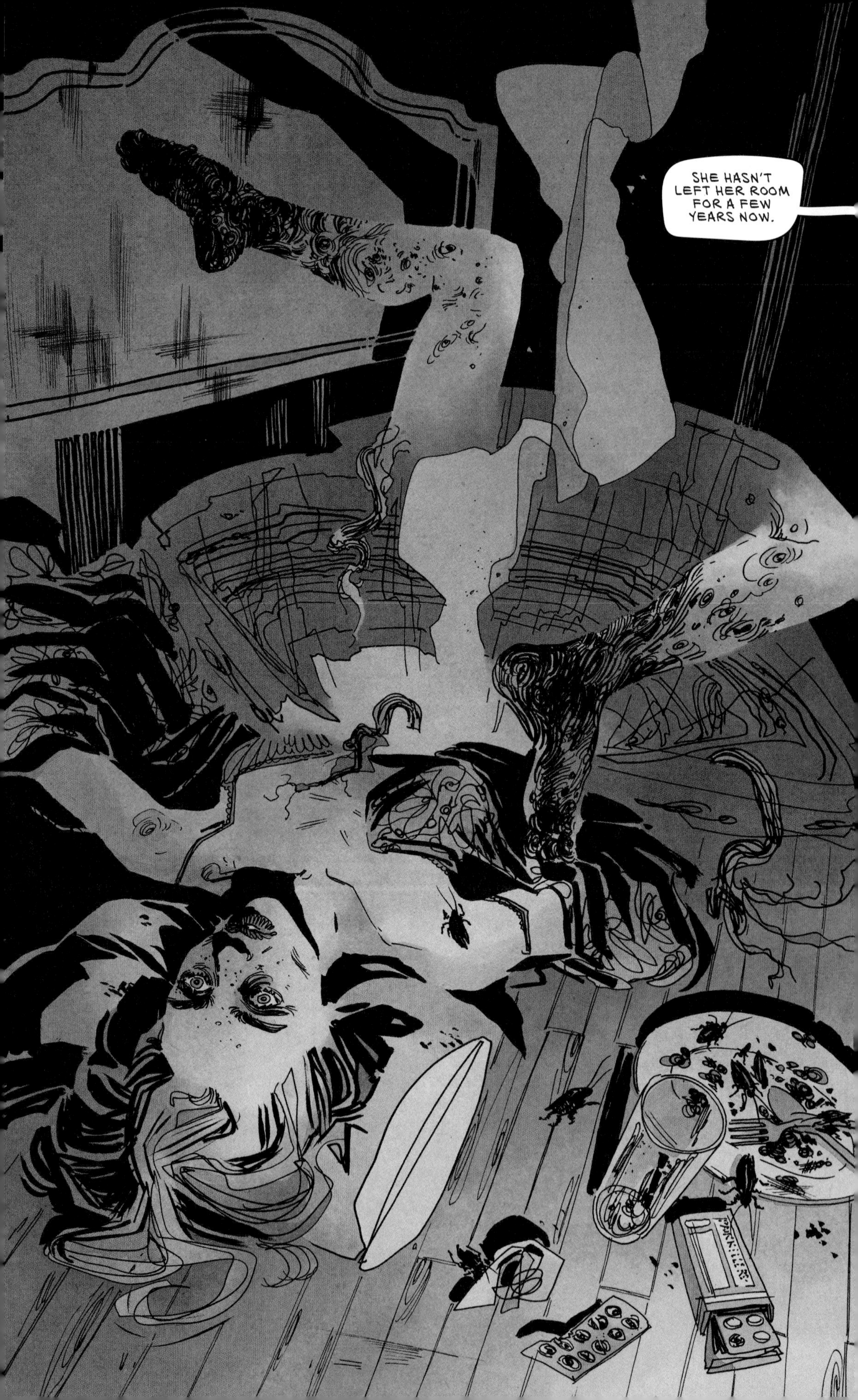
SHE HASN'T LEFT HER ROOM FOR A FEW YEARS NOW.

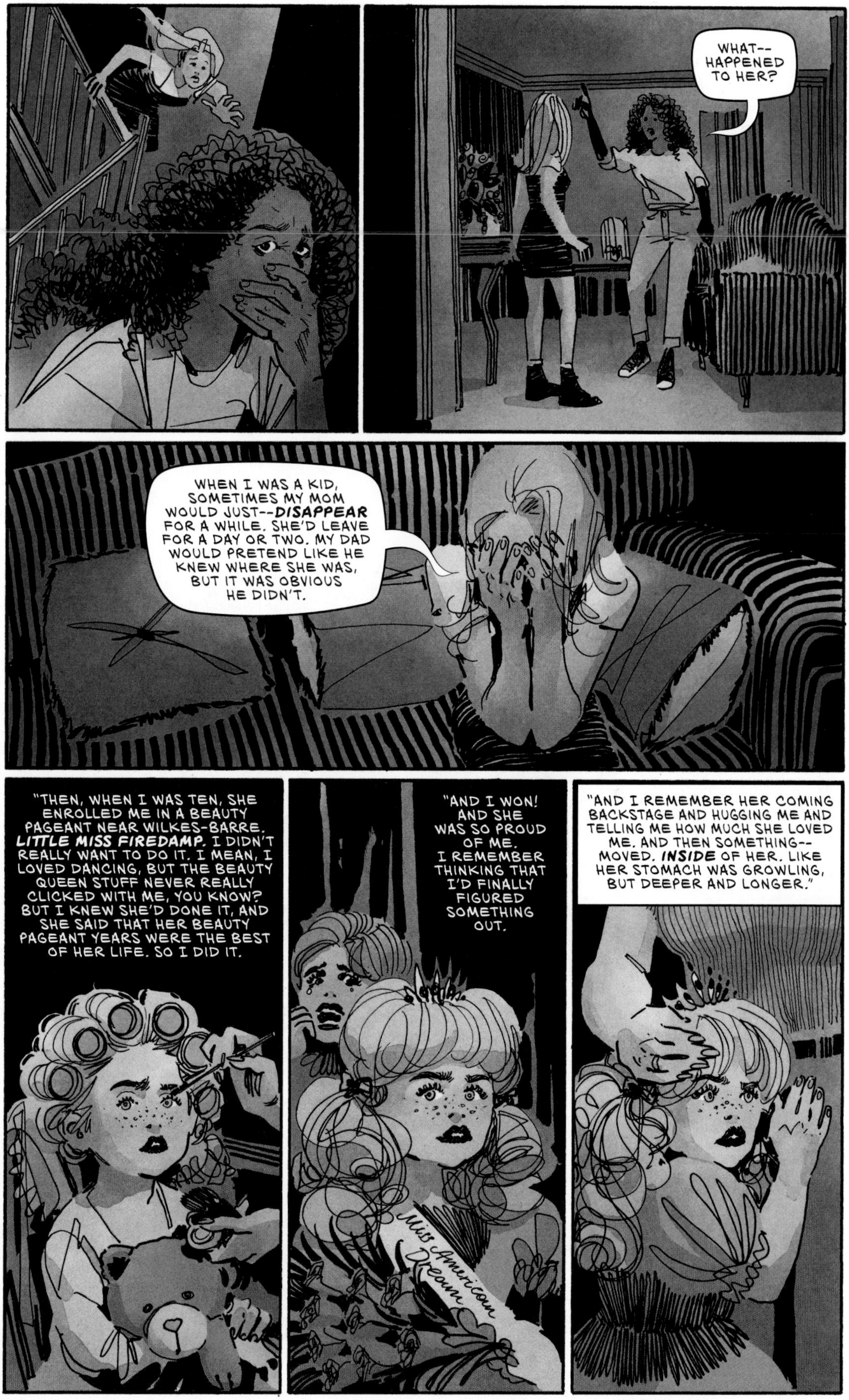
WHAT--
HAPPENED
TO HER?
WHEN I WAS A KID, SOMETIMES MY MOM WOULD JUST--*DISAPPEAR* FOR A WHILE. SHE'D LEAVE FOR A DAY OR TWO. MY DAD WOULD PRETEND LIKE HE KNEW WHERE SHE WAS, BUT IT WAS OBVIOUS HE DIDN'T.
"THEN, WHEN I WAS TEN, SHE ENROLLED ME IN A BEAUTY PAGEANT NEAR WILKES-BARRE. *LITTLE MISS FIREDAMP.* I DIDN'T REALLY WANT TO DO IT. I MEAN, I LOVED DANCING, BUT THE BEAUTY QUEEN STUFF NEVER REALLY CLICKED WITH ME, YOU KNOW? BUT I KNEW SHE'D DONE IT, AND SHE SAID THAT HER BEAUTY PAGEANT YEARS WERE THE BEST OF HER LIFE. SO I DID IT.
"AND I WON! AND SHE WAS SO PROUD OF ME. I REMEMBER THINKING THAT I'D FINALLY FIGURED SOMETHING OUT.
Miss American Dream
"AND I REMEMBER HER COMING BACKSTAGE AND HUGGING ME AND TELLING ME HOW MUCH SHE LOVED ME. AND THEN SOMETHING--MOVED. *INSIDE* OF HER. LIKE HER STOMACH WAS GROWLING, BUT DEEPER AND LONGER."

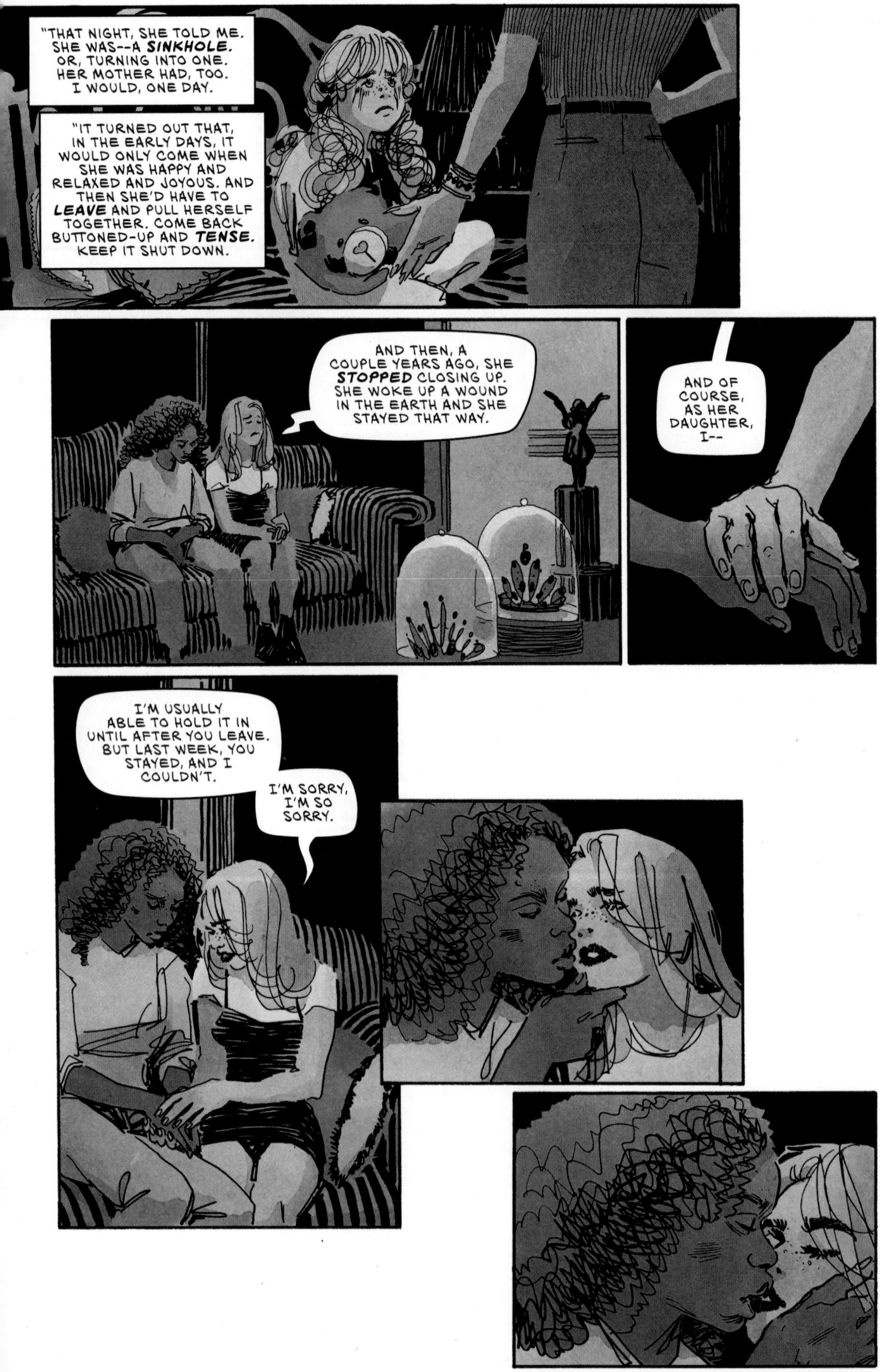
"THAT NIGHT, SHE TOLD ME. SHE WAS--A SINKHOLE. OR, TURNING INTO ONE. HER MOTHER HAD, TOO. I WOULD, ONE DAY.
"IT TURNED OUT THAT, IN THE EARLY DAYS, IT WOULD ONLY COME WHEN SHE WAS HAPPY AND RELAXED AND JOYOUS. AND THEN SHE'D HAVE TO LEAVE AND PULL HERSELF TOGETHER. COME BACK BUTTONED-UP AND TENSE. KEEP IT SHUT DOWN.
AND THEN, A COUPLE YEARS AGO, SHE STOPPED CLOSING UP. SHE WOKE UP A WOUND IN THE EARTH AND SHE STAYED THAT WAY.
AND OF COURSE, AS HER DAUGHTER, I--
I'M USUALLY ABLE TO HOLD IT IN UNTIL AFTER YOU LEAVE. BUT LAST WEEK, YOU STAYED, AND I COULDN'T.
I'M SORRY, I'M SO SORRY.

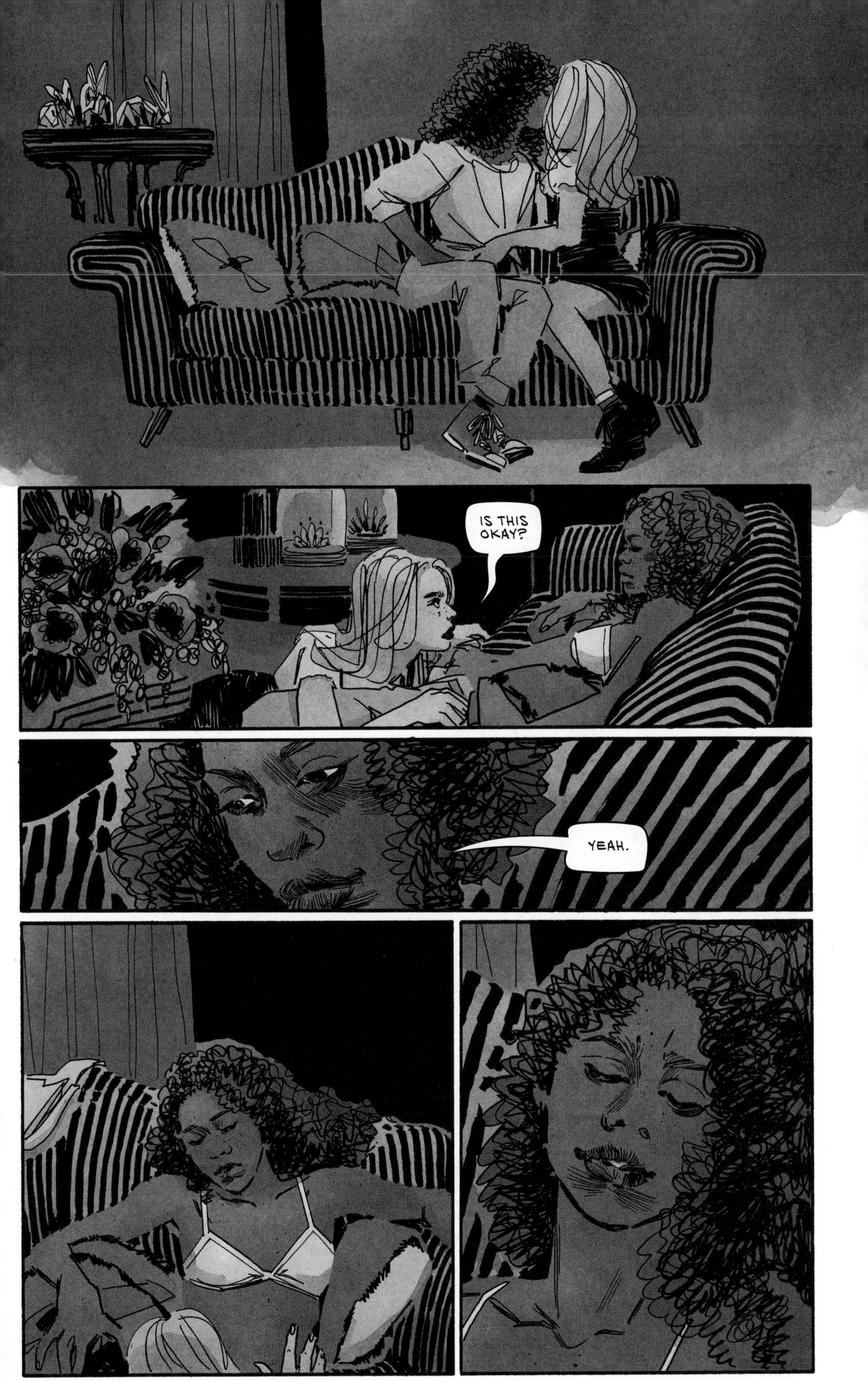
IS THIS OKAY?
YEAH.

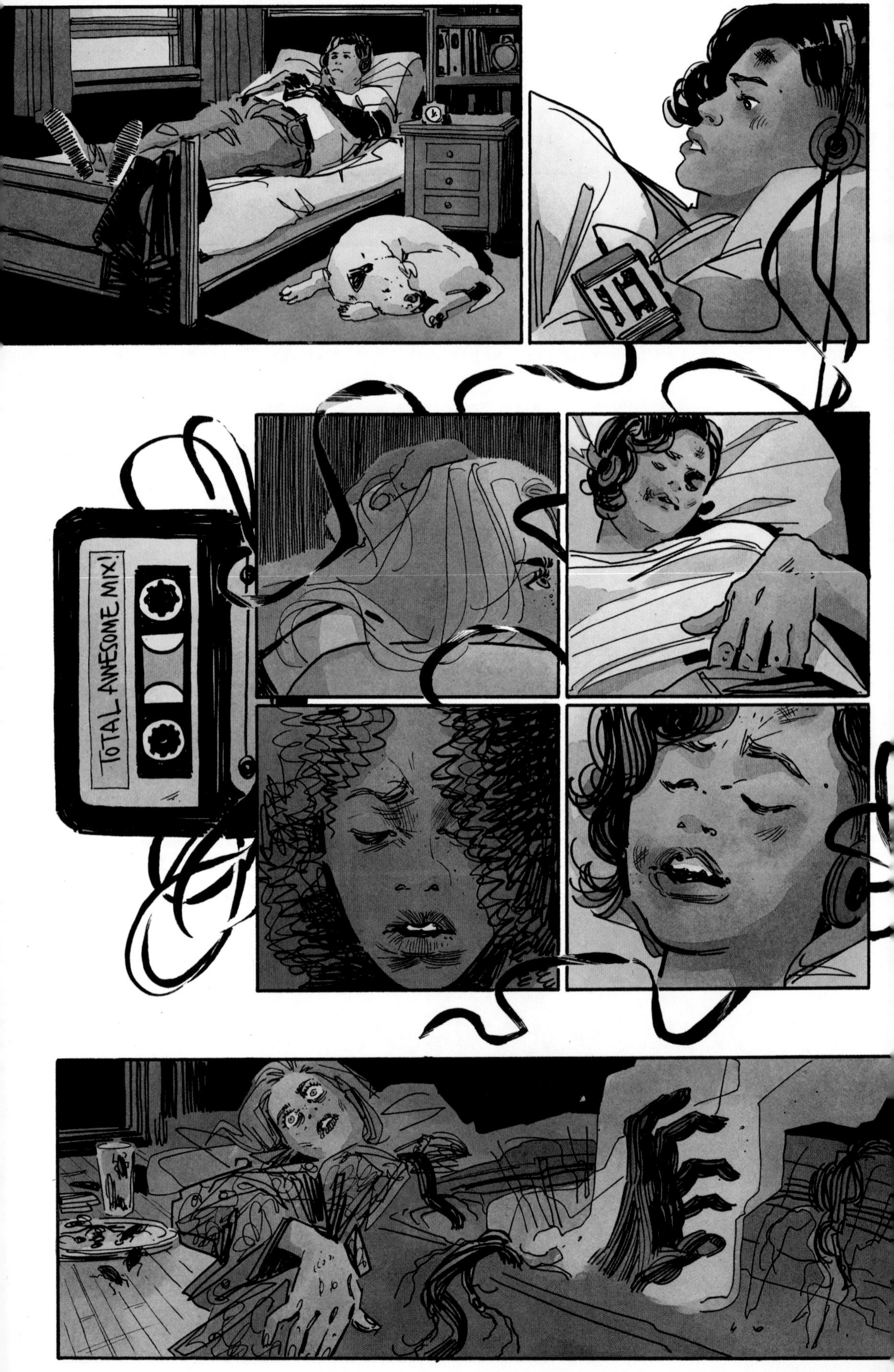
TOTAL AWESOME MIX!

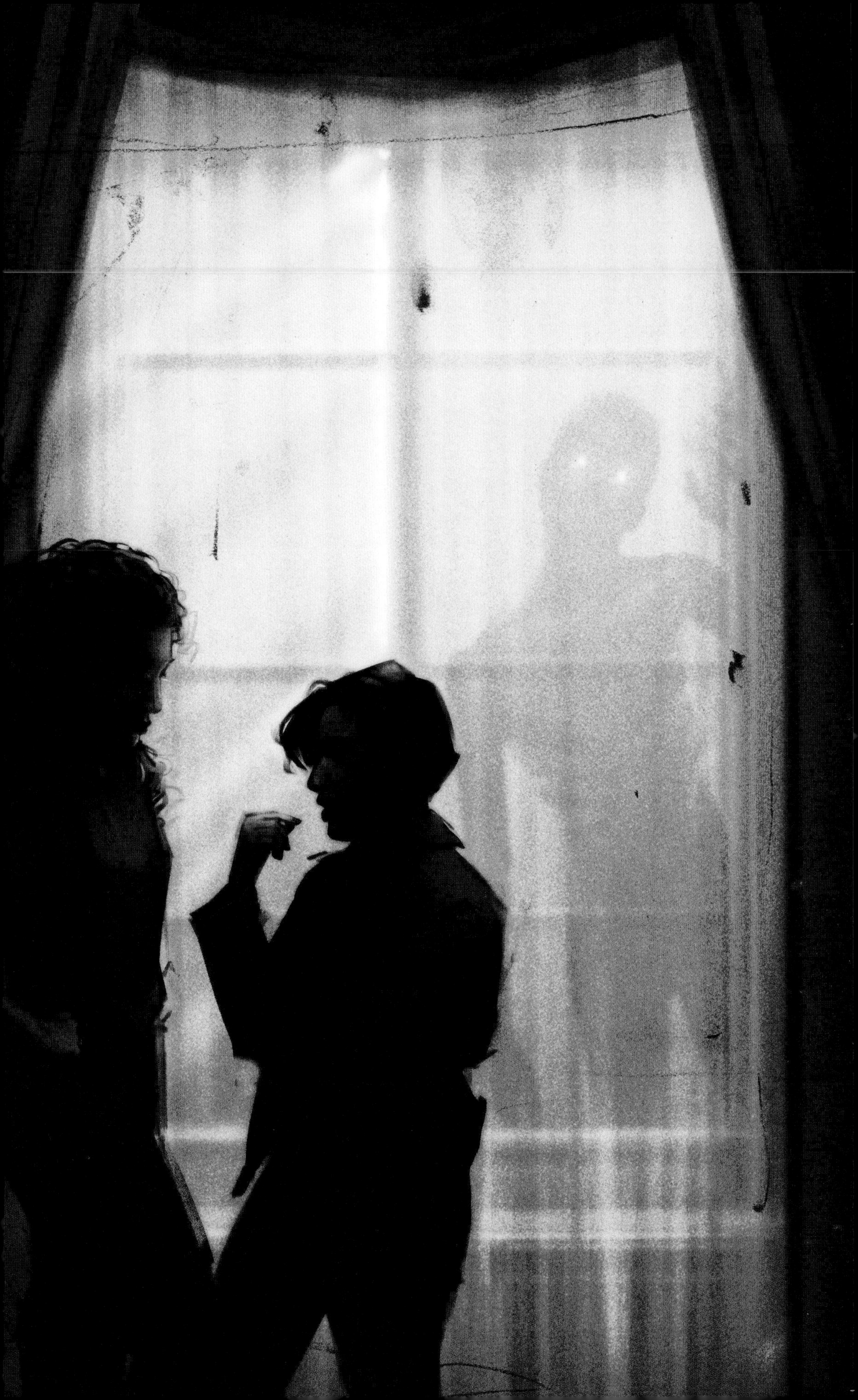

Einstein on the Beach

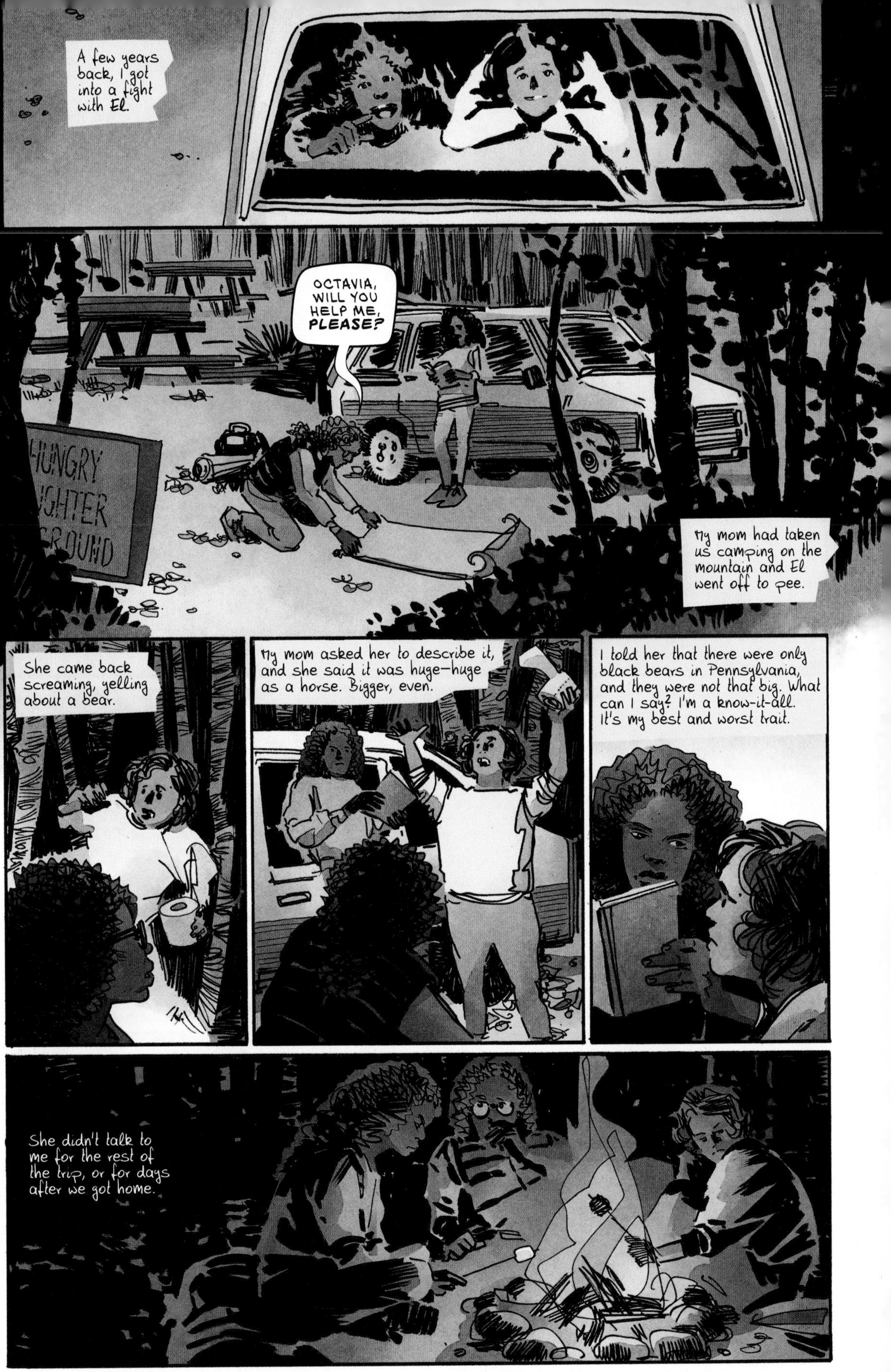

A few years back, I got into a fight with El.
OCTAVIA, WILL YOU HELP ME, **PLEASE?**
HUNGRY
IGHTER
GROUND
My mom had taken us camping on the mountain and El went off to pee.
She came back screaming, yelling about a bear.
My mom asked her to describe it, and she said it was huge—huge as a horse. Bigger, even.
I told her that there were only black bears in Pennsylvania, and they were not that big. What can I say? I'm a know-it-all. It's my best and worst trait.
She didn't talk to me for the rest of the trip, or for days after we got home.

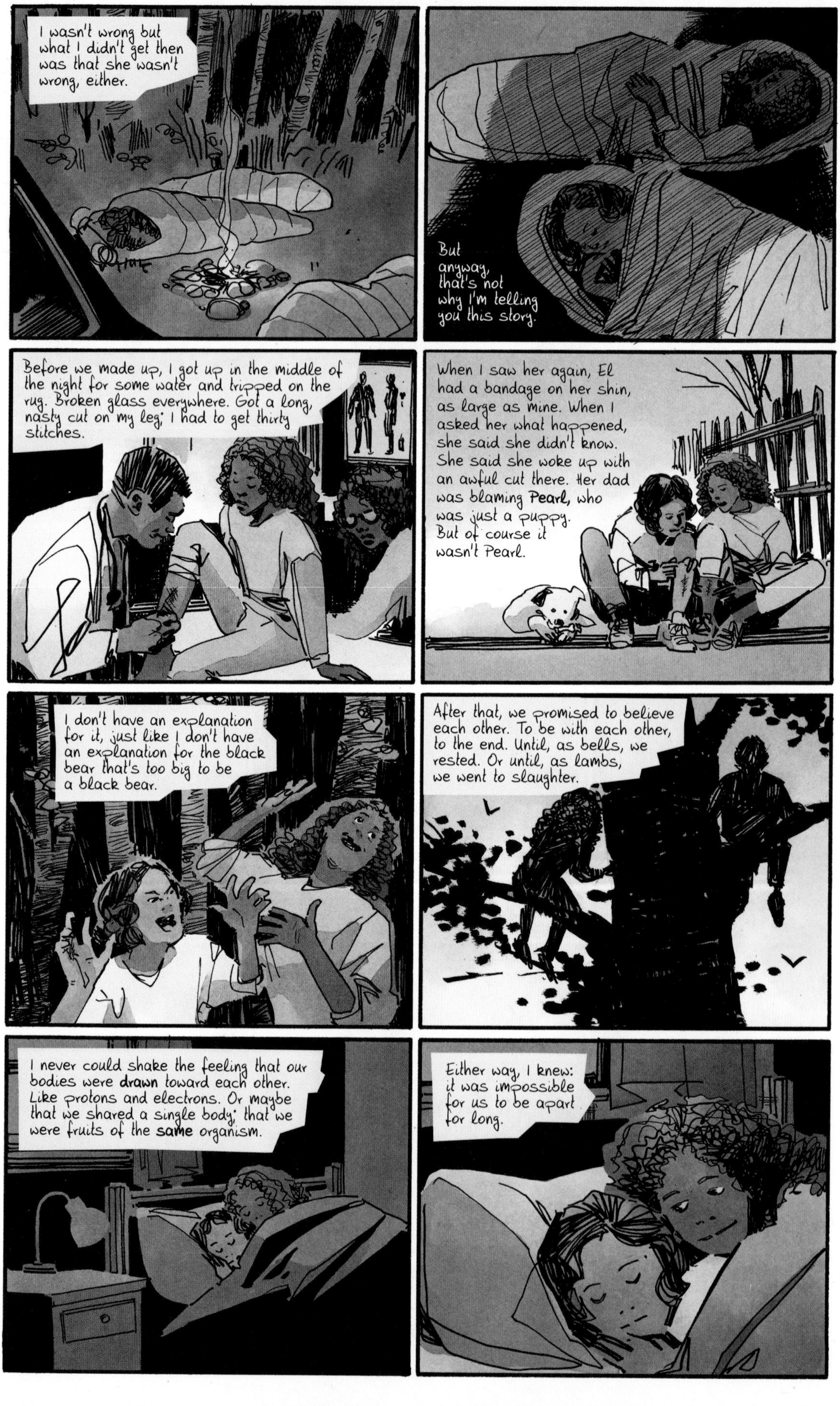
I wasn't wrong but what I didn't get then was that she wasn't wrong, either.
But anyway, that's not why I'm telling you this story.
Before we made up, I got up in the middle of the night for some water and tripped on the rug. Broken glass everywhere. Got a long, nasty cut on my leg; I had to get thirty stitches.
When I saw her again, El had a bandage on her shin, as large as mine. When I asked her what happened, she said she didn't know. She said she woke up with an awful cut there. Her dad was blaming **Pearl**, who was just a puppy. But of course it wasn't Pearl.
I don't have an explanation for it, just like I don't have an explanation for the black bear that's too big to be a black bear.
After that, we promised to believe each other. To be with each other, to the end. Until, as bells, we rested. Or until, as lambs, we went to slaughter.
I never could shake the feeling that our bodies were **drawn** toward each other. Like protons and electrons. Or maybe that we shared a single body; that we were fruits of the **same** organism.
Either way, I **knew**: it was impossible for us to be apart for long.

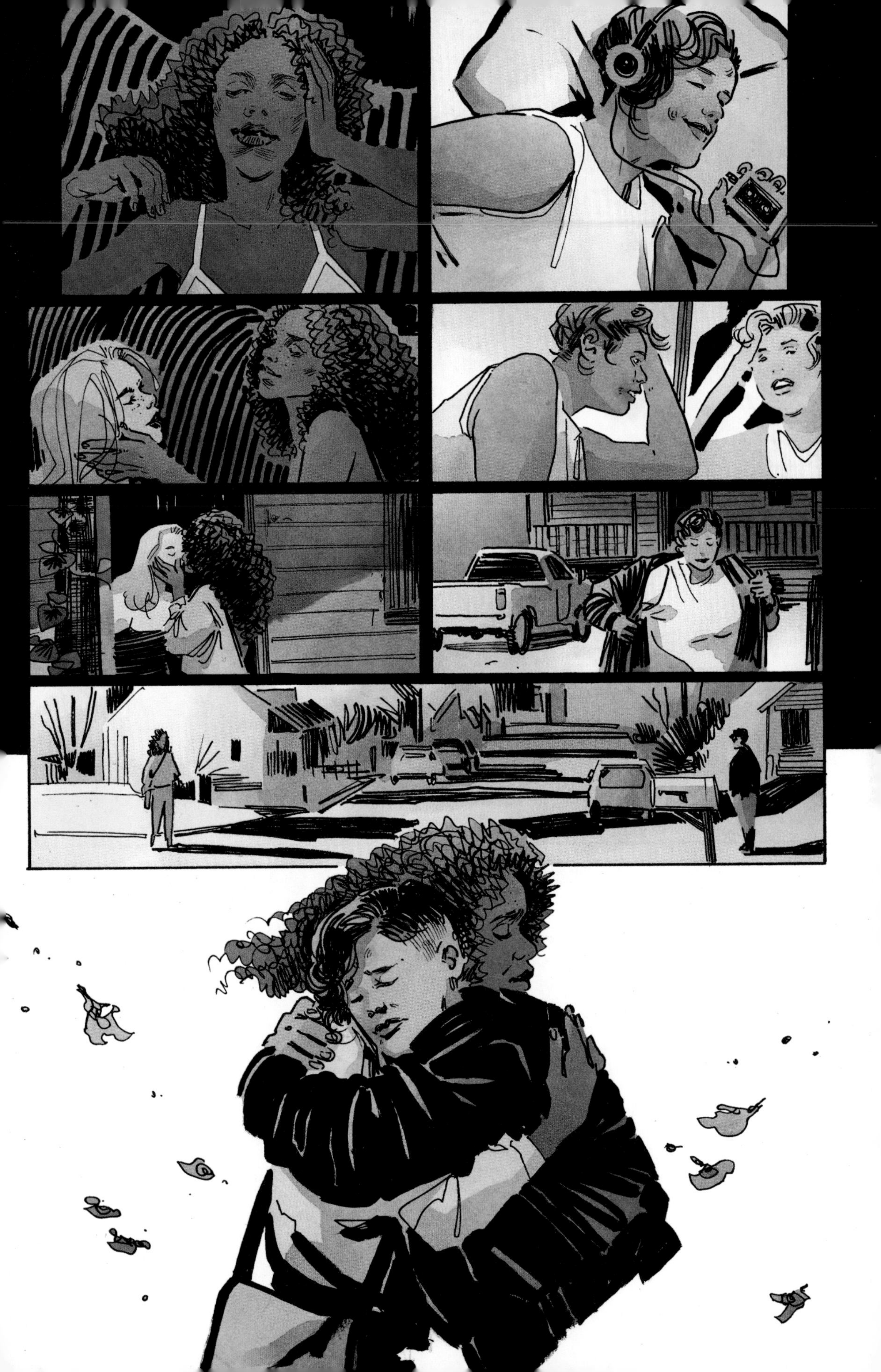

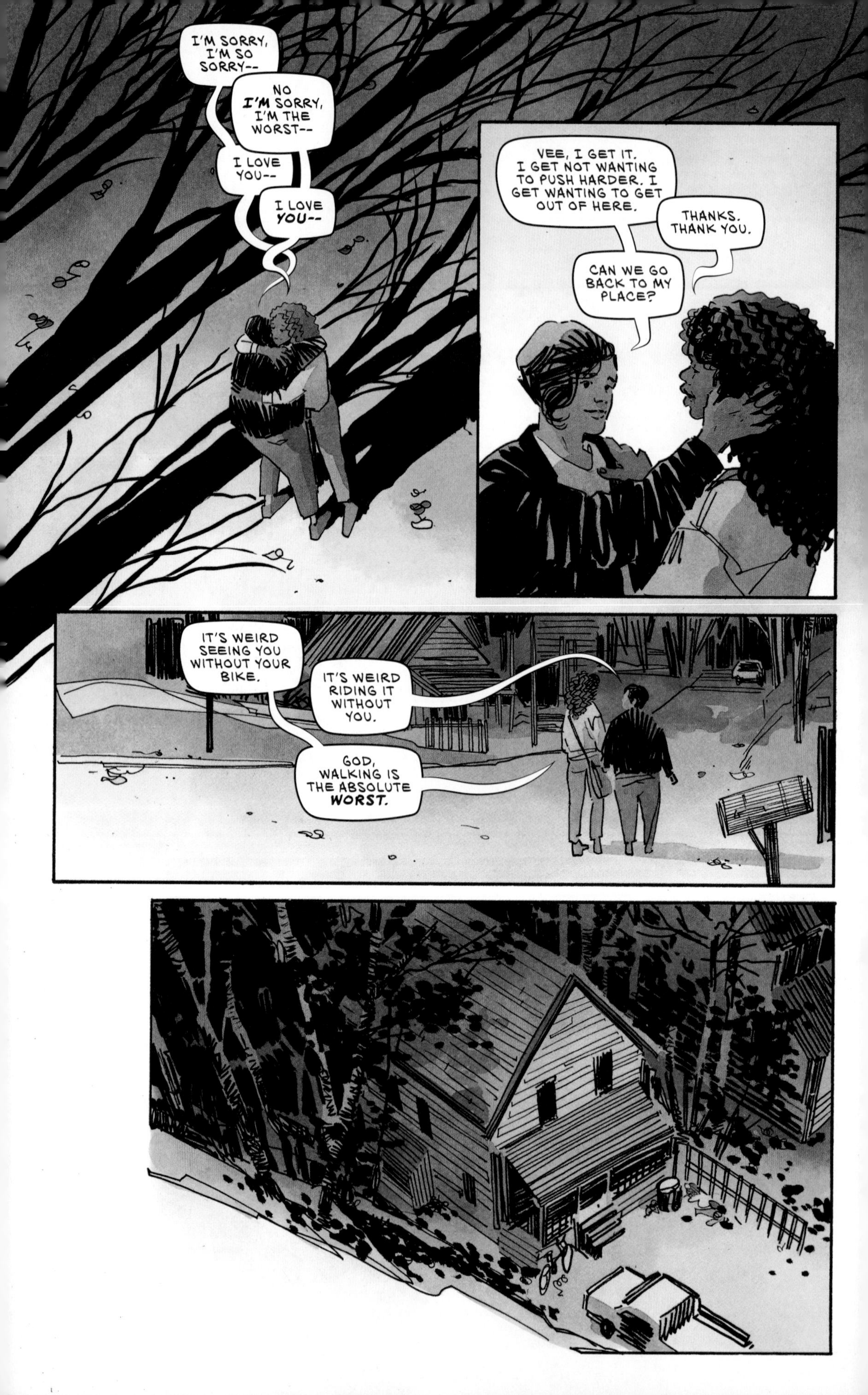
I'M SORRY, I'M SO SORRY--
NO I'M SORRY, I'M THE WORST--
I LOVE YOU--
I LOVE YOU--
VEE, I GET IT. I GET NOT WANTING TO PUSH HARDER. I GET WANTING TO GET OUT OF HERE.
THANKS. THANK YOU.
CAN WE GO BACK TO MY PLACE?
IT'S WEIRD SEEING YOU WITHOUT YOUR BIKE.
IT'S WEIRD RIDING IT WITHOUT YOU.
GOD, WALKING IS THE ABSOLUTE WORST.

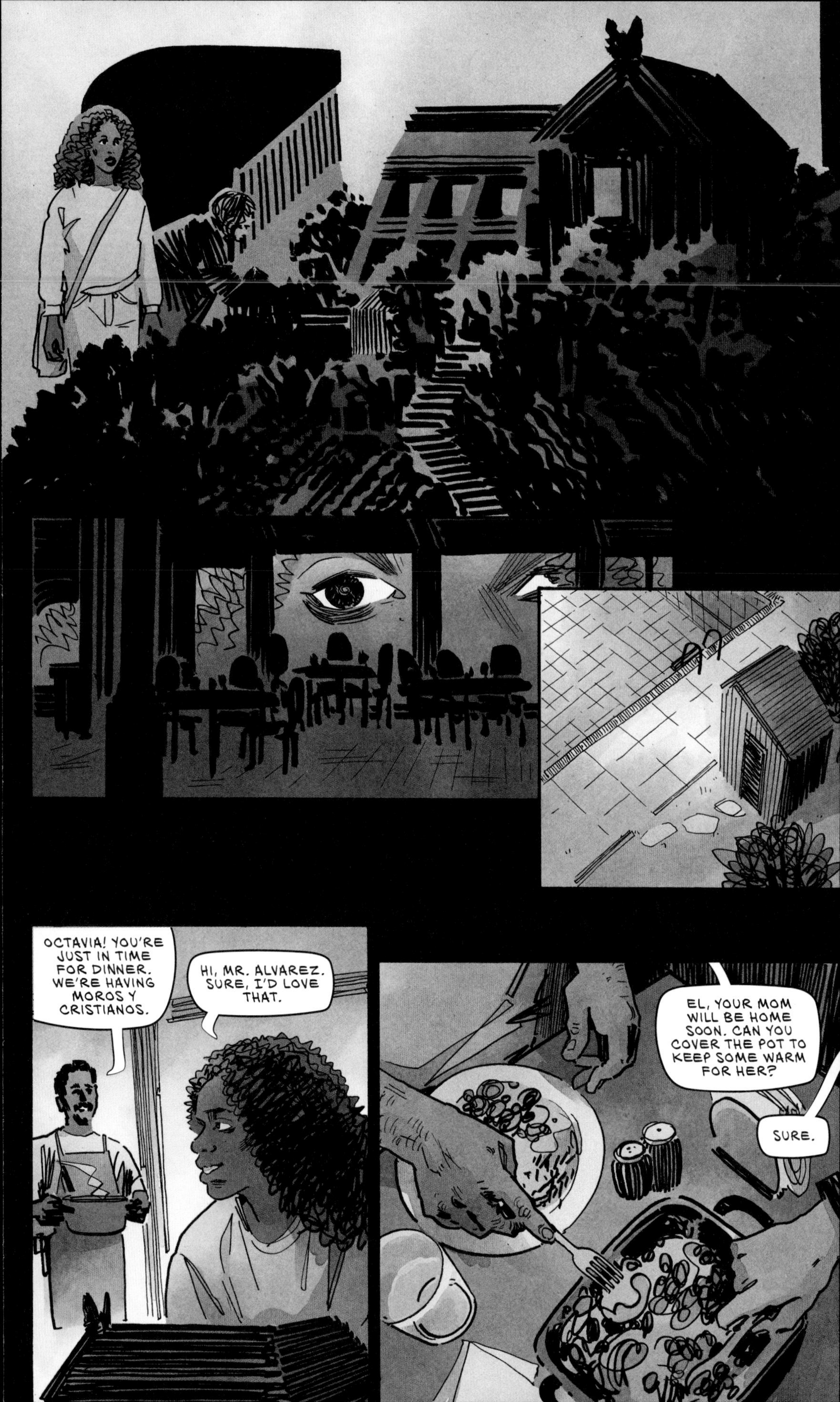
OCTAVIA! YOU'RE JUST IN TIME FOR DINNER. WE'RE HAVING MOROS Y CRISTIANOS.
HI, MR. ALVAREZ. SURE, I'D LOVE THAT.
EL, YOUR MOM WILL BE HOME SOON. CAN YOU COVER THE POT TO KEEP SOME WARM FOR HER?
SURE.

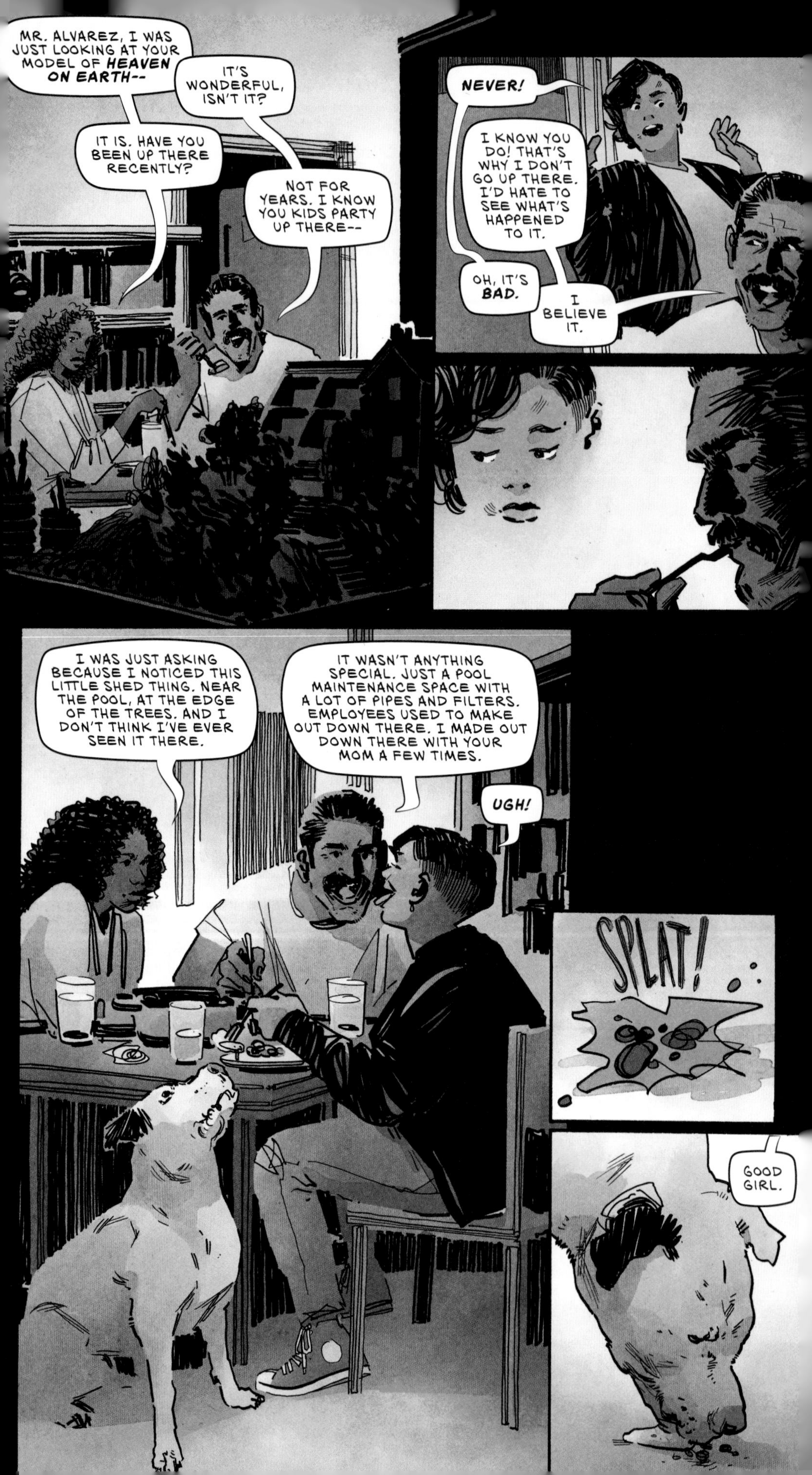
MR. ALVAREZ, I WAS JUST LOOKING AT YOUR MODEL OF **HEAVEN ON EARTH**--
IT'S WONDERFUL, ISN'T IT?
IT IS. HAVE YOU BEEN UP THERE RECENTLY?
NOT FOR YEARS. I KNOW YOU KIDS PARTY UP THERE--
NEVER!
I KNOW YOU DO! THAT'S WHY I DON'T GO UP THERE. I'D HATE TO SEE WHAT'S HAPPENED TO IT.
OH, IT'S **BAD.**
I BELIEVE IT.
I WAS JUST ASKING BECAUSE I NOTICED THIS LITTLE SHED THING. NEAR THE POOL, AT THE EDGE OF THE TREES. AND I DON'T THINK I'VE EVER SEEN IT THERE.
IT WASN'T ANYTHING SPECIAL. JUST A POOL MAINTENANCE SPACE WITH A LOT OF PIPES AND FILTERS. EMPLOYEES USED TO MAKE OUT DOWN THERE. I MADE OUT DOWN THERE WITH YOUR MOM A FEW TIMES.
UGH!
SPLAT!
GOOD GIRL.

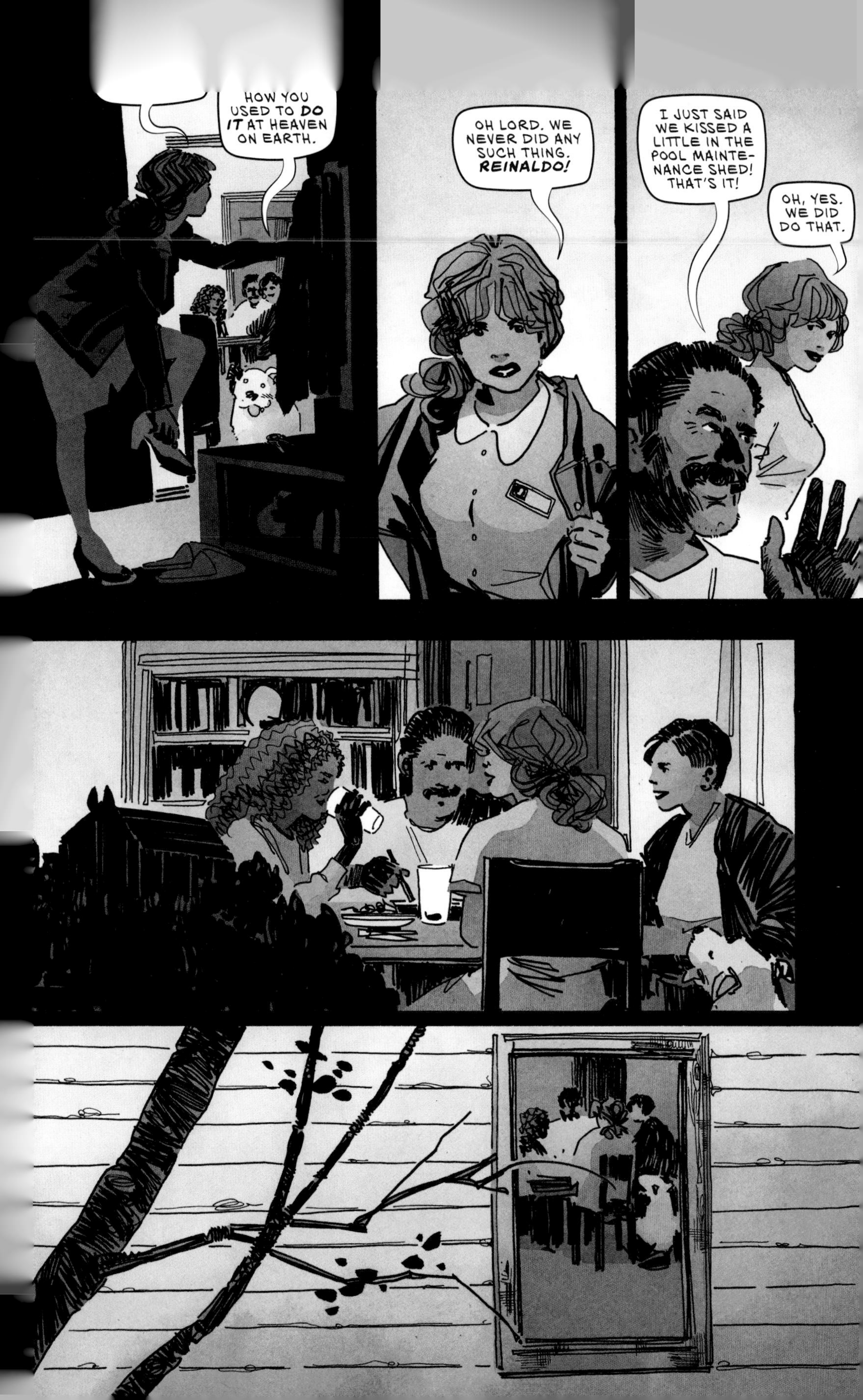
HOW YOU USED TO DO IT AT HEAVEN ON EARTH.
OH LORD. WE NEVER DID ANY SUCH THING. REINALDO!
I JUST SAID WE KISSED A LITTLE IN THE POOL MAINTE-NANCE SHED! THAT'S IT!
OH, YES. WE DID DO THAT.

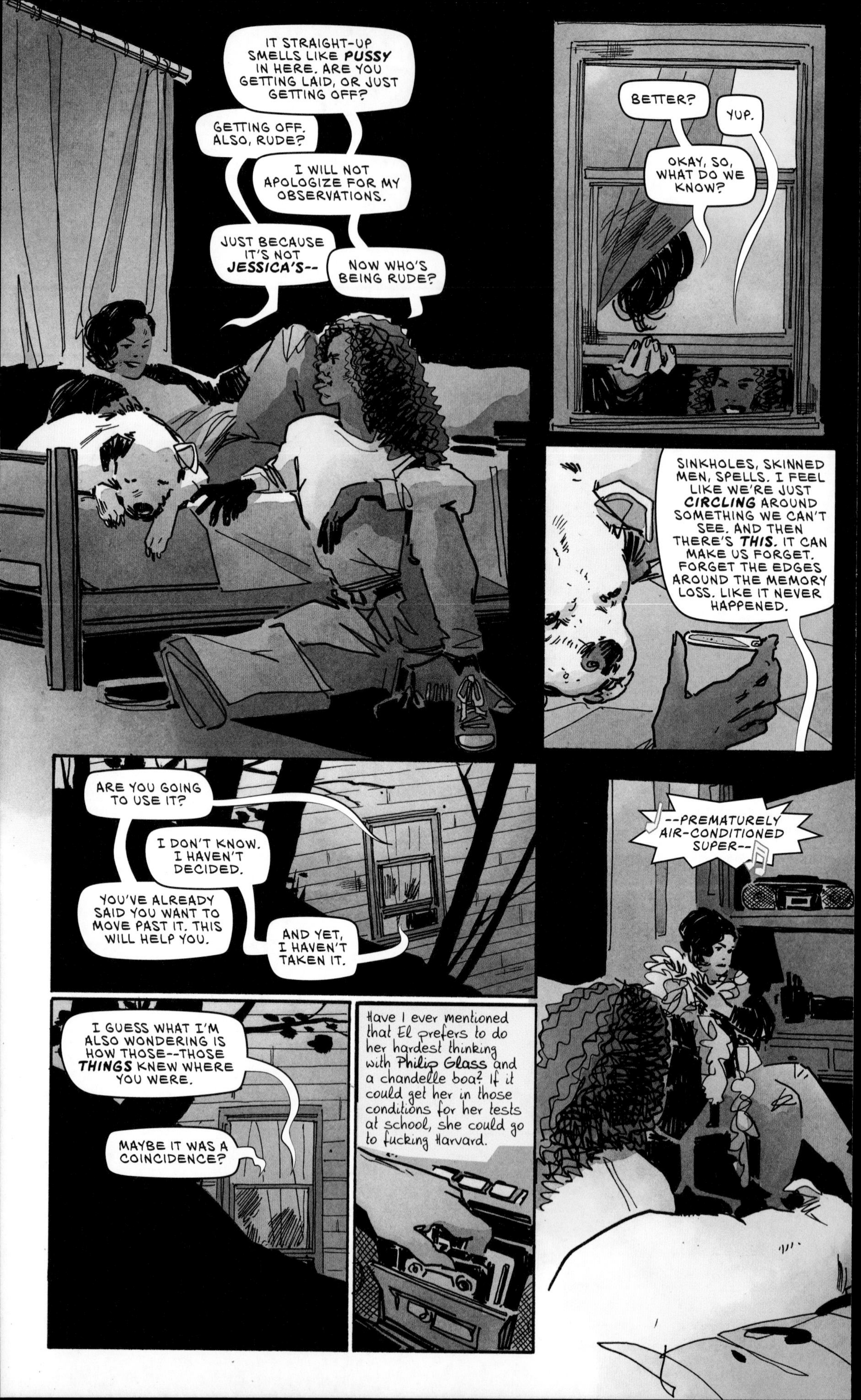
IT STRAIGHT-UP SMELLS LIKE PUSSY IN HERE. ARE YOU GETTING LAID, OR JUST GETTING OFF?
GETTING OFF. ALSO, RUDE?
I WILL NOT APOLOGIZE FOR MY OBSERVATIONS.
JUST BECAUSE IT'S NOT JESSICA'S--
NOW WHO'S BEING RUDE?
BETTER?
YUP.
OKAY, SO, WHAT DO WE KNOW?
SINKHOLES, SKINNED MEN, SPELLS. I FEEL LIKE WE'RE JUST CIRCLING AROUND SOMETHING WE CAN'T SEE. AND THEN THERE'S THIS. IT CAN MAKE US FORGET. FORGET THE EDGES AROUND THE MEMORY LOSS. LIKE IT NEVER HAPPENED.
ARE YOU GOING TO USE IT?
I DON'T KNOW. I HAVEN'T DECIDED.
YOU'VE ALREADY SAID YOU WANT TO MOVE PAST IT. THIS WILL HELP YOU.
AND YET, I HAVEN'T TAKEN IT.
I GUESS WHAT I'M ALSO WONDERING IS HOW THOSE--THOSE THINGS KNEW WHERE YOU WERE.
MAYBE IT WAS A COINCIDENCE?
Have I ever mentioned that El prefers to do her hardest thinking with Philip Glass and a chandelle boa? If it could get her in those conditions for her tests at school, she could go to fucking Harvard.
--PREMATURELY AIR-CONDITIONED SUPER--

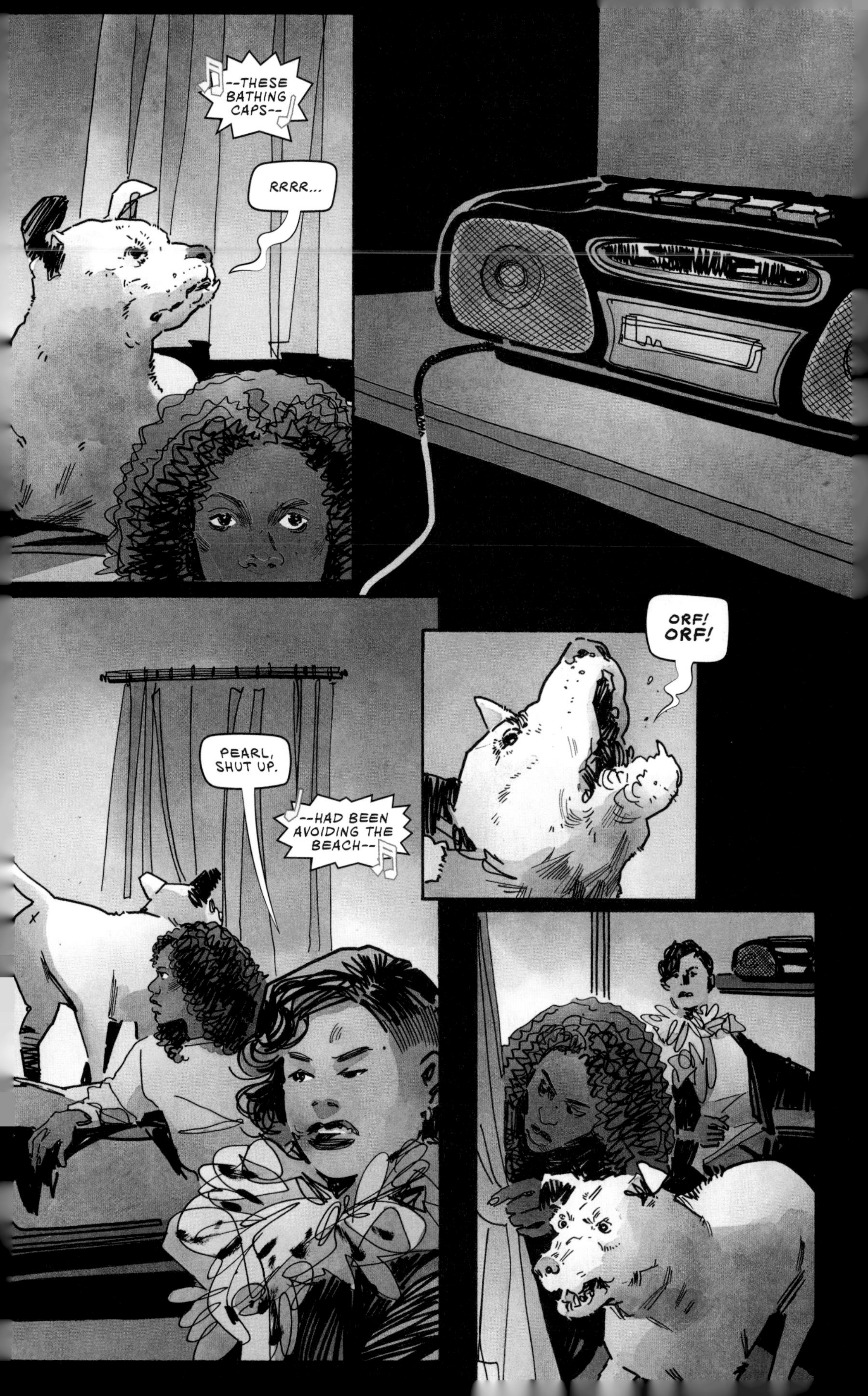
--THESE BATHING CAPS--
RRRR...
ORF! ORF!
PEARL, SHUT UP.
--HAD BEEN AVOIDING THE BEACH--

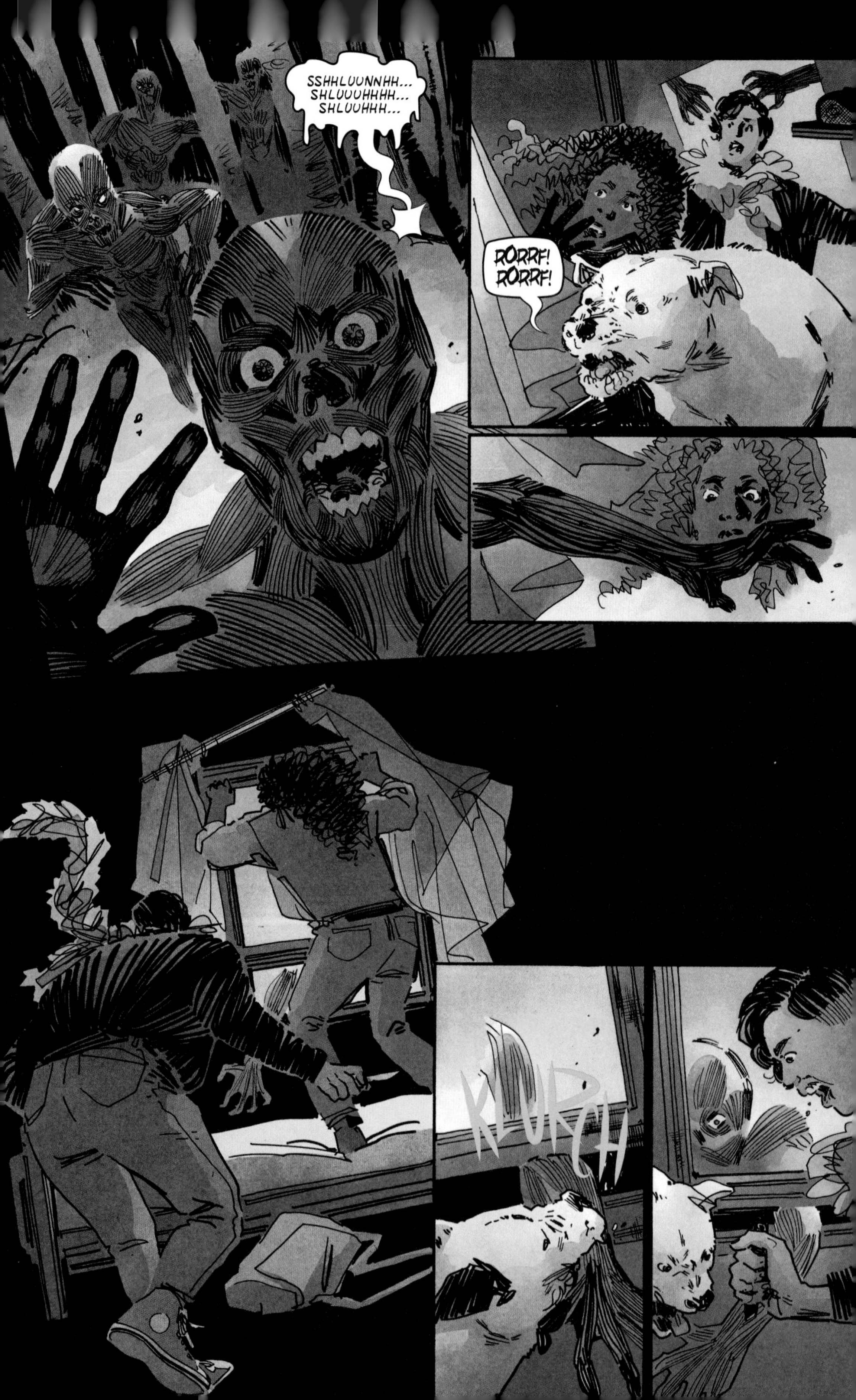
SSHHLUUNNHH...
SHLUUUHHHH...
SHLUUHHH...
RORRF! RORRF!
KLURCH

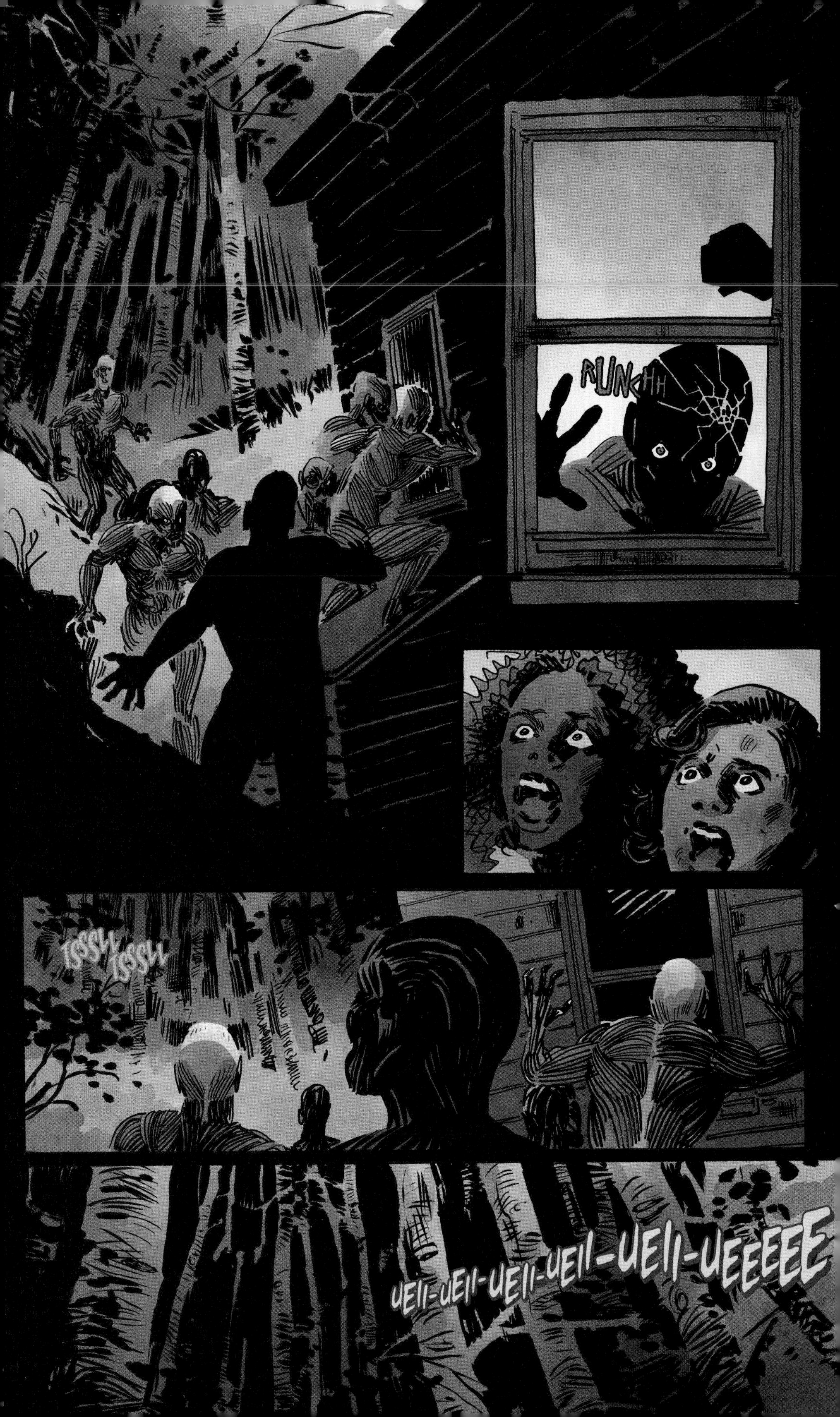
RUNCHH
TSSSLL TSSSLL
UEII-UEII-UEII-UEII-UEII-UEEEEE

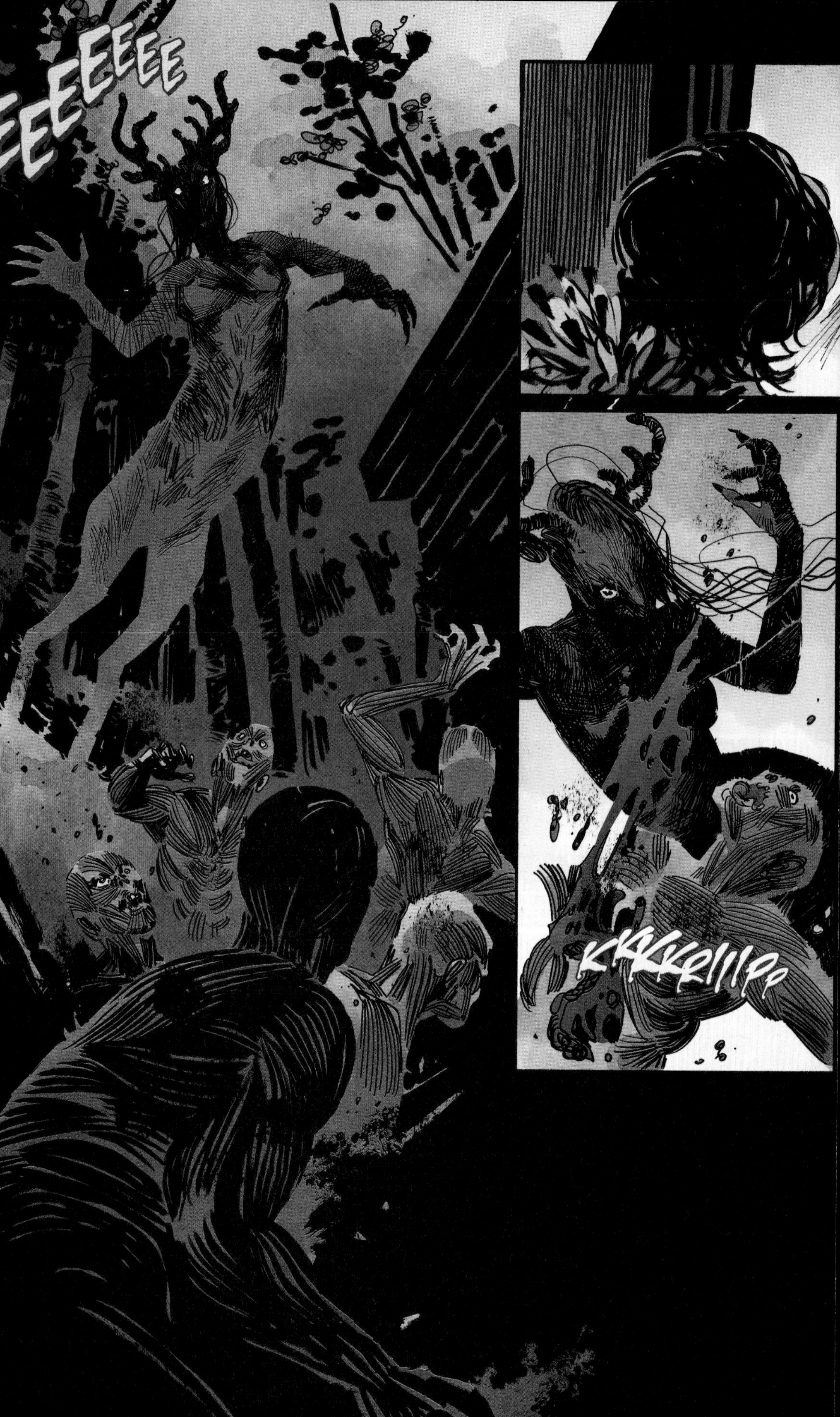
EEEEEEEE
KKKKRIIIPP

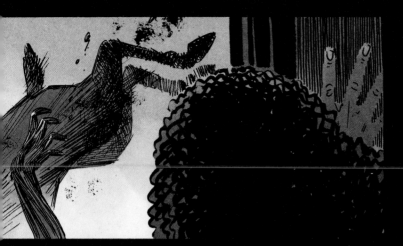

RRRAKKT

SPLURK

KLORCH

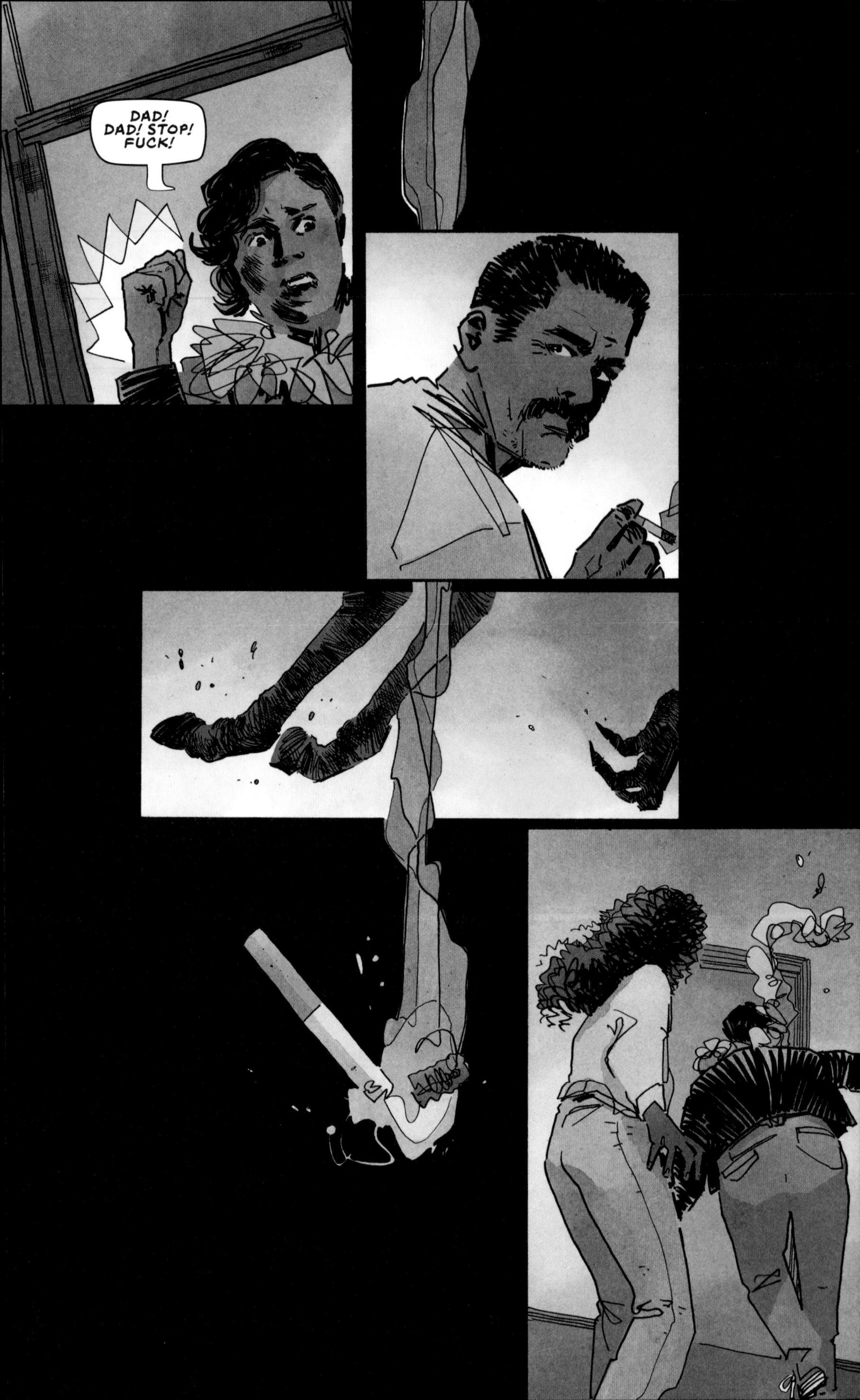
DAD! DAD! STOP! FUCK!

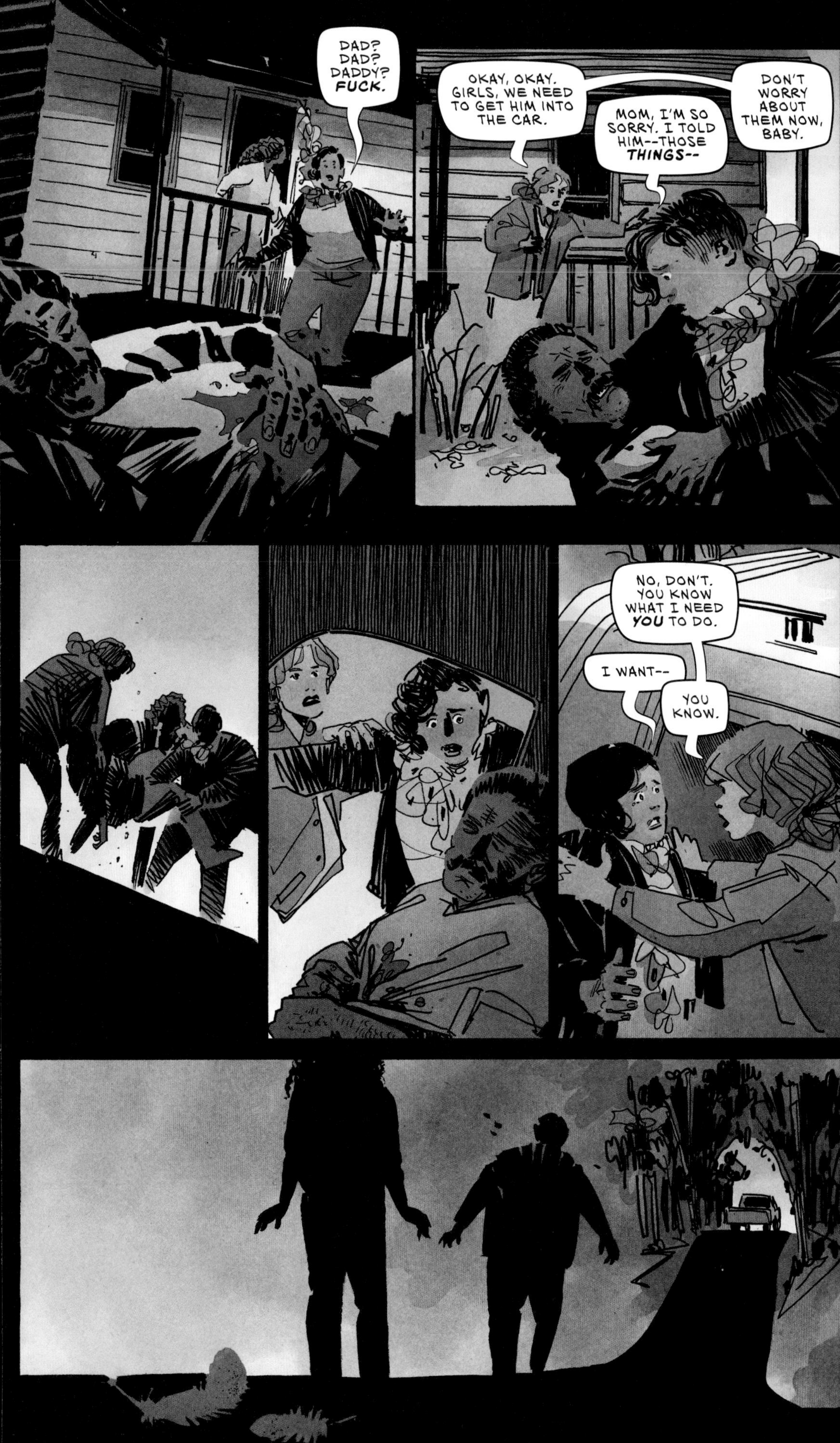
DAD? DAD? DADDY? FUCK.
OKAY, OKAY. GIRLS, WE NEED TO GET HIM INTO THE CAR.
MOM, I'M SO SORRY. I TOLD HIM--THOSE THINGS--
DON'T WORRY ABOUT THEM NOW, BABY.
NO, DON'T. YOU KNOW WHAT I NEED YOU TO DO.
I WANT--
YOU KNOW.

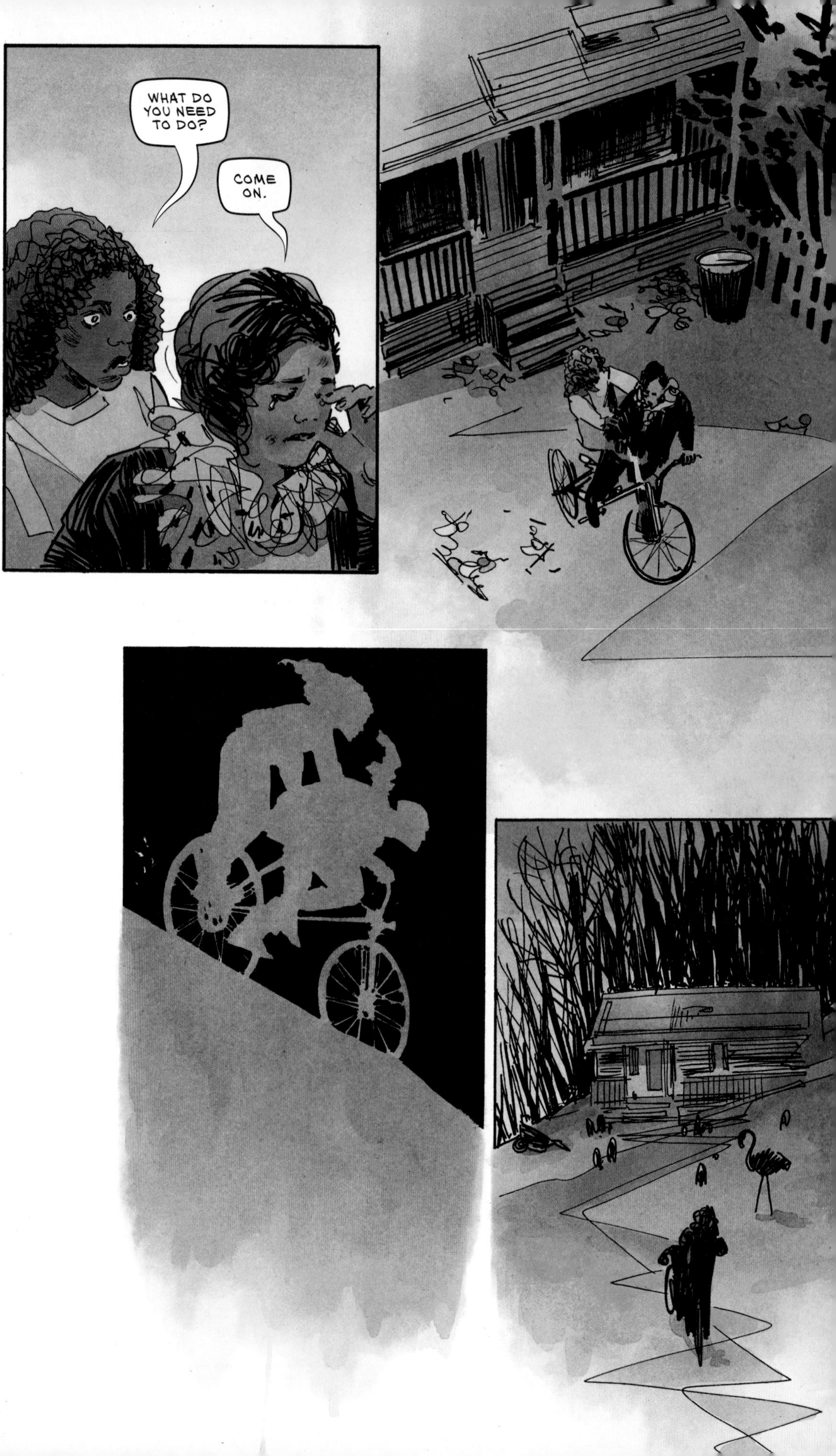
WHAT DO YOU NEED TO DO?
COME ON.

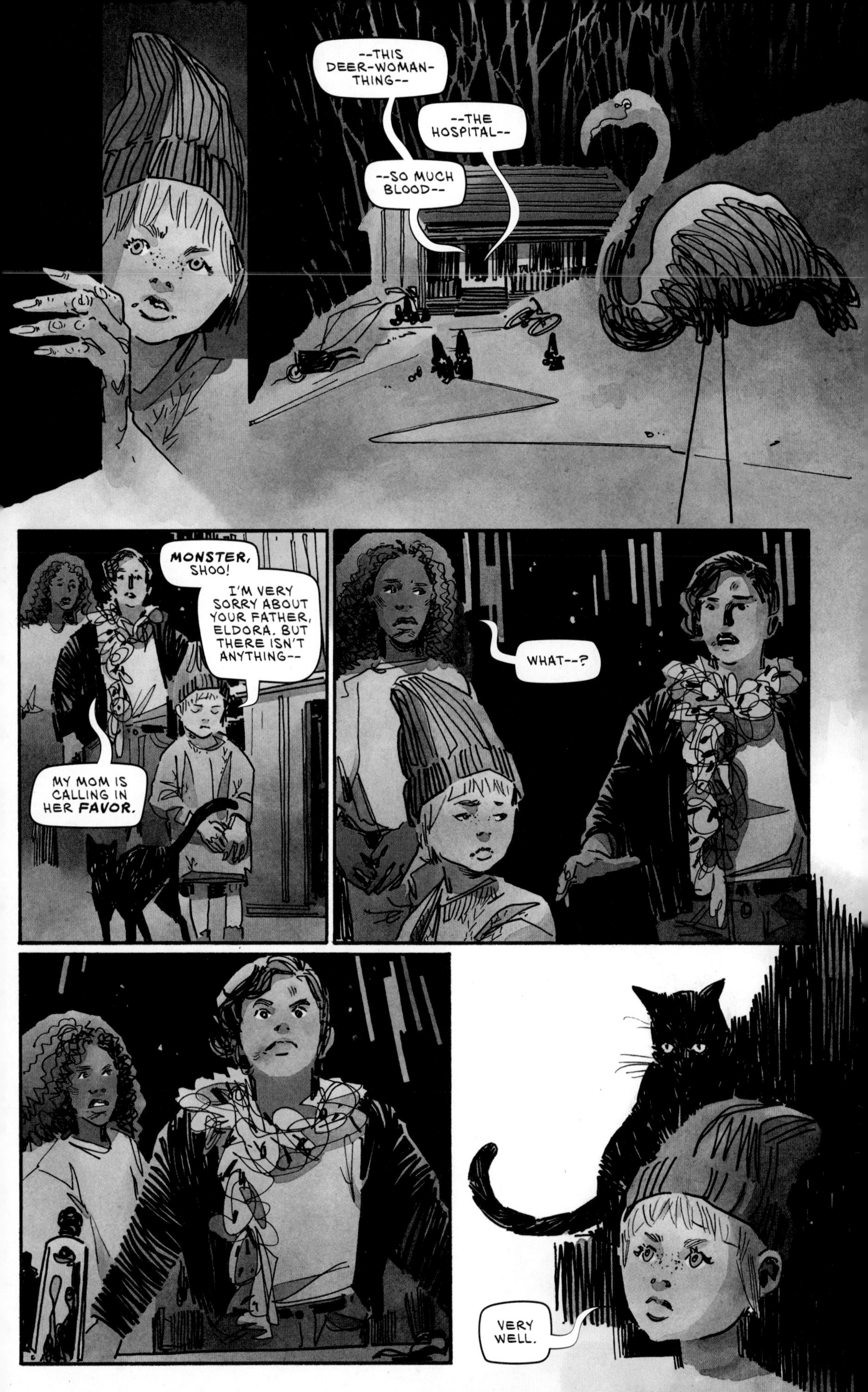
--THIS DEER-WOMAN-THING--
--THE HOSPITAL--
--SO MUCH BLOOD--
MONSTER, SHOO!
I'M VERY SORRY ABOUT YOUR FATHER, ELDORA. BUT THERE ISN'T ANYTHING--
MY MOM IS CALLING IN HER FAVOR.
WHAT--?
VERY WELL.

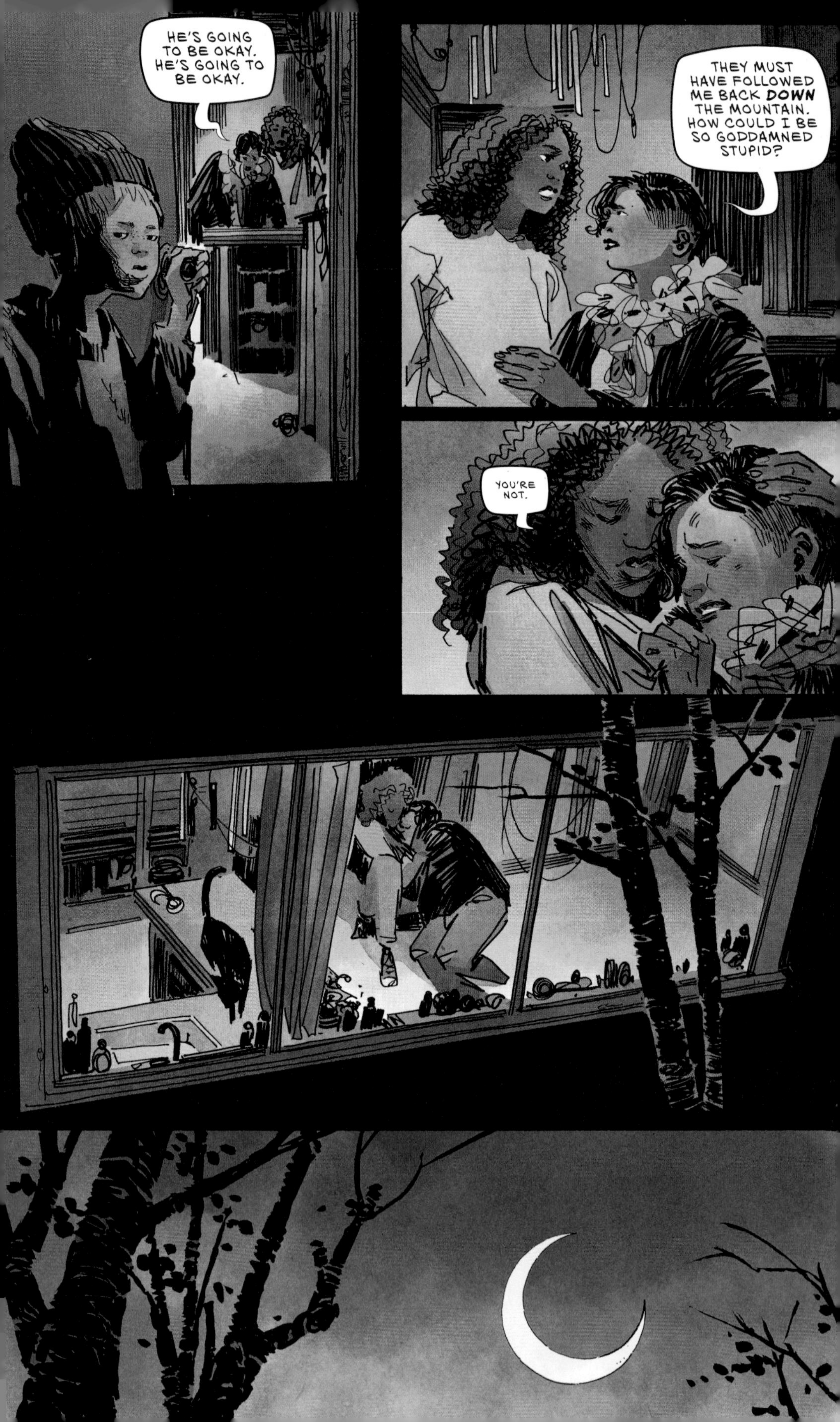
HE'S GOING TO BE OKAY. HE'S GOING TO BE OKAY.
THEY MUST HAVE FOLLOWED ME BACK **DOWN** THE MOUNTAIN. HOW COULD I BE SO GODDAMNED STUPID?
YOU'RE NOT.

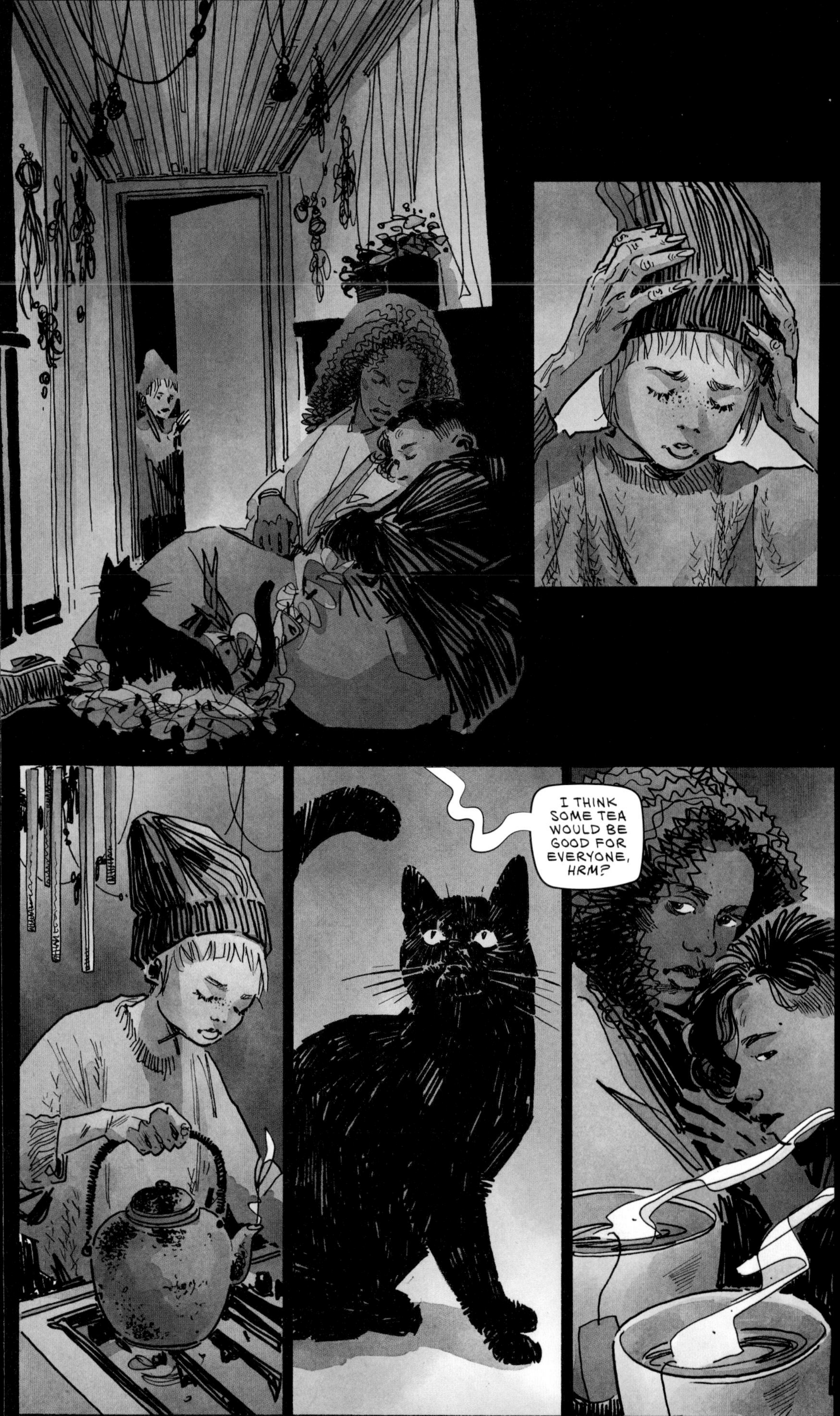
I THINK SOME TEA WOULD BE GOOD FOR EVERYONE, HRM?

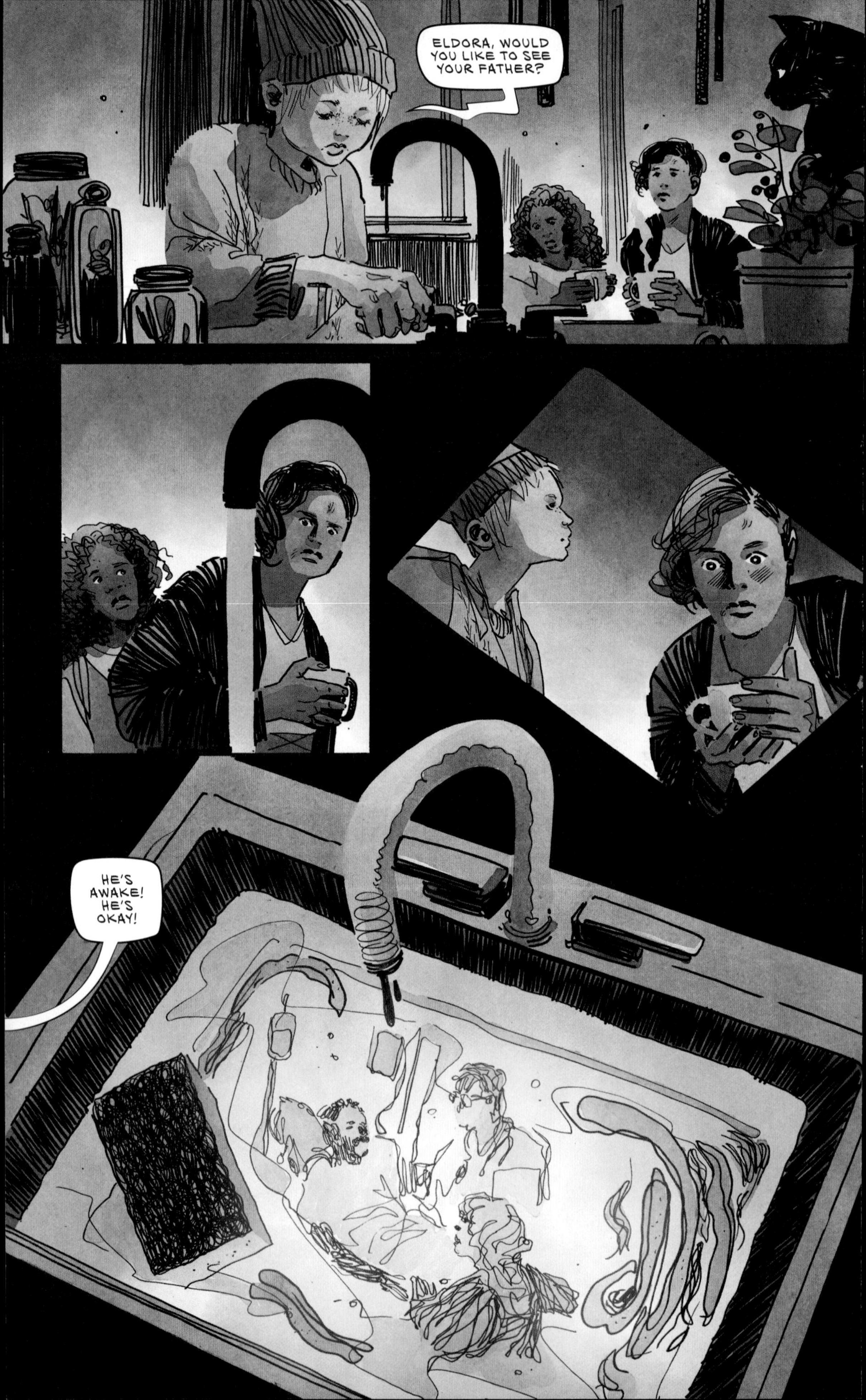
ELDORA, WOULD YOU LIKE TO SEE YOUR FATHER?
HE'S AWAKE! HE'S OKAY!

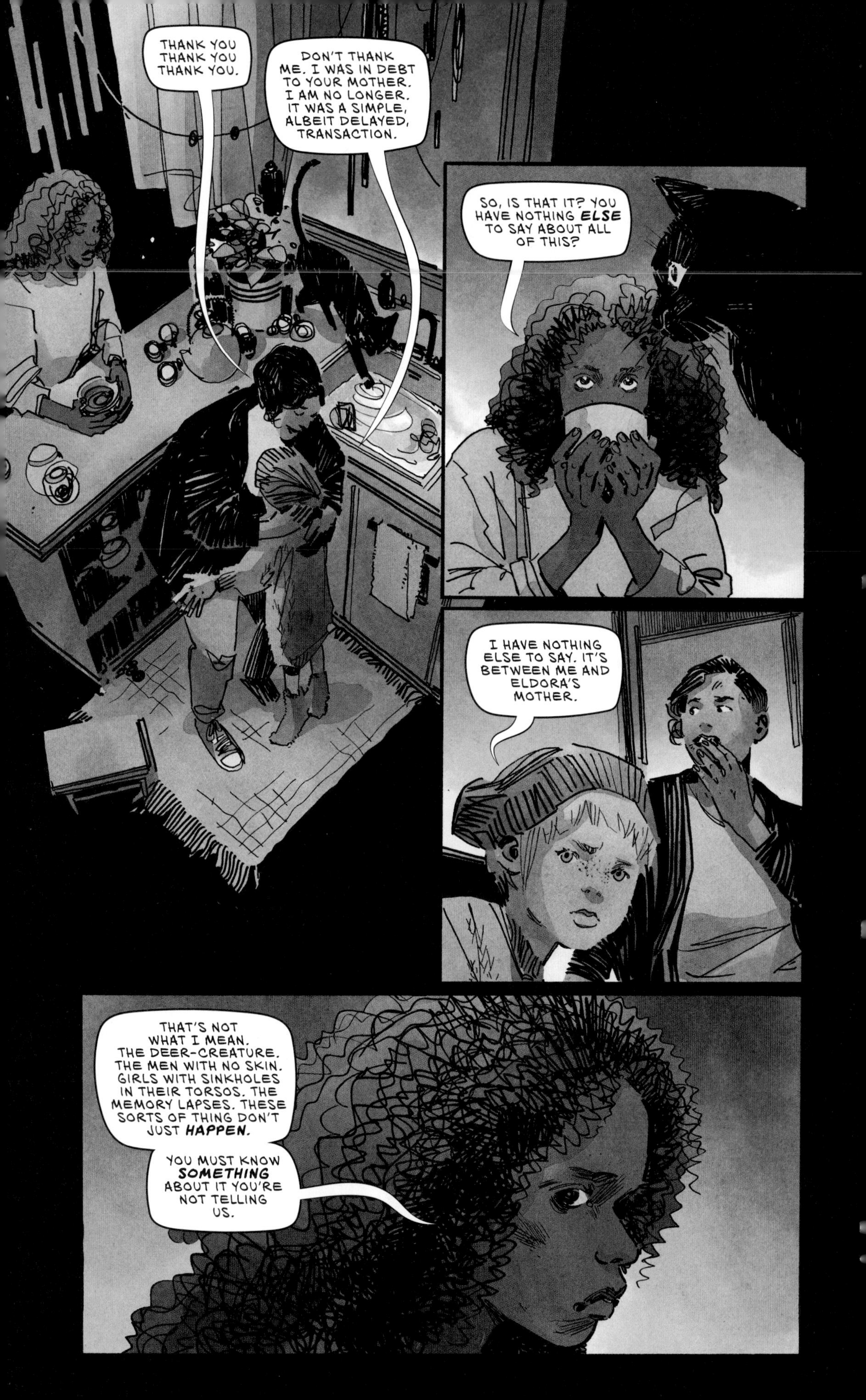
THANK YOU THANK YOU THANK YOU.
DON'T THANK ME. I WAS IN DEBT TO YOUR MOTHER. I AM NO LONGER. IT WAS A SIMPLE, ALBEIT DELAYED, TRANSACTION.
SO, IS THAT IT? YOU HAVE NOTHING ELSE TO SAY ABOUT ALL OF THIS?
I HAVE NOTHING ELSE TO SAY. IT'S BETWEEN ME AND ELDORA'S MOTHER.
THAT'S NOT WHAT I MEAN. THE DEER-CREATURE. THE MEN WITH NO SKIN. GIRLS WITH SINKHOLES IN THEIR TORSOS. THE MEMORY LAPSES. THESE SORTS OF THING DON'T JUST HAPPEN.
YOU MUST KNOW SOMETHING ABOUT IT YOU'RE NOT TELLING US.

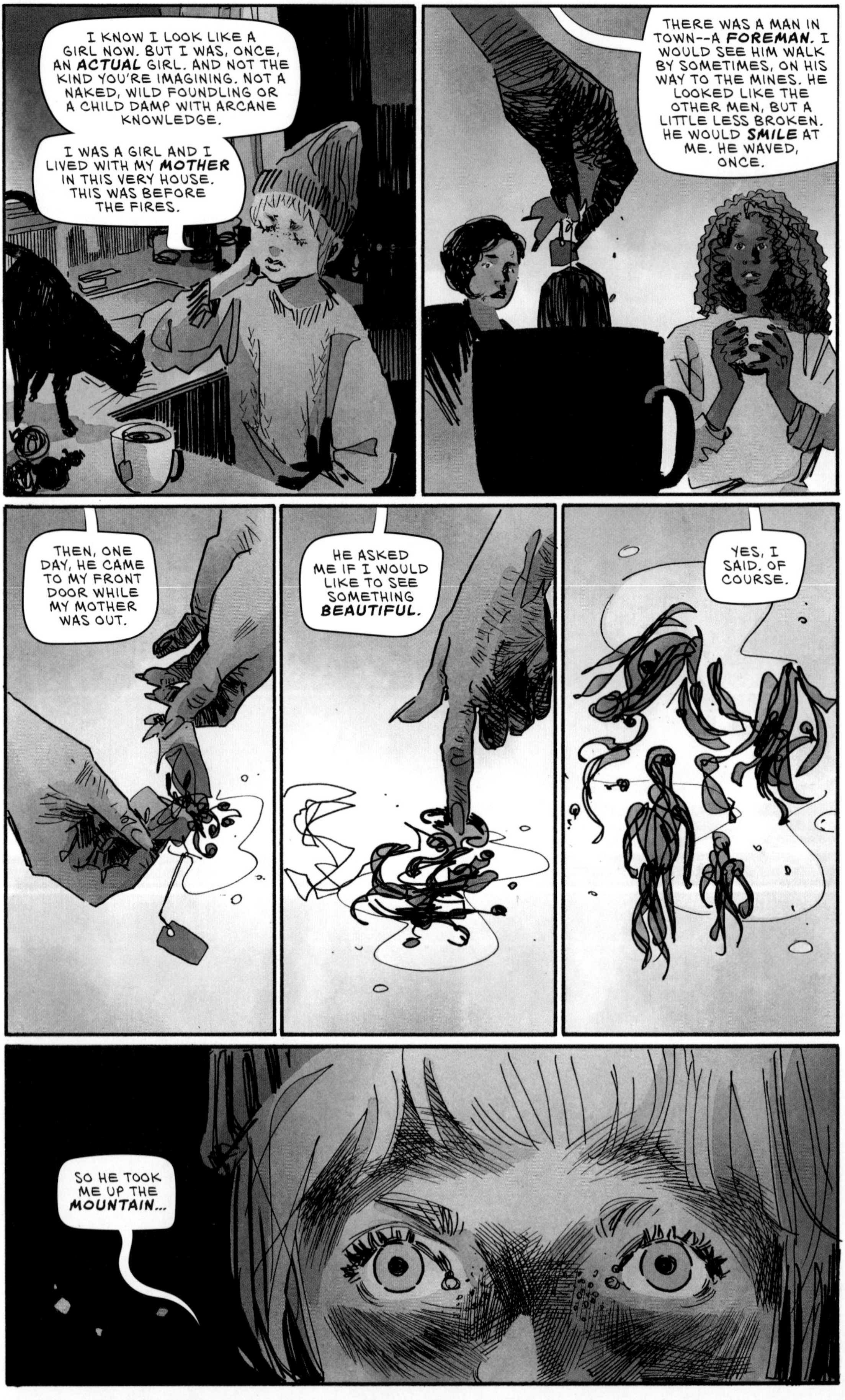
I KNOW I LOOK LIKE A GIRL NOW. BUT I WAS, ONCE, AN ACTUAL GIRL. AND NOT THE KIND YOU'RE IMAGINING. NOT A NAKED, WILD FOUNDLING OR A CHILD DAMP WITH ARCANE KNOWLEDGE.
I WAS A GIRL AND I LIVED WITH MY MOTHER IN THIS VERY HOUSE. THIS WAS BEFORE THE FIRES.
THERE WAS A MAN IN TOWN--A FOREMAN. I WOULD SEE HIM WALK BY SOMETIMES, ON HIS WAY TO THE MINES. HE LOOKED LIKE THE OTHER MEN, BUT A LITTLE LESS BROKEN. HE WOULD SMILE AT ME. HE WAVED, ONCE.
THEN, ONE DAY, HE CAME TO MY FRONT DOOR WHILE MY MOTHER WAS OUT.
HE ASKED ME IF I WOULD LIKE TO SEE SOMETHING BEAUTIFUL.
YES, I SAID. OF COURSE.
SO HE TOOK ME UP THE MOUNTAIN...

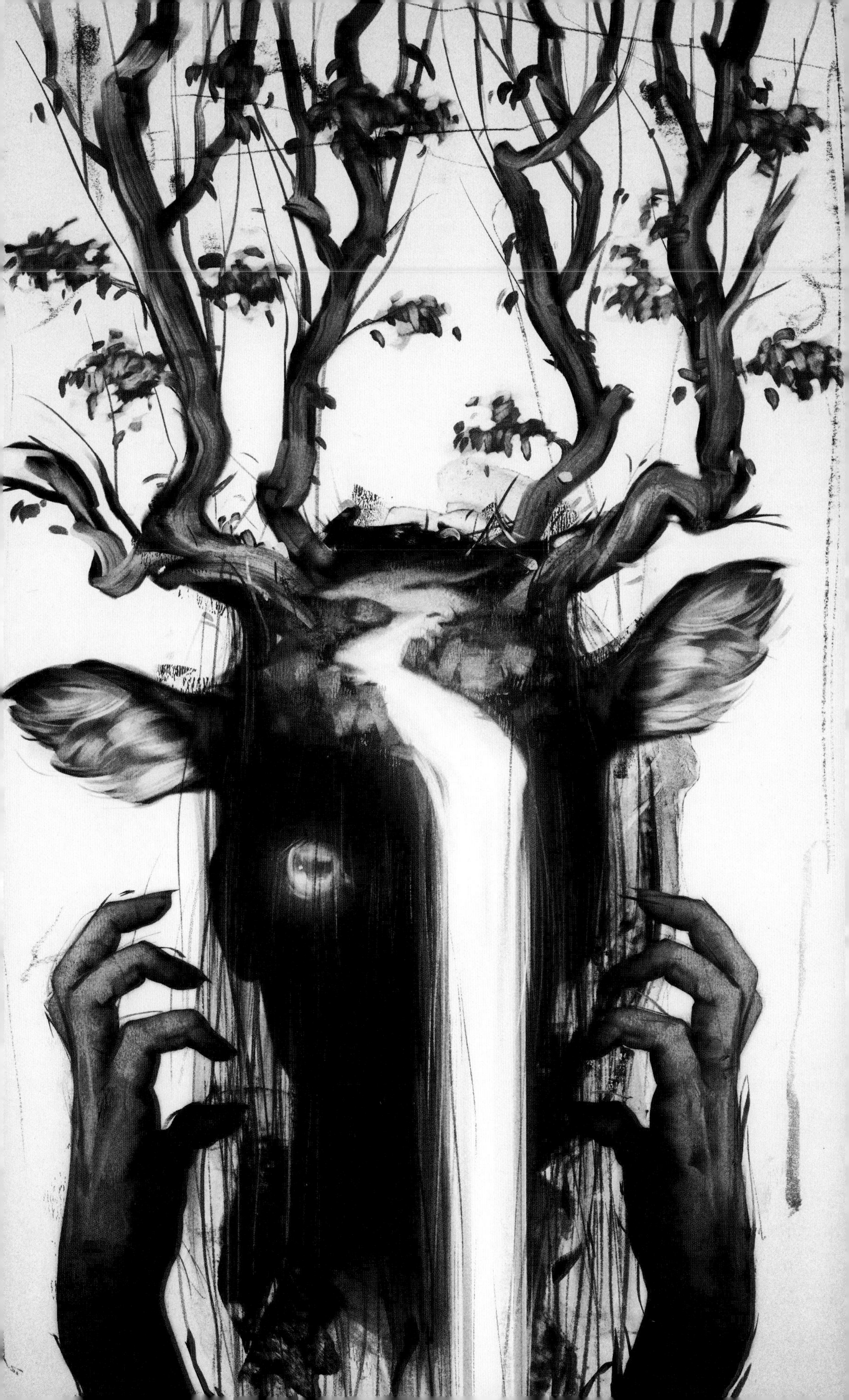

The Witch's Tale

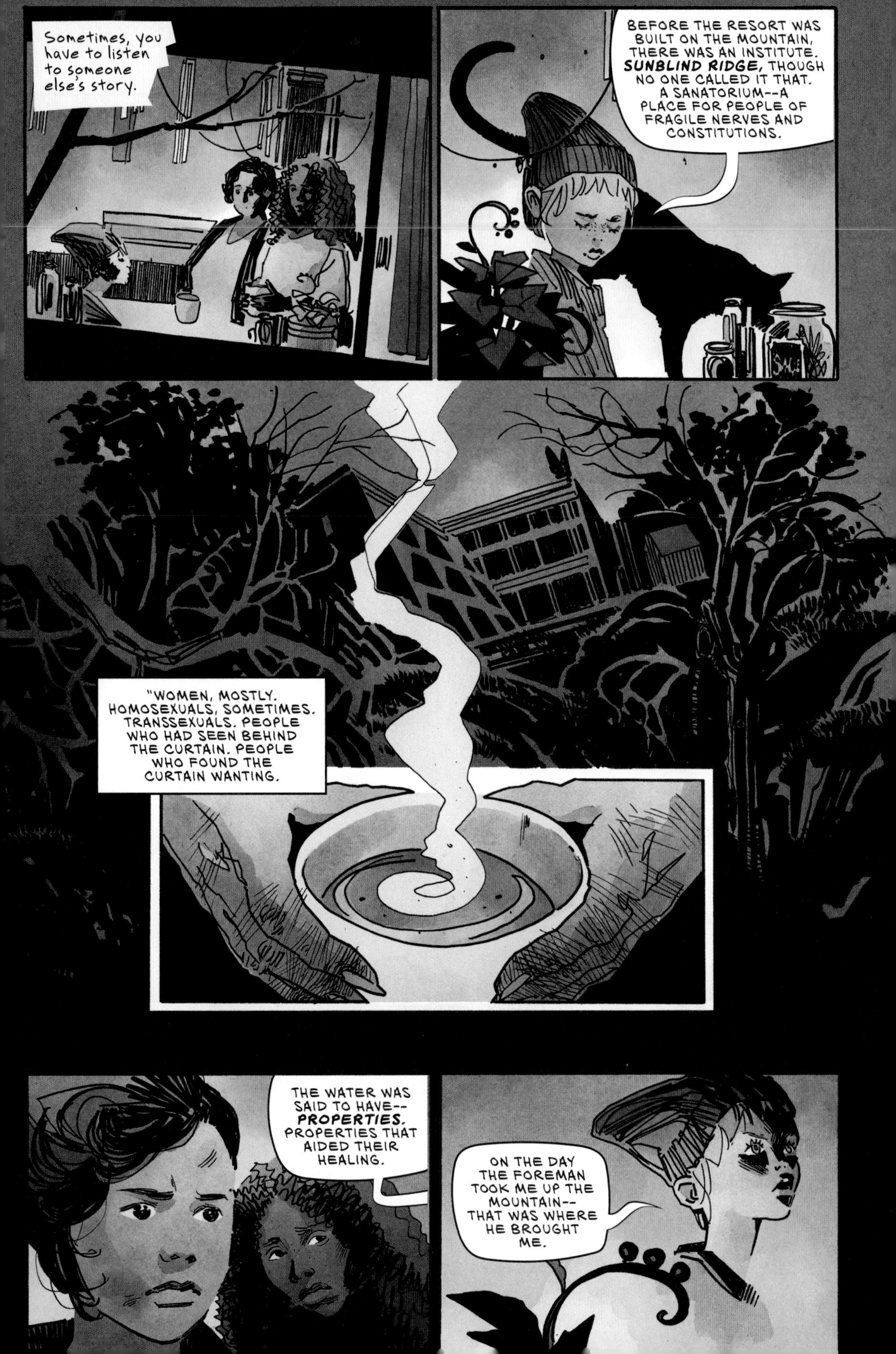

Sometimes, you have to listen to someone else's story.
BEFORE THE RESORT WAS BUILT ON THE MOUNTAIN, THERE WAS AN INSTITUTE. SUNBLIND RIDGE, THOUGH NO ONE CALLED IT THAT. A SANATORIUM--A PLACE FOR PEOPLE OF FRAGILE NERVES AND CONSTITUTIONS.
"WOMEN, MOSTLY. HOMOSEXUALS, SOMETIMES. TRANSSEXUALS. PEOPLE WHO HAD SEEN BEHIND THE CURTAIN. PEOPLE WHO FOUND THE CURTAIN WANTING.
THE WATER WAS SAID TO HAVE-- PROPERTIES. PROPERTIES THAT AIDED THEIR HEALING.
ON THE DAY THE FOREMAN TOOK ME UP THE MOUNTAIN-- THAT WAS WHERE HE BROUGHT ME.

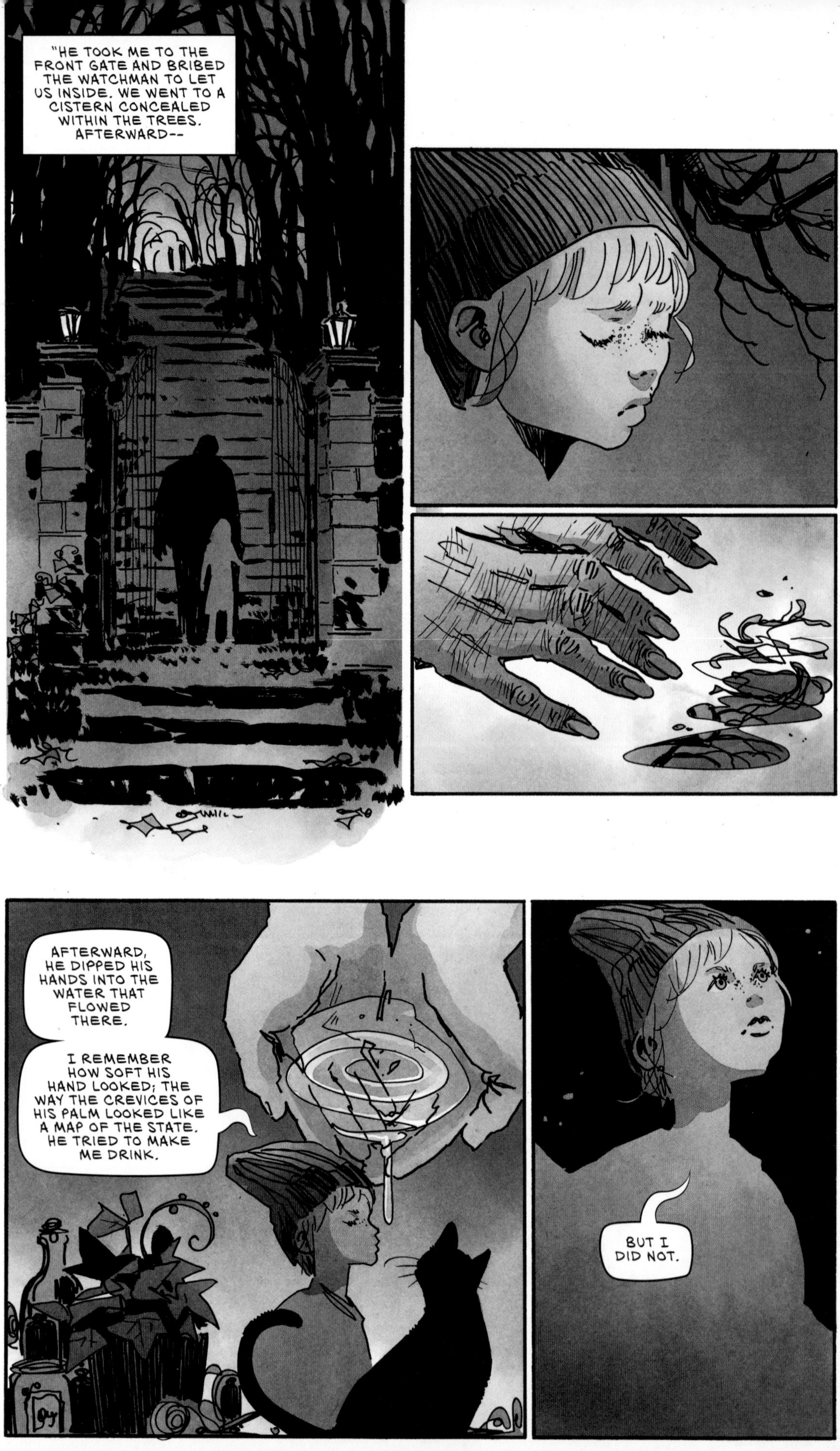
"HE TOOK ME TO THE FRONT GATE AND BRIBED THE WATCHMAN TO LET US INSIDE. WE WENT TO A CISTERN CONCEALED WITHIN THE TREES. AFTERWARD--
AFTERWARD, HE DIPPED HIS HANDS INTO THE WATER THAT FLOWED THERE.
I REMEMBER HOW SOFT HIS HAND LOOKED; THE WAY THE CREVICES OF HIS PALM LOOKED LIKE A MAP OF THE STATE. HE TRIED TO MAKE ME DRINK.
BUT I DID NOT.

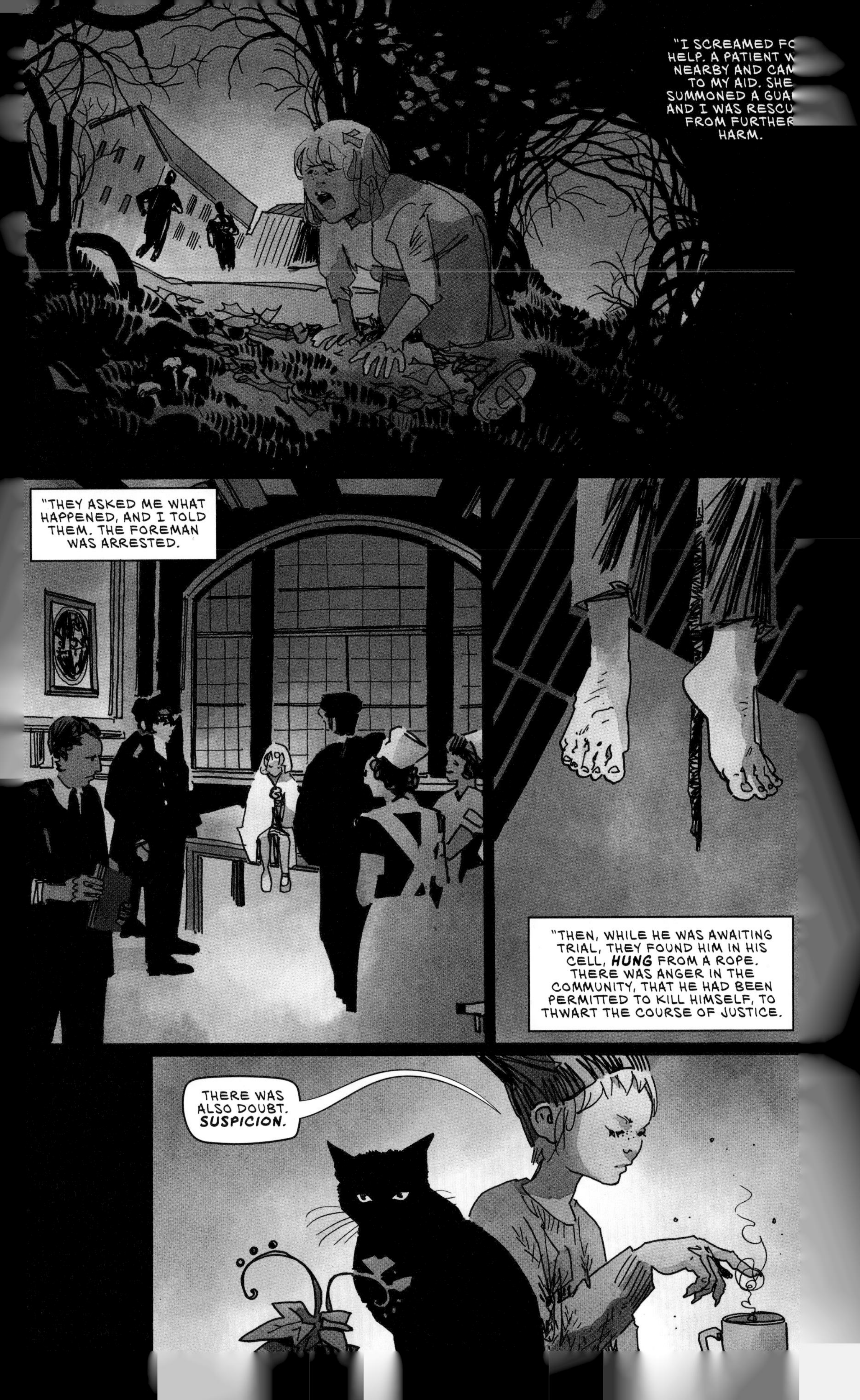
"I SCREAMED FO
HELP. A PATIENT W
NEARBY AND CAM
TO MY AID. SHE
SUMMONED A GUA
AND I WAS RESCU
FROM FURTHER
HARM.
"THEY ASKED ME WHAT HAPPENED, AND I TOLD THEM. THE FOREMAN WAS ARRESTED.
"THEN, WHILE HE WAS AWAITING TRIAL, THEY FOUND HIM IN HIS CELL, HUNG FROM A ROPE. THERE WAS ANGER IN THE COMMUNITY, THAT HE HAD BEEN PERMITTED TO KILL HIMSELF, TO THWART THE COURSE OF JUSTICE.
THERE WAS ALSO DOUBT. SUSPICION.

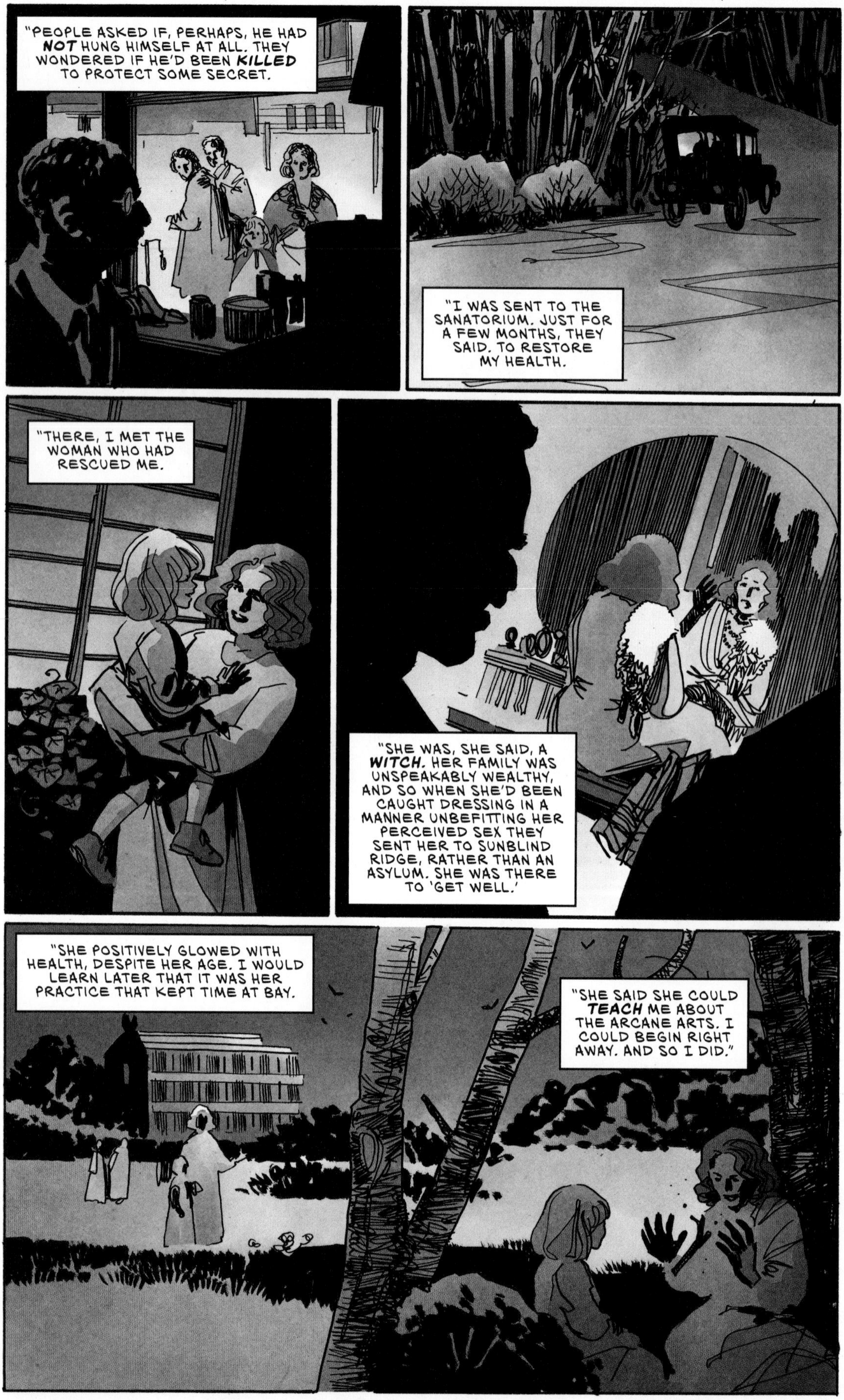
"PEOPLE ASKED IF, PERHAPS, HE HAD NOT HUNG HIMSELF AT ALL. THEY WONDERED IF HE'D BEEN KILLED TO PROTECT SOME SECRET.
"I WAS SENT TO THE SANATORIUM. JUST FOR A FEW MONTHS, THEY SAID. TO RESTORE MY HEALTH.
"THERE, I MET THE WOMAN WHO HAD RESCUED ME.
"SHE WAS, SHE SAID, A WITCH. HER FAMILY WAS UNSPEAKABLY WEALTHY, AND SO WHEN SHE'D BEEN CAUGHT DRESSING IN A MANNER UNBEFITTING HER PERCEIVED SEX THEY SENT HER TO SUNBLIND RIDGE, RATHER THAN AN ASYLUM. SHE WAS THERE TO 'GET WELL.'
"SHE POSITIVELY GLOWED WITH HEALTH, DESPITE HER AGE. I WOULD LEARN LATER THAT IT WAS HER PRACTICE THAT KEPT TIME AT BAY.
"SHE SAID SHE COULD TEACH ME ABOUT THE ARCANE ARTS. I COULD BEGIN RIGHT AWAY. AND SO I DID."

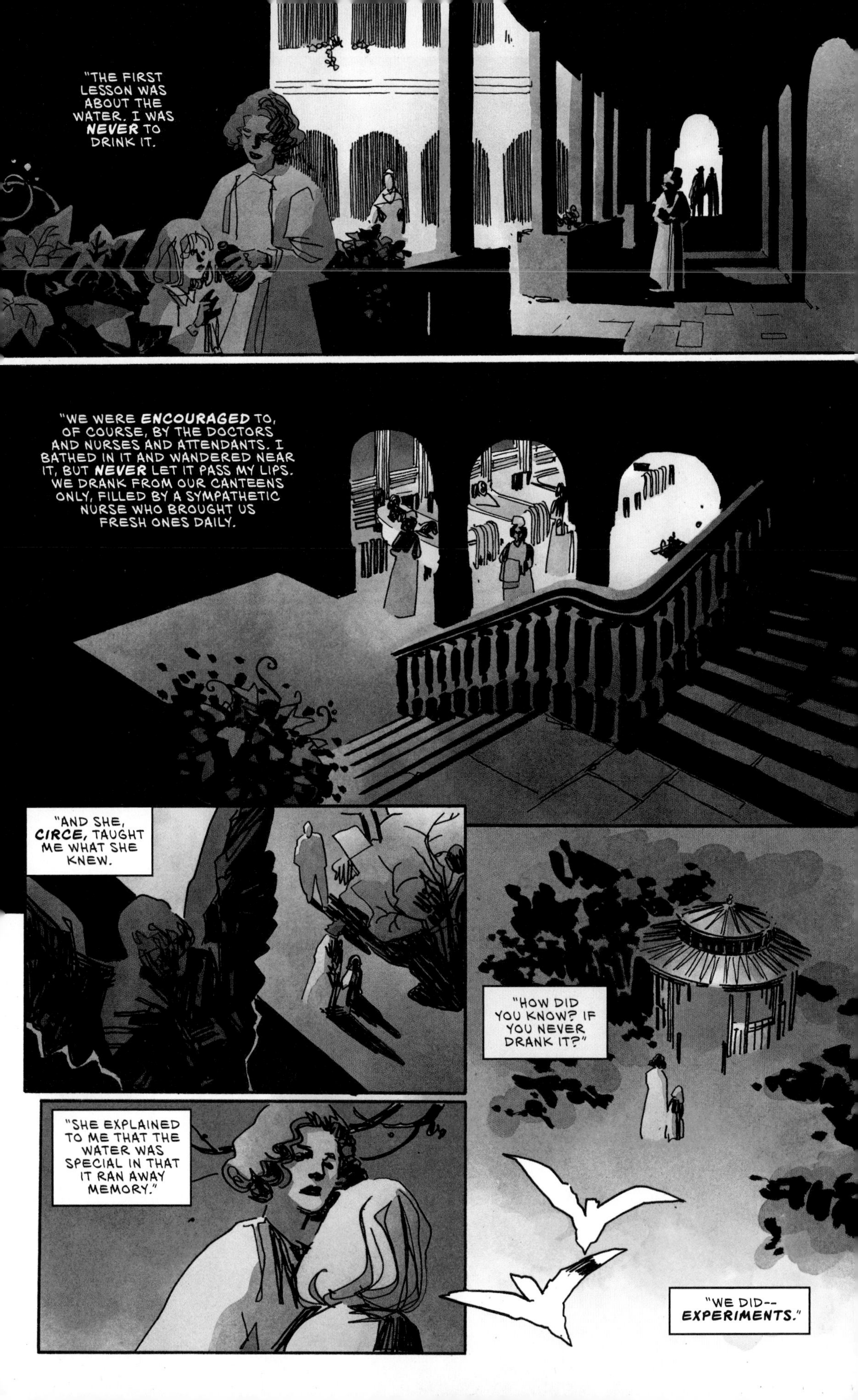
"THE FIRST LESSON WAS ABOUT THE WATER. I WAS NEVER TO DRINK IT.
"WE WERE ENCOURAGED TO, OF COURSE, BY THE DOCTORS AND NURSES AND ATTENDANTS. I BATHED IN IT AND WANDERED NEAR IT, BUT NEVER LET IT PASS MY LIPS. WE DRANK FROM OUR CANTEENS ONLY, FILLED BY A SYMPATHETIC NURSE WHO BROUGHT US FRESH ONES DAILY.
"AND SHE, CIRCE, TAUGHT ME WHAT SHE KNEW.
"SHE EXPLAINED TO ME THAT THE WATER WAS SPECIAL IN THAT IT RAN AWAY MEMORY."
"HOW DID YOU KNOW? IF YOU NEVER DRANK IT?"
"WE DID-- EXPERIMENTS."

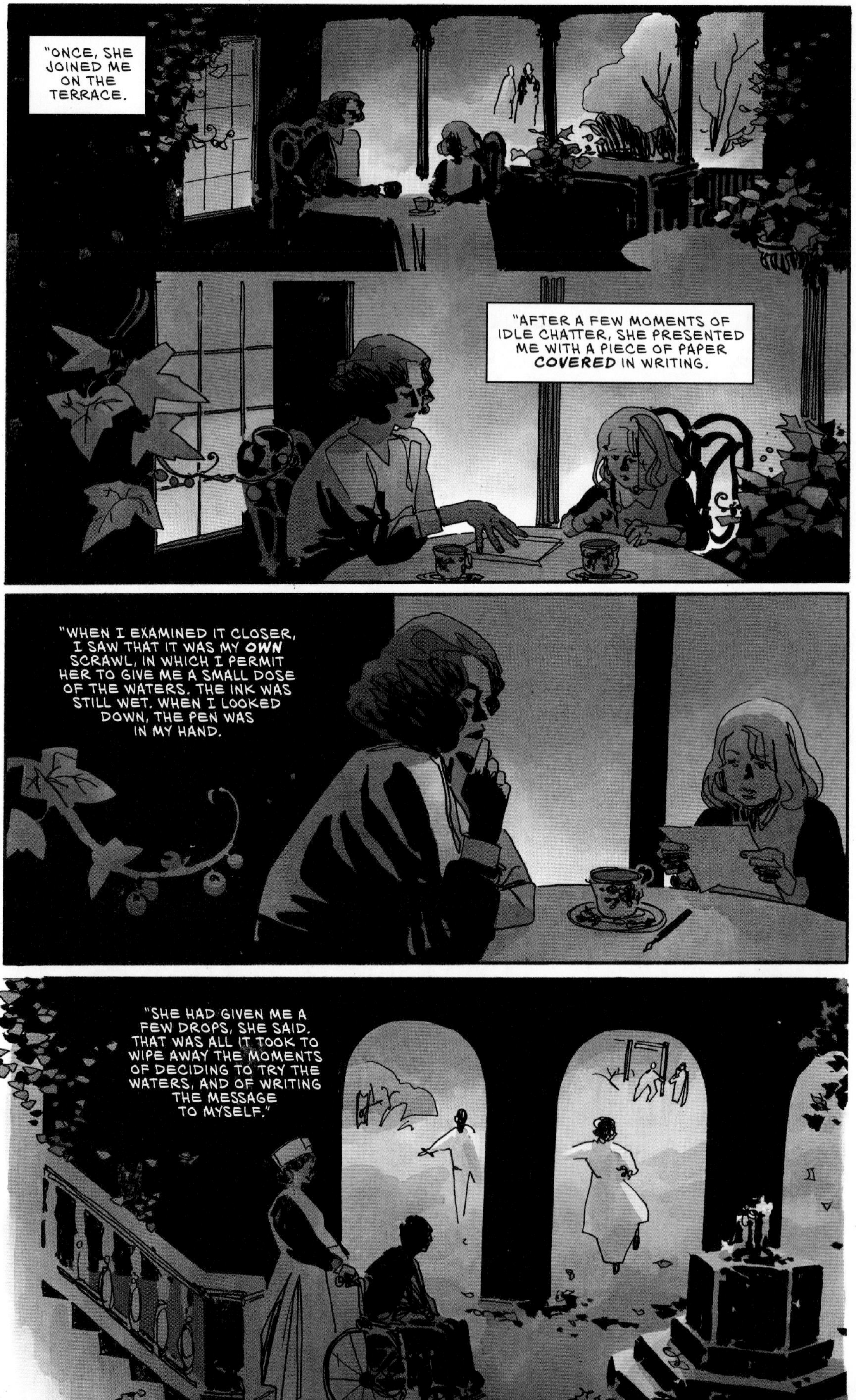
"ONCE, SHE JOINED ME ON THE TERRACE.
"AFTER A FEW MOMENTS OF IDLE CHATTER, SHE PRESENTED ME WITH A PIECE OF PAPER **COVERED** IN WRITING.
"WHEN I EXAMINED IT CLOSER, I SAW THAT IT WAS MY ***OWN*** SCRAWL, IN WHICH I PERMIT HER TO GIVE ME A SMALL DOSE OF THE WATERS. THE INK WAS STILL WET. WHEN I LOOKED DOWN, THE PEN WAS IN MY HAND.
"SHE HAD GIVEN ME A FEW DROPS, SHE SAID. THAT WAS ALL IT TOOK TO WIPE AWAY THE MOMENTS OF DECIDING TO TRY THE WATERS, AND OF WRITING THE MESSAGE TO MYSELF."

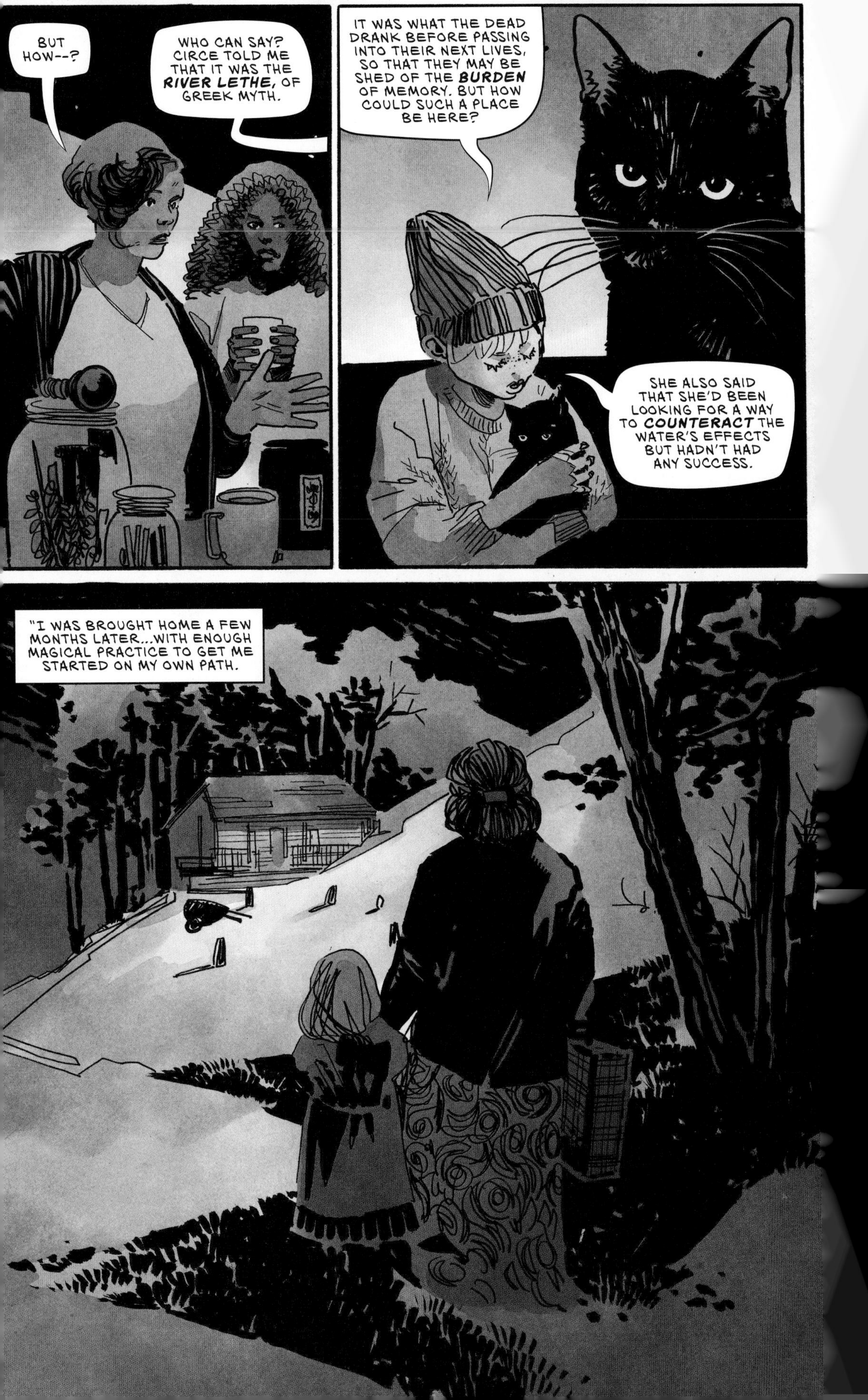
BUT HOW--?
WHO CAN SAY? CIRCE TOLD ME THAT IT WAS THE **RIVER LETHE,** OF GREEK MYTH.
IT WAS WHAT THE DEAD DRANK BEFORE PASSING INTO THEIR NEXT LIVES, SO THAT THEY MAY BE SHED OF THE **BURDEN** OF MEMORY. BUT HOW COULD SUCH A PLACE BE HERE?
SHE ALSO SAID THAT SHE'D BEEN LOOKING FOR A WAY TO **COUNTERACT** THE WATER'S EFFECTS BUT HADN'T HAD ANY SUCCESS.
"I WAS BROUGHT HOME A FEW MONTHS LATER...WITH ENOUGH MAGICAL PRACTICE TO GET ME STARTED ON MY OWN PATH.

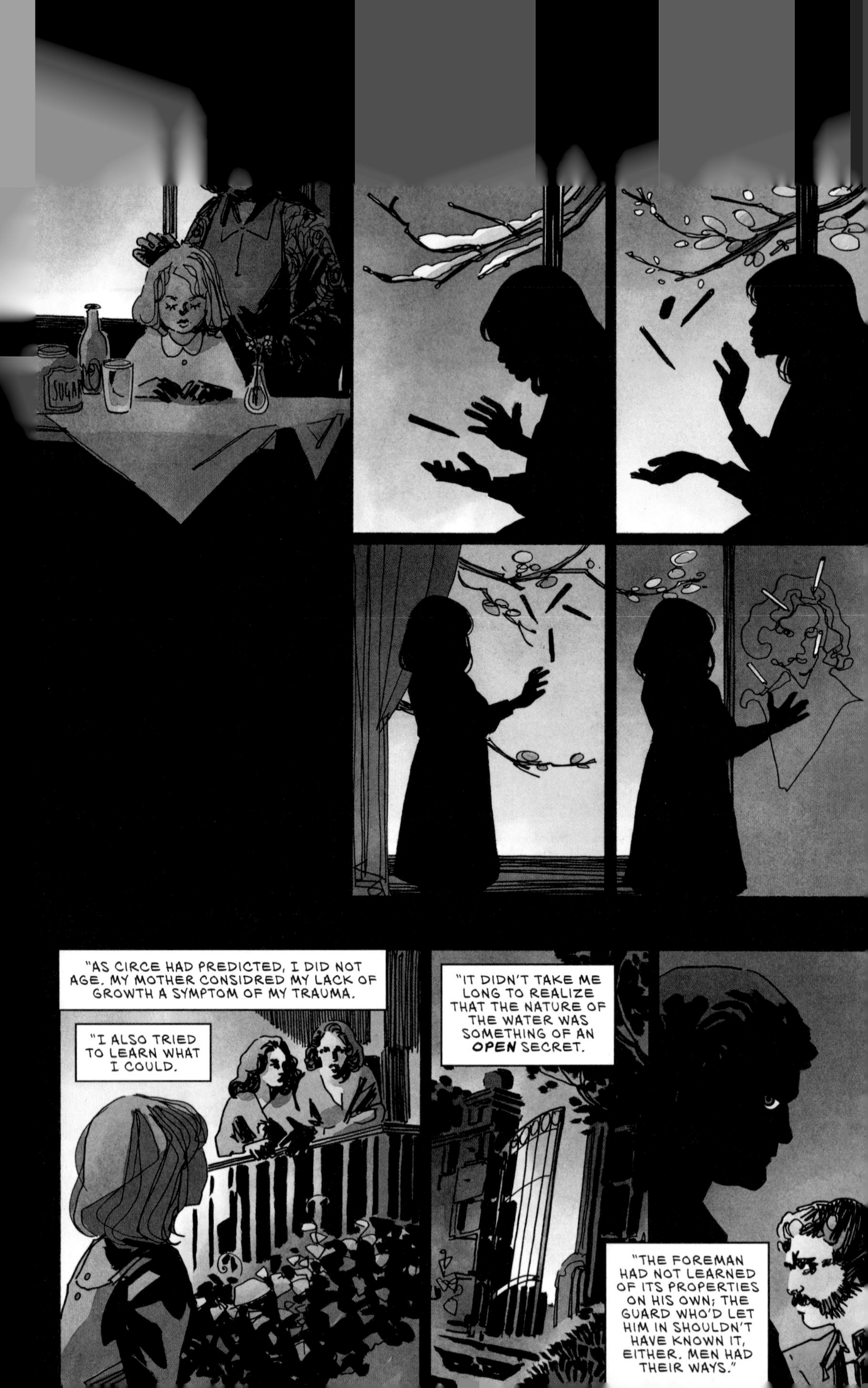
"AS CIRCE HAD PREDICTED, I DID NOT AGE. MY MOTHER CONSIDRED MY LACK OF GROWTH A SYMPTOM OF MY TRAUMA.
"I ALSO TRIED TO LEARN WHAT I COULD.
"IT DIDN'T TAKE ME LONG TO REALIZE THAT THE NATURE OF THE WATER WAS SOMETHING OF AN OPEN SECRET.
"THE FOREMAN HAD NOT LEARNED OF ITS PROPERTIES ON HIS OWN; THE GUARD WHO'D LET HIM IN SHOULDN'T HAVE KNOWN IT, EITHER. MEN HAD THEIR WAYS."

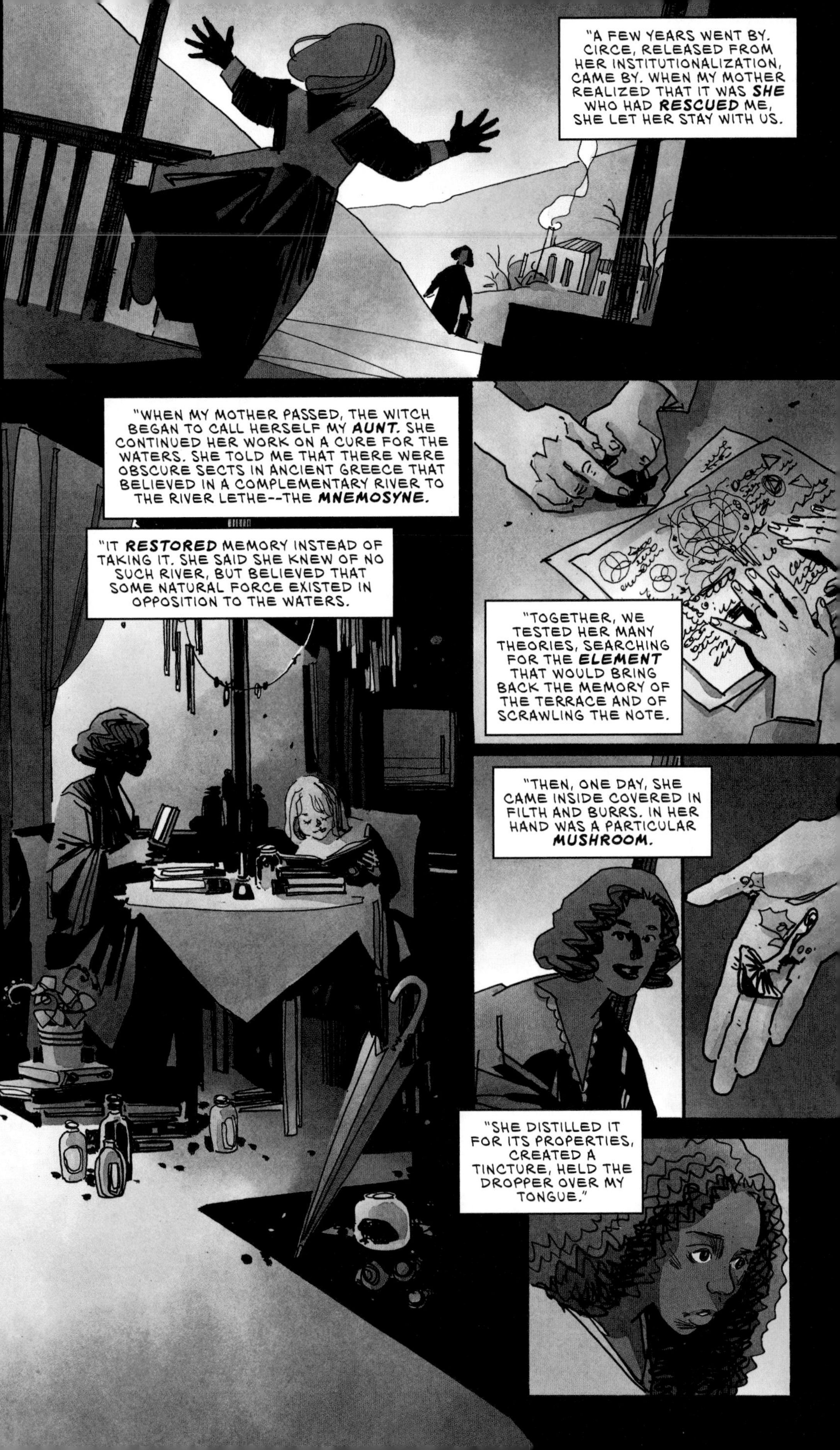
"A FEW YEARS WENT BY. CIRCE, RELEASED FROM HER INSTITUTIONALIZATION, CAME BY. WHEN MY MOTHER REALIZED THAT IT WAS SHE WHO HAD RESCUED ME, SHE LET HER STAY WITH US.
"WHEN MY MOTHER PASSED, THE WITCH BEGAN TO CALL HERSELF MY AUNT. SHE CONTINUED HER WORK ON A CURE FOR THE WATERS. SHE TOLD ME THAT THERE WERE OBSCURE SECTS IN ANCIENT GREECE THAT BELIEVED IN A COMPLEMENTARY RIVER TO THE RIVER LETHE--THE MNEMOSYNE.
"IT RESTORED MEMORY INSTEAD OF TAKING IT. SHE SAID SHE KNEW OF NO SUCH RIVER, BUT BELIEVED THAT SOME NATURAL FORCE EXISTED IN OPPOSITION TO THE WATERS.
"TOGETHER, WE TESTED HER MANY THEORIES, SEARCHING FOR THE ELEMENT THAT WOULD BRING BACK THE MEMORY OF THE TERRACE AND OF SCRAWLING THE NOTE.
"THEN, ONE DAY, SHE CAME INSIDE COVERED IN FILTH AND BURRS. IN HER HAND WAS A PARTICULAR MUSHROOM.
"SHE DISTILLED IT FOR ITS PROPERTIES, CREATED A TINCTURE, HELD THE DROPPER OVER MY TONGUE."

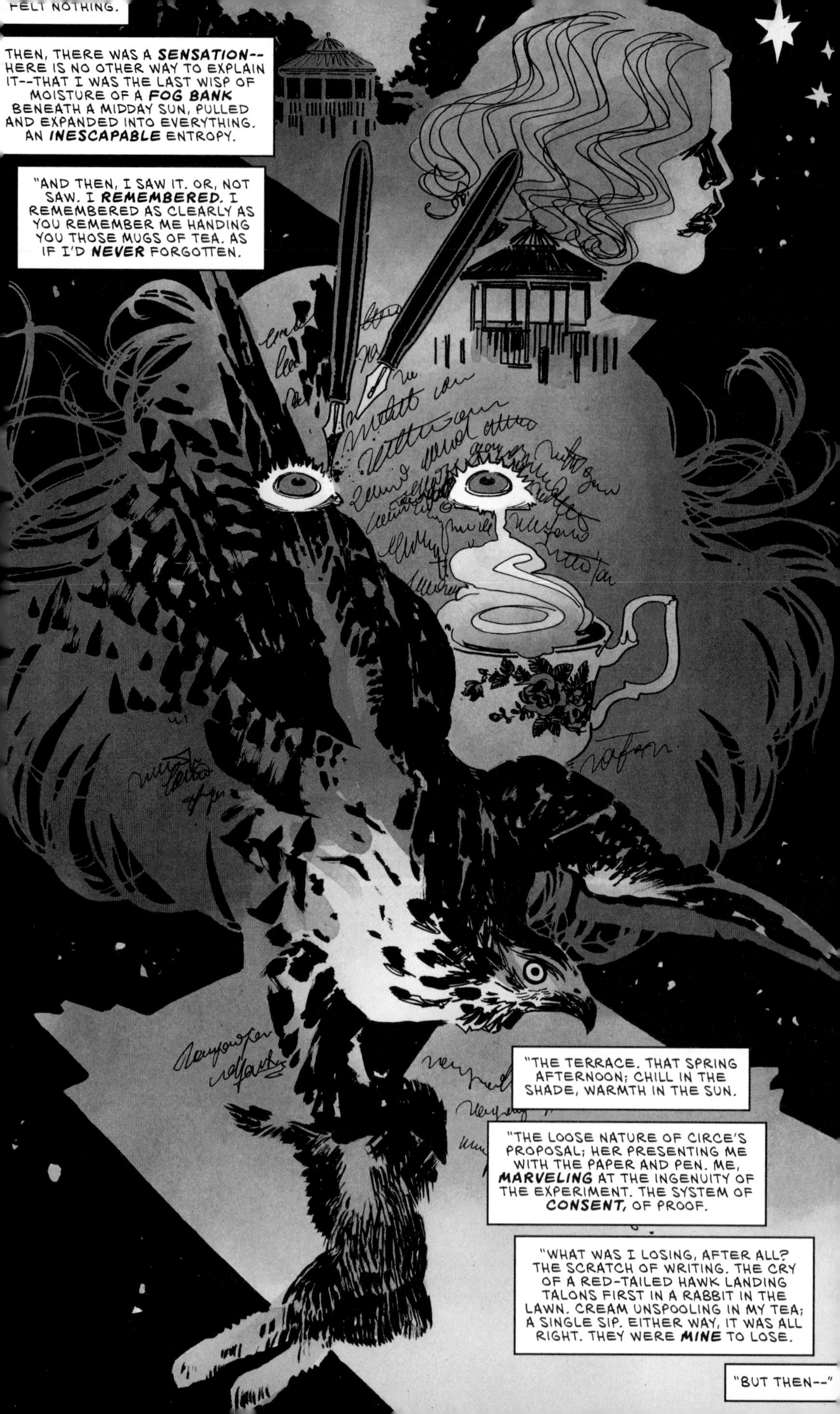
FELT NOTHING.
THEN, THERE WAS A SENSATION-- HERE IS NO OTHER WAY TO EXPLAIN IT--THAT I WAS THE LAST WISP OF MOISTURE OF A FOG BANK BENEATH A MIDDAY SUN, PULLED AND EXPANDED INTO EVERYTHING. AN INESCAPABLE ENTROPY.
"AND THEN, I SAW IT. OR, NOT SAW. I REMEMBERED. I REMEMBERED AS CLEARLY AS YOU REMEMBER ME HANDING YOU THOSE MUGS OF TEA. AS IF I'D NEVER FORGOTTEN.
"THE TERRACE. THAT SPRING AFTERNOON; CHILL IN THE SHADE, WARMTH IN THE SUN.
"THE LOOSE NATURE OF CIRCE'S PROPOSAL; HER PRESENTING ME WITH THE PAPER AND PEN. ME, MARVELING AT THE INGENUITY OF THE EXPERIMENT. THE SYSTEM OF CONSENT, OF PROOF.
"WHAT WAS I LOSING, AFTER ALL? THE SCRATCH OF WRITING. THE CRY OF A RED-TAILED HAWK LANDING TALONS FIRST IN A RABBIT IN THE LAWN. CREAM UNSPOOLING IN MY TEA; A SINGLE SIP. EITHER WAY, IT WAS ALL RIGHT. THEY WERE MINE TO LOSE.
"BUT THEN--"

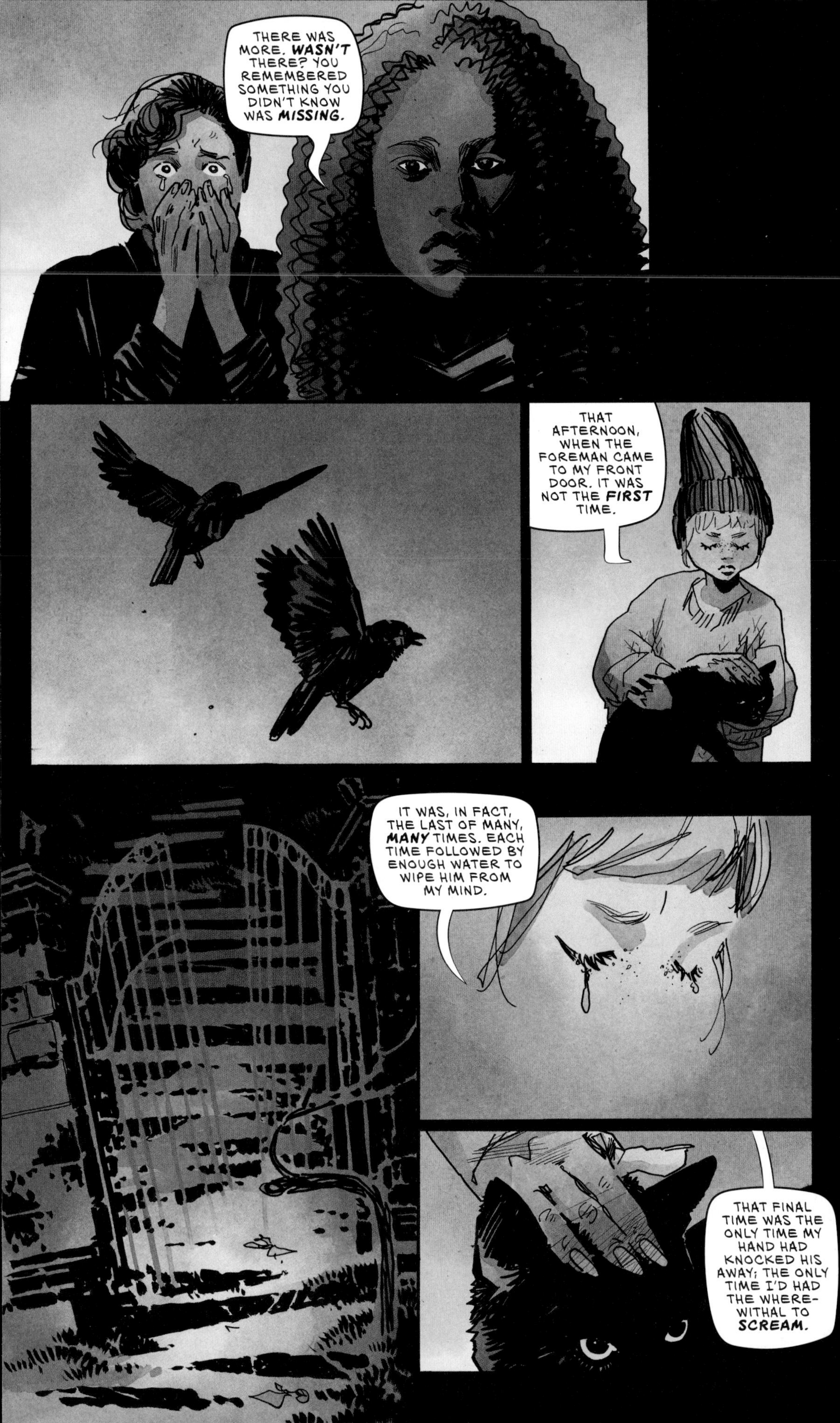
THERE WAS MORE. WASN'T THERE? YOU REMEMBERED SOMETHING YOU DIDN'T KNOW WAS MISSING.
THAT AFTERNOON, WHEN THE FOREMAN CAME TO MY FRONT DOOR, IT WAS NOT THE FIRST TIME.
IT WAS, IN FACT, THE LAST OF MANY, MANY TIMES. EACH TIME FOLLOWED BY ENOUGH WATER TO WIPE HIM FROM MY MIND.
THAT FINAL TIME WAS THE ONLY TIME MY HAND HAD KNOCKED HIS AWAY; THE ONLY TIME I'D HAD THE WHERE-WITHAL TO SCREAM.

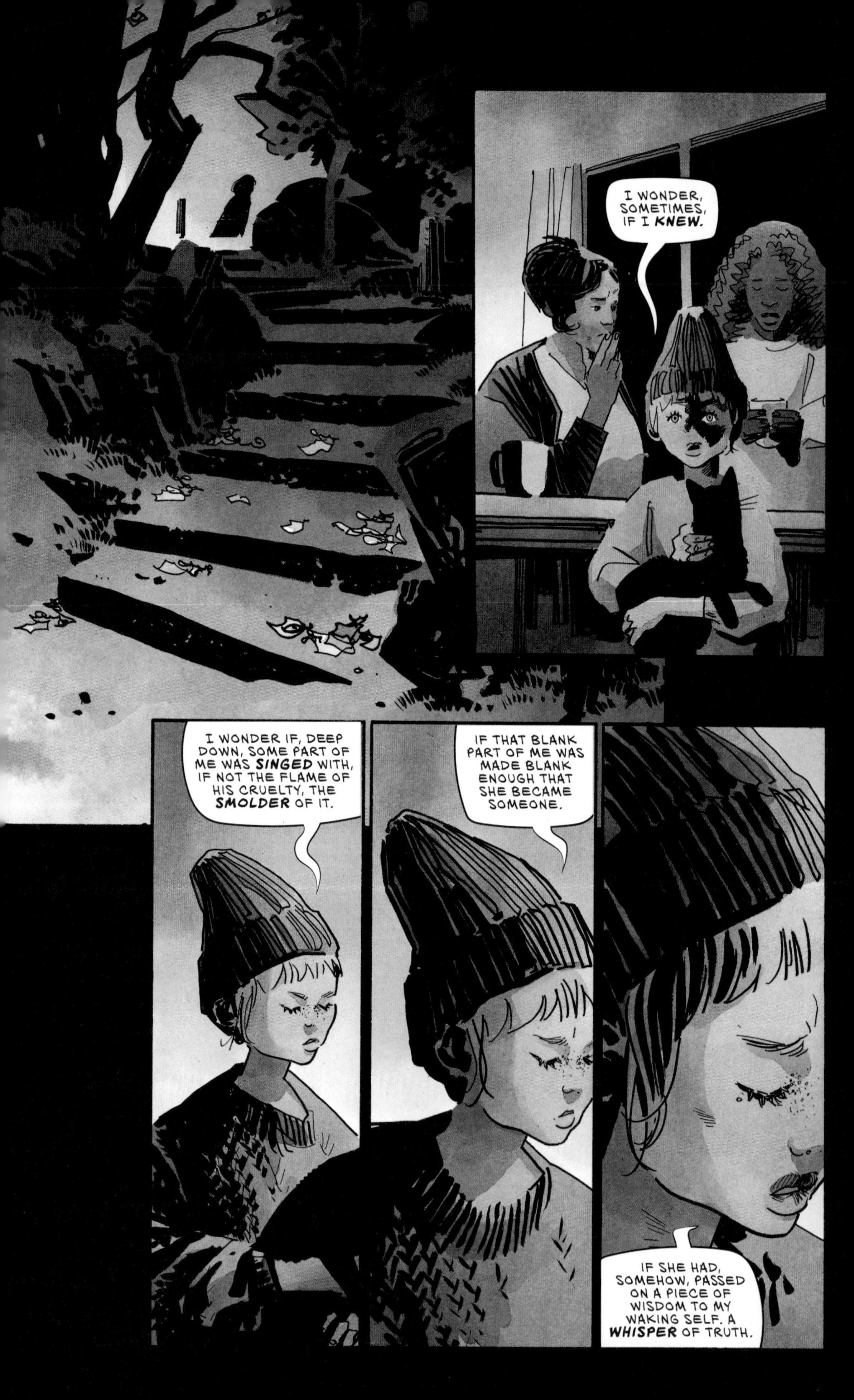
I WONDER, SOMETIMES, IF I KNEW.
I WONDER IF, DEEP DOWN, SOME PART OF ME WAS SINGED WITH, IF NOT THE FLAME OF HIS CRUELTY, THE SMOLDER OF IT.
IF THAT BLANK PART OF ME WAS MADE BLANK ENOUGH THAT SHE BECAME SOMEONE.
IF SHE HAD, SOMEHOW, PASSED ON A PIECE OF WISDOM TO MY WAKING SELF. A WHISPER OF TRUTH.

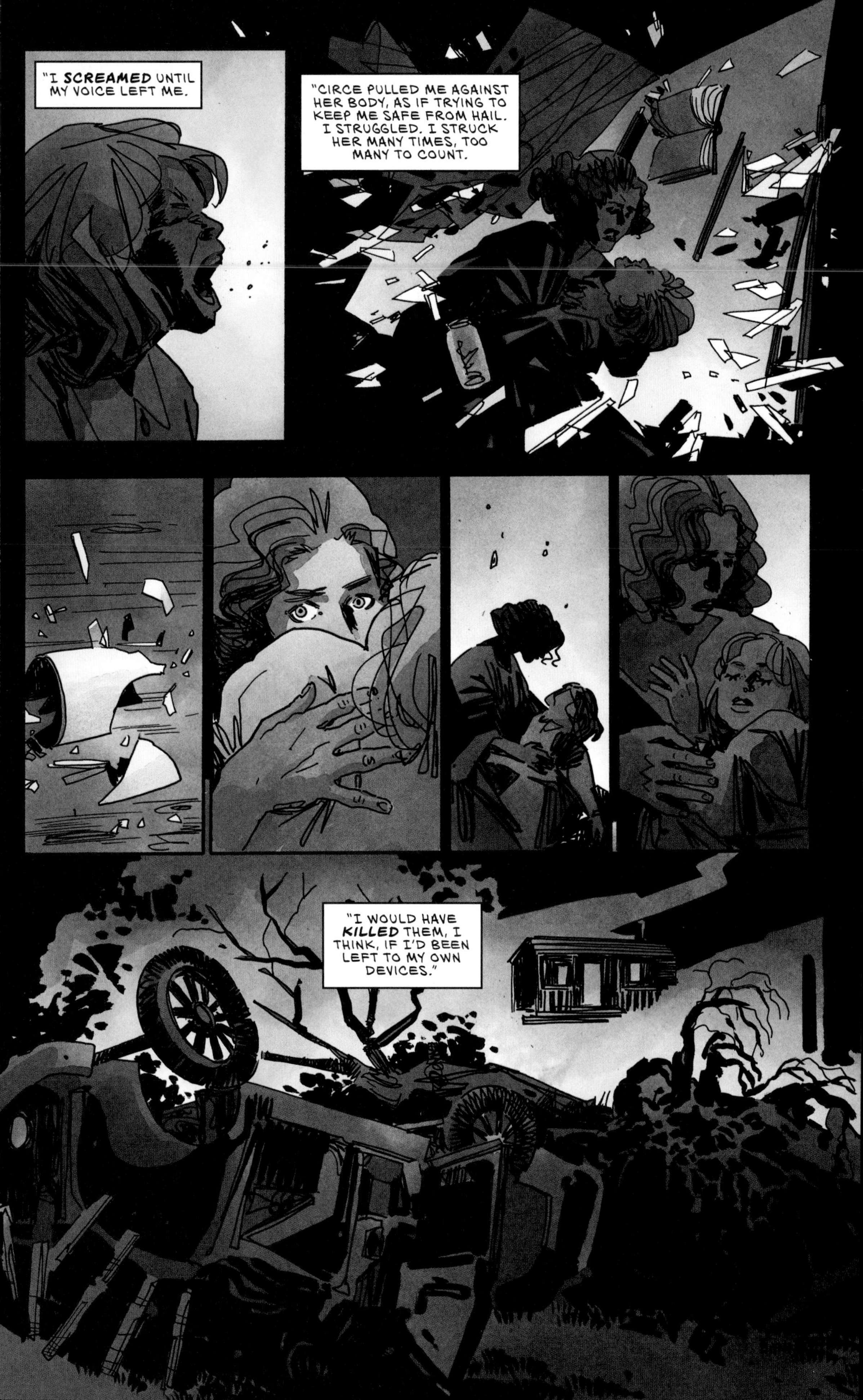
"I **SCREAMED** UNTIL MY VOICE LEFT ME.
"CIRCE PULLED ME AGAINST HER BODY, AS IF TRYING TO KEEP ME SAFE FROM HAIL. I STRUGGLED. I STRUCK HER MANY TIMES, TOO MANY TO COUNT.
"I WOULD HAVE **KILLED** THEM, I THINK, IF I'D BEEN LEFT TO MY OWN DEVICES."

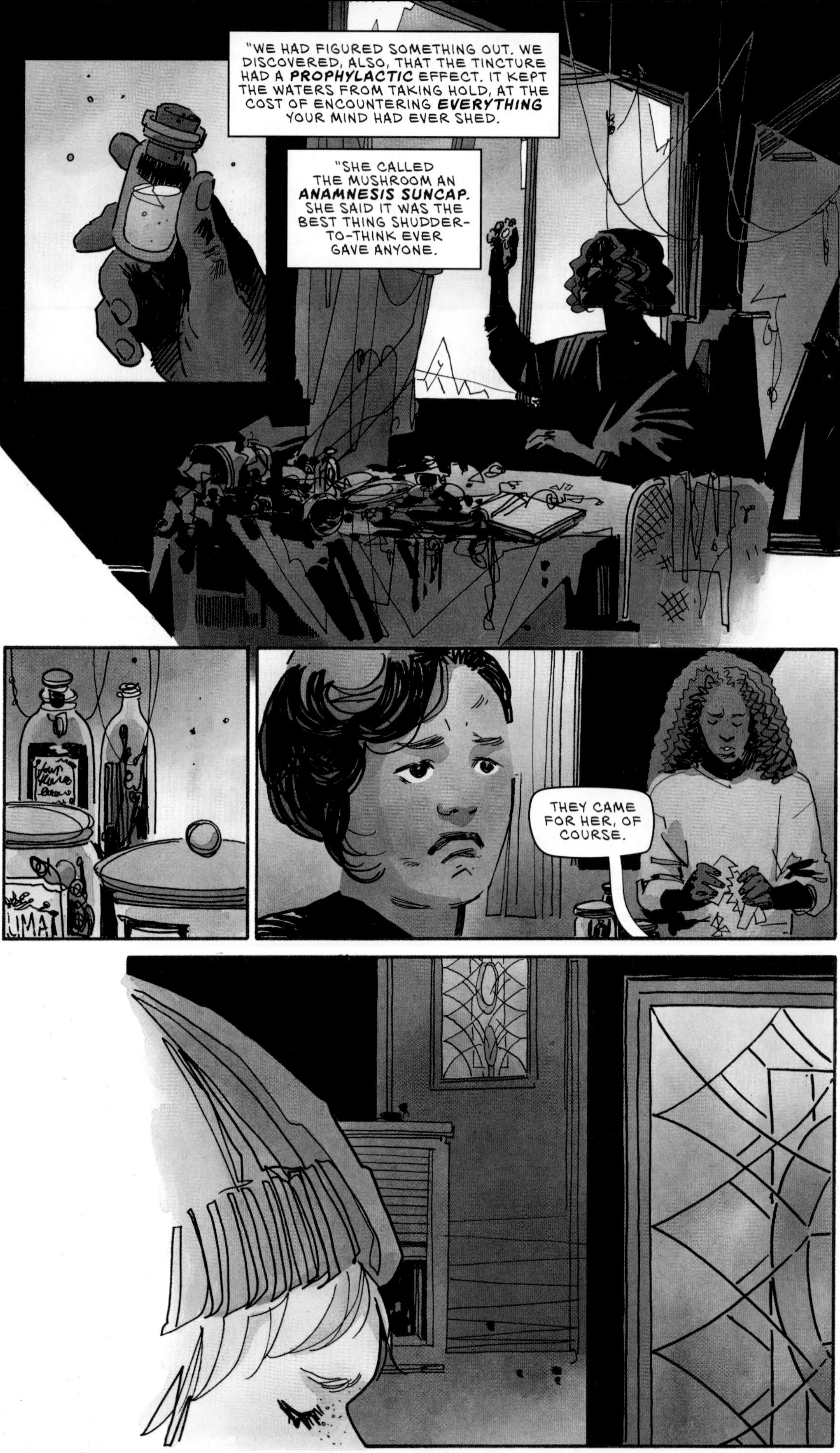
"WE HAD FIGURED SOMETHING OUT. WE DISCOVERED, ALSO, THAT THE TINCTURE HAD A **PROPHYLACTIC** EFFECT. IT KEPT THE WATERS FROM TAKING HOLD, AT THE COST OF ENCOUNTERING **EVERYTHING** YOUR MIND HAD EVER SHED.
"SHE CALLED THE MUSHROOM AN **ANAMNESIS SUNCAP.** SHE SAID IT WAS THE BEST THING SHUDDER-TO-THINK EVER GAVE ANYONE.
THEY CAME FOR HER, OF COURSE.

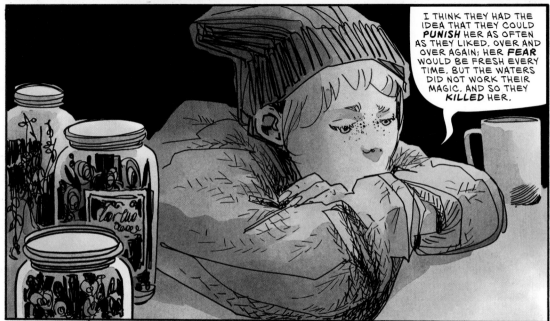

I THINK THEY HAD THE IDEA THAT THEY COULD *PUNISH* HER AS OFTEN AS THEY LIKED, OVER AND OVER AGAIN; HER *FEAR* WOULD BE FRESH EVERY TIME. BUT THE WATERS DID NOT WORK THEIR MAGIC. AND SO THEY *KILLED* HER.

"THEY WENT AMOK AFTER THAT. THEY WERE AFRAID OF NO ONE.

"THE WOMEN WERE GIVEN THE WATERS SO MUCH THEY BEGAN TO SUFFER. SCHOOLGIRLS WOULD *SCREAM* AT THEIR DESKS. GROWN WOMEN WOULD FALL *SILENT* MID-SENTENCE AND STAY THAT WAY FOR HOURS.

"THEY GOT SLOPPY. INSTEAD OF RETURNING WOMEN TO THEIR BEDS, THEY SIMPLY *LEFT* THEM WHERE THEY FELL.

"HE SPELL *I* DID AS NOT SUPPOSED TO REATE *FIRE*. IT WAS O SEND THE MEN--ANY AN WHOSE HANDS HAD OUCHED THAT CIPHER-- ENEATH THE EARTH. IMAGINED THEM RITHING IN THOSE ATERS, *DROWNING* D THEN COMING ACK AND THEN ROWNING AIN. OREVER.

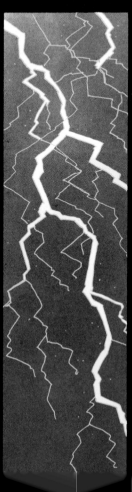

"BUT SOMETHING WENT WRONG."

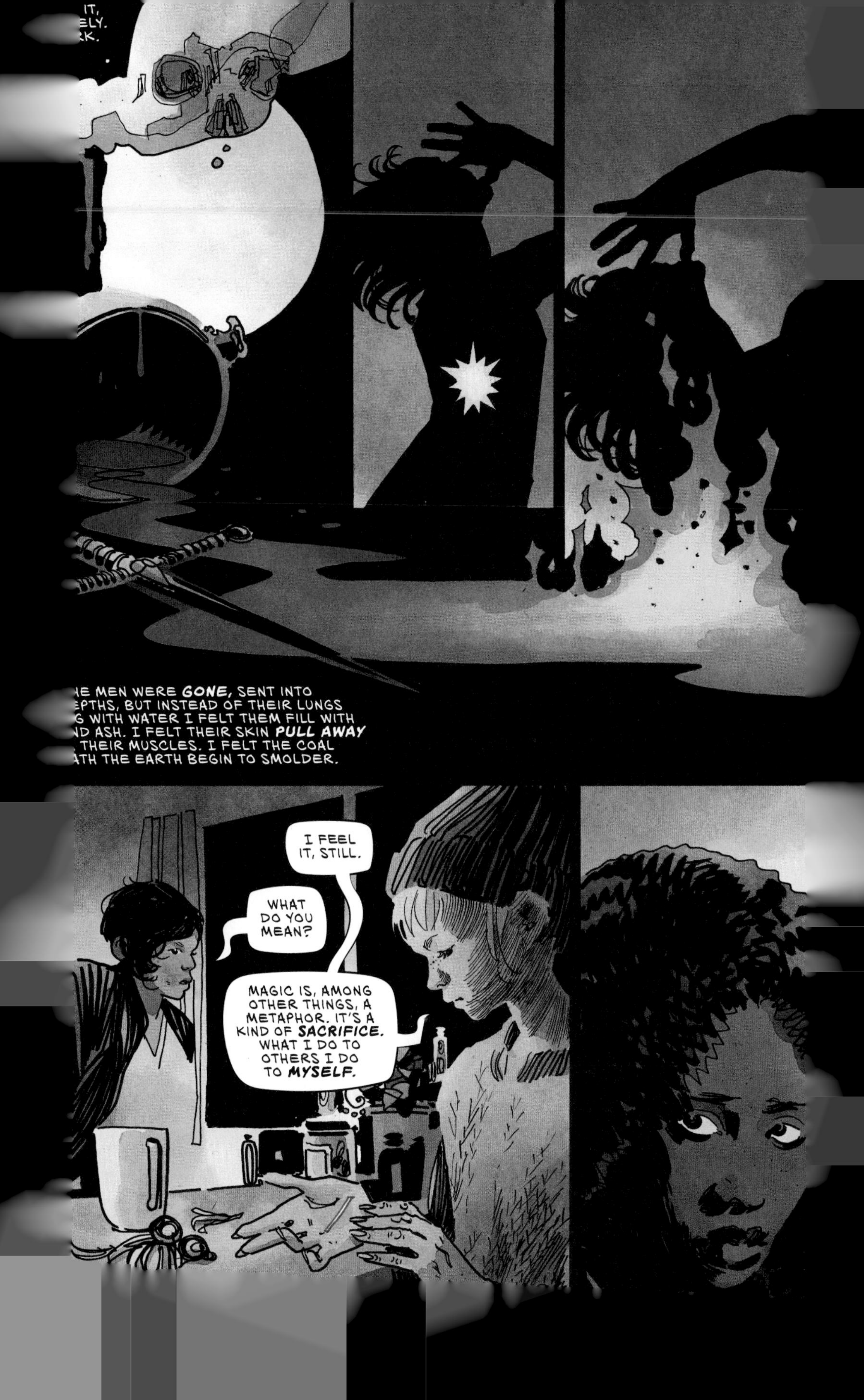

IT,
HE MEN WERE GONE, SENT INTO
EPTHS, BUT INSTEAD OF THEIR LUNGS
G WITH WATER I FELT THEM FILL WITH
ND ASH. I FELT THEIR SKIN PULL AWAY
THEIR MUSCLES. I FELT THE COAL
ATH THE EARTH BEGIN TO SMOLDER.
I FEEL IT, STILL.
WHAT DO YOU MEAN?
MAGIC IS, AMONG OTHER THINGS, A METAPHOR. IT'S A KIND OF SACRIFICE. WHAT I DO TO OTHERS I DO TO MYSELF.

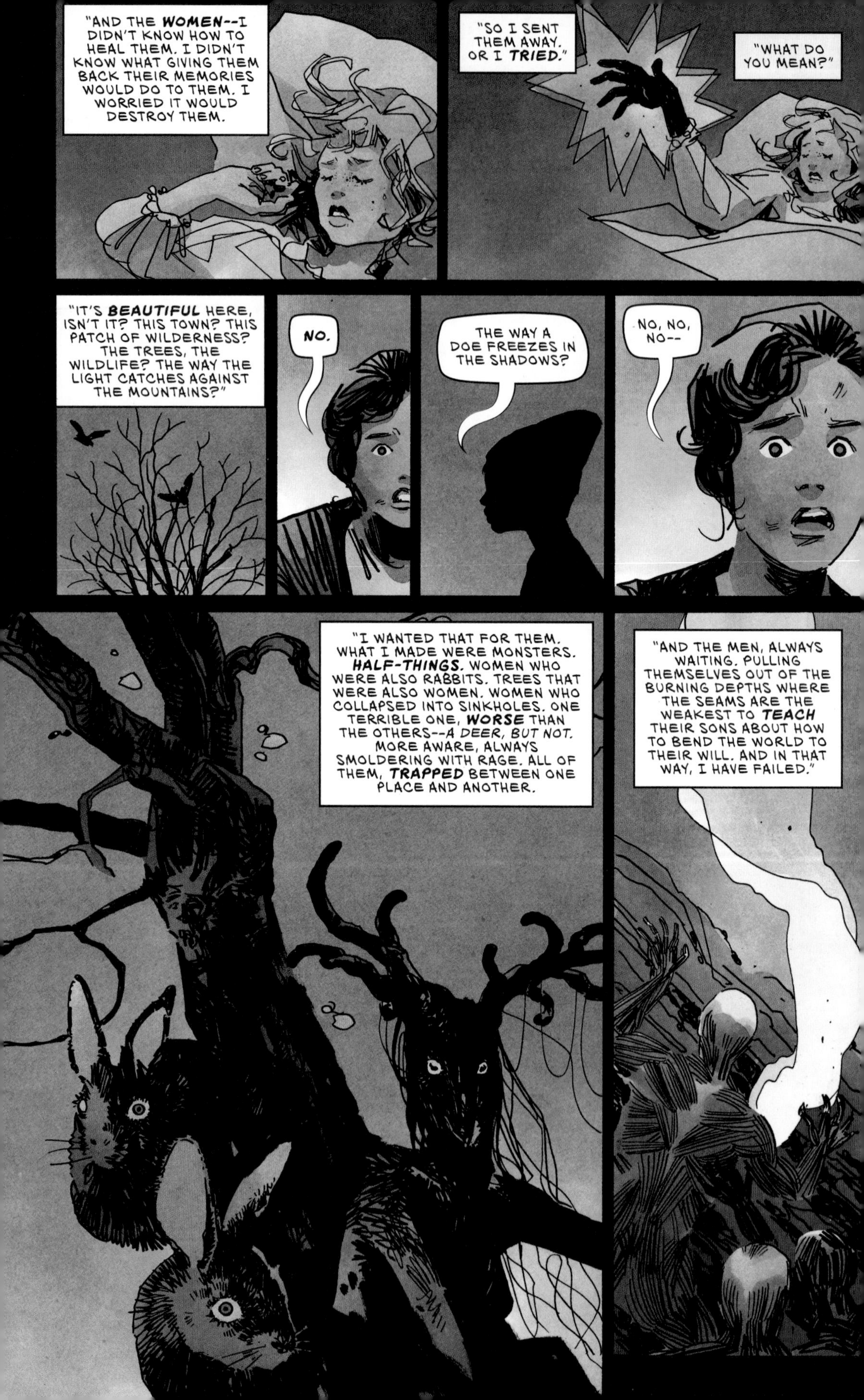
"AND THE WOMEN--I DIDN'T KNOW HOW TO HEAL THEM. I DIDN'T KNOW WHAT GIVING THEM BACK THEIR MEMORIES WOULD DO TO THEM. I WORRIED IT WOULD DESTROY THEM.
"SO I SENT THEM AWAY. OR I TRIED."
"WHAT DO YOU MEAN?"
"IT'S BEAUTIFUL HERE, ISN'T IT? THIS TOWN? THIS PATCH OF WILDERNESS? THE TREES, THE WILDLIFE? THE WAY THE LIGHT CATCHES AGAINST THE MOUNTAINS?"
NO.
THE WAY A DOE FREEZES IN THE SHADOWS?
NO, NO, NO--
"I WANTED THAT FOR THEM. WHAT I MADE WERE MONSTERS. HALF-THINGS. WOMEN WHO WERE ALSO RABBITS. TREES THAT WERE ALSO WOMEN. WOMEN WHO COLLAPSED INTO SINKHOLES. ONE TERRIBLE ONE, WORSE THAN THE OTHERS--A DEER, BUT NOT. MORE AWARE, ALWAYS SMOLDERING WITH RAGE. ALL OF THEM, TRAPPED BETWEEN ONE PLACE AND ANOTHER.
"AND THE MEN, ALWAYS WAITING. PULLING THEMSELVES OUT OF THE BURNING DEPTHS WHERE THE SEAMS ARE THE WEAKEST TO TEACH THEIR SONS ABOUT HOW TO BEND THE WORLD TO THEIR WILL. AND IN THAT WAY, I HAVE FAILED."

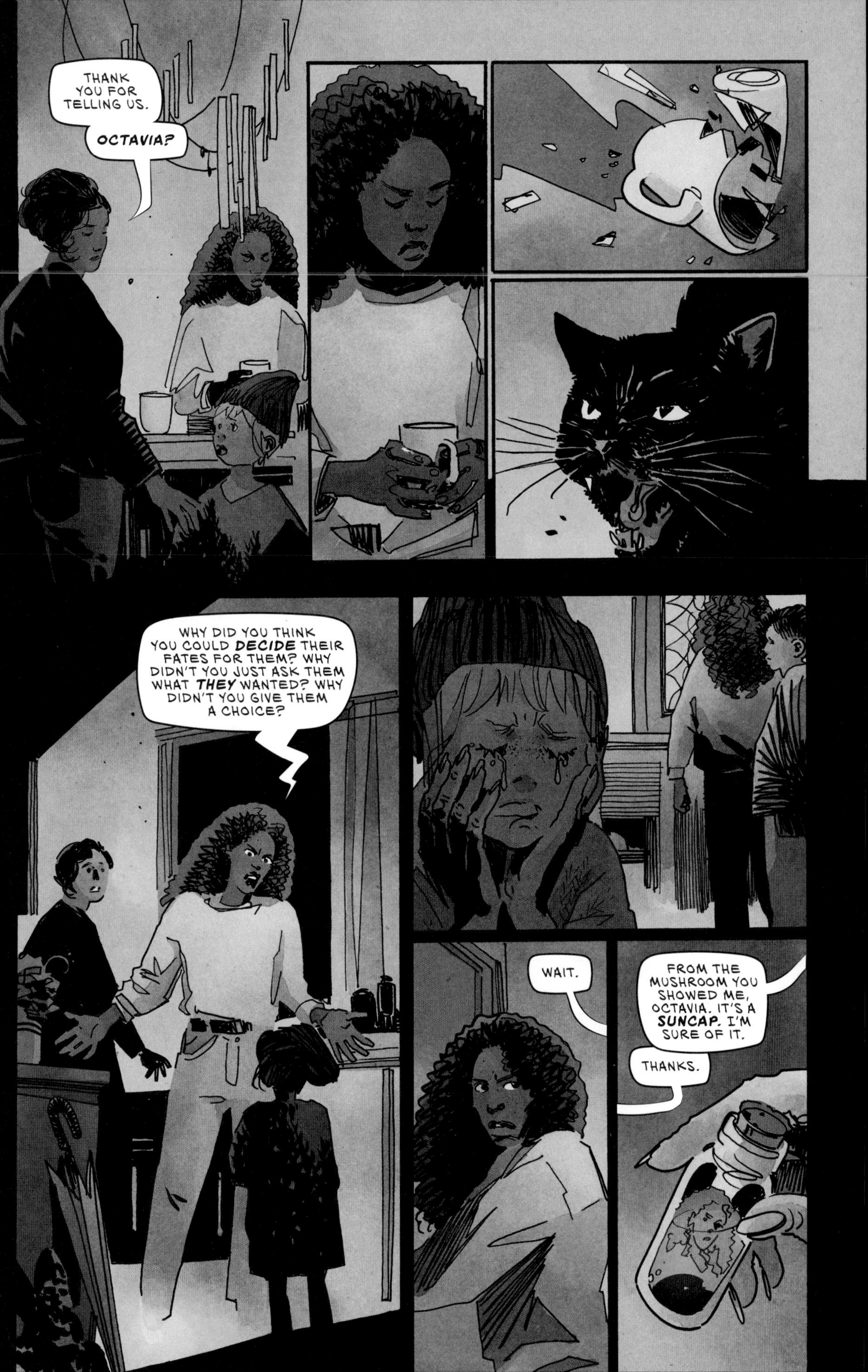
THANK YOU FOR TELLING US.
OCTAVIA?
WHY DID YOU THINK YOU COULD DECIDE THEIR FATES FOR THEM? WHY DIDN'T YOU JUST ASK THEM WHAT THEY WANTED? WHY DIDN'T YOU GIVE THEM A CHOICE?
WAIT.
FROM THE MUSHROOM YOU SHOWED ME, OCTAVIA. IT'S A SUNCAP. I'M SURE OF IT.
THANKS.

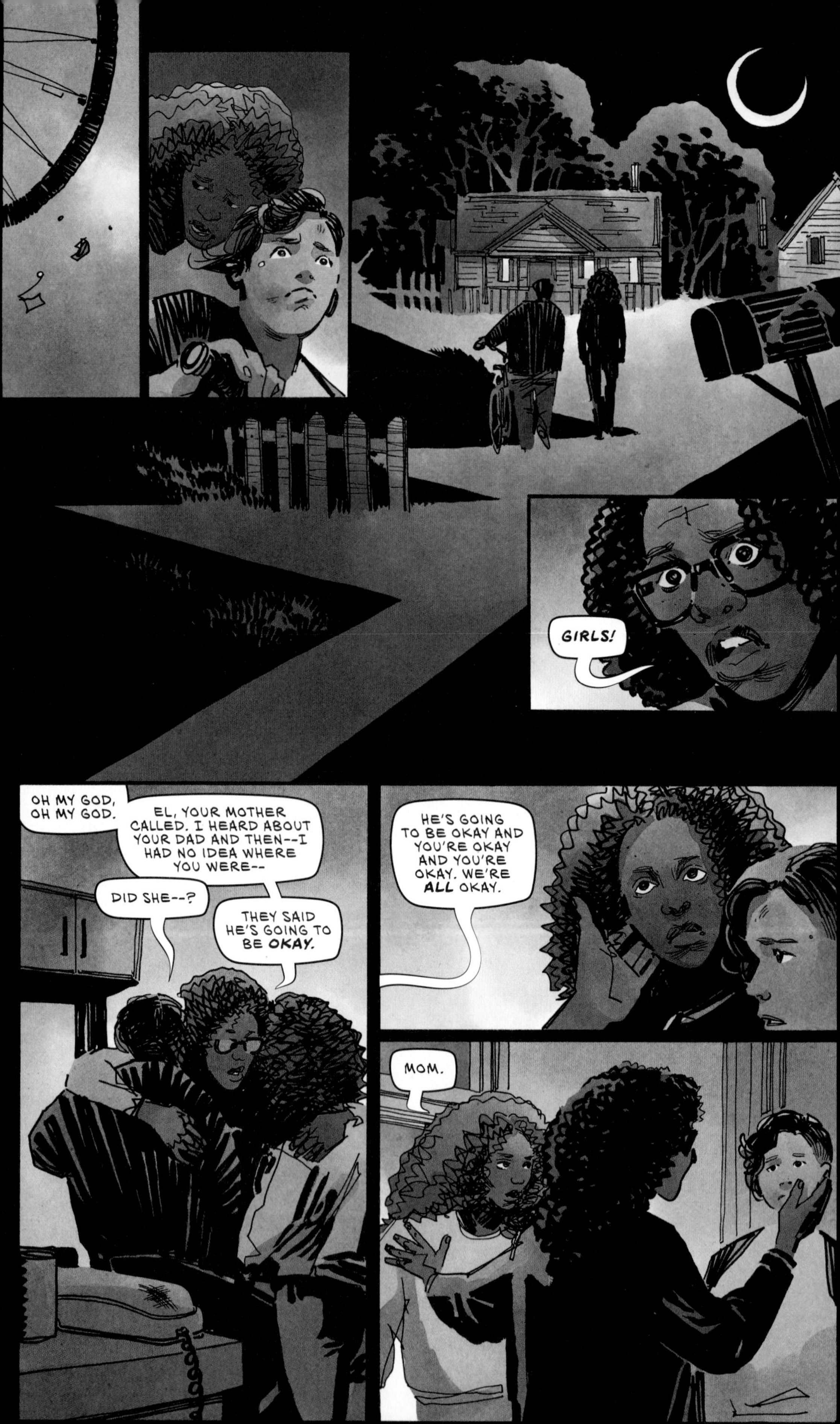
GIRLS!
OH MY GOD, OH MY GOD.
EL, YOUR MOTHER CALLED. I HEARD ABOUT YOUR DAD AND THEN--I HAD NO IDEA WHERE YOU WERE--
DID SHE--?
THEY SAID HE'S GOING TO BE OKAY.
HE'S GOING TO BE OKAY AND YOU'RE OKAY AND YOU'RE OKAY. WE'RE ALL OKAY.
MOM.

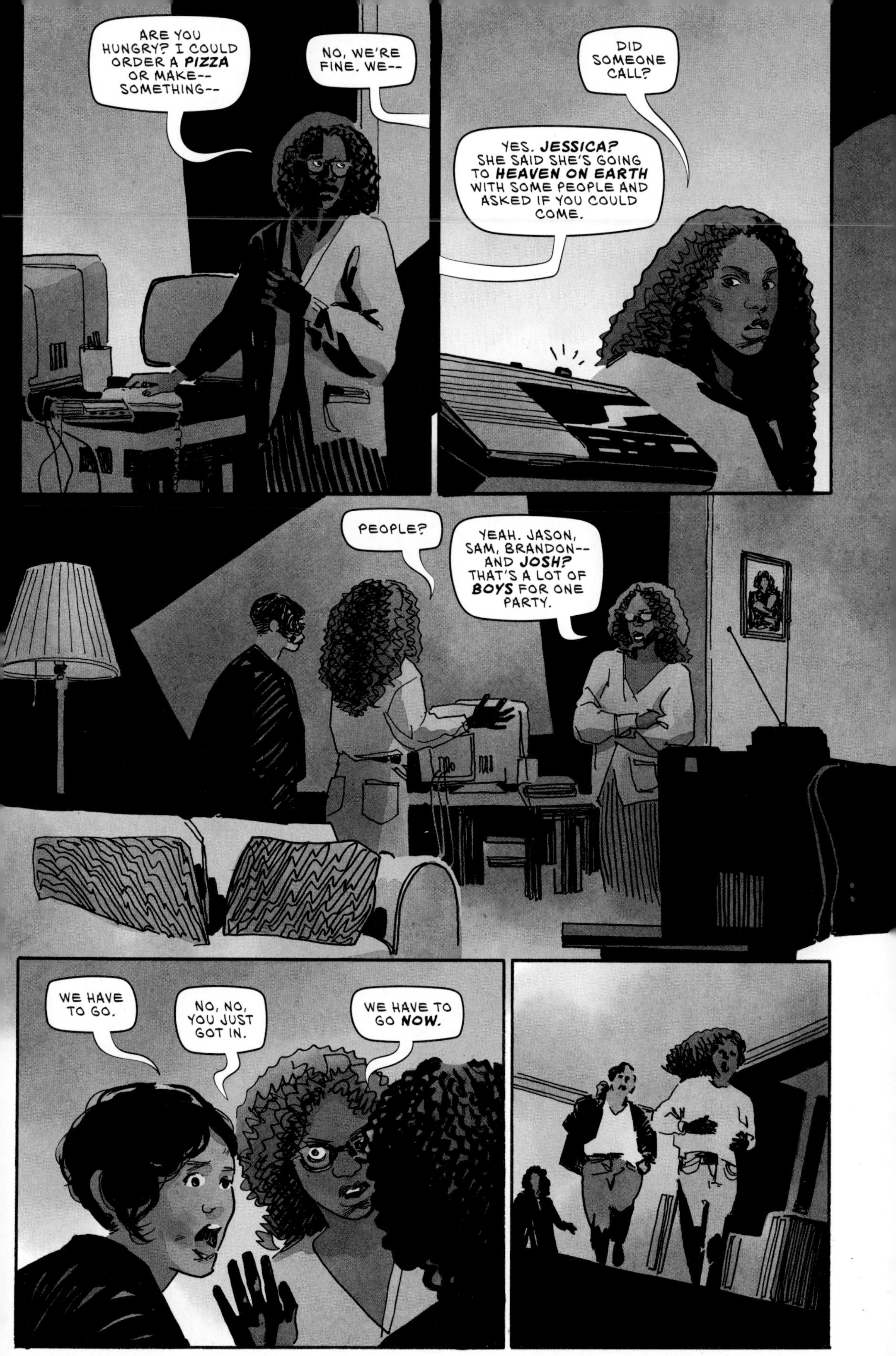
ARE YOU HUNGRY? I COULD ORDER A **PIZZA** OR MAKE-- SOMETHING--
NO, WE'RE FINE. WE--
DID SOMEONE CALL?
YES. **JESSICA?** SHE SAID SHE'S GOING TO **HEAVEN ON EARTH** WITH SOME PEOPLE AND ASKED IF YOU COULD COME.
PEOPLE?
YEAH. JASON, SAM, BRANDON-- AND **JOSH?** THAT'S A LOT OF **BOYS** FOR ONE PARTY.
WE HAVE TO GO.
NO, NO, YOU JUST GOT IN.
WE HAVE TO GO **NOW.**

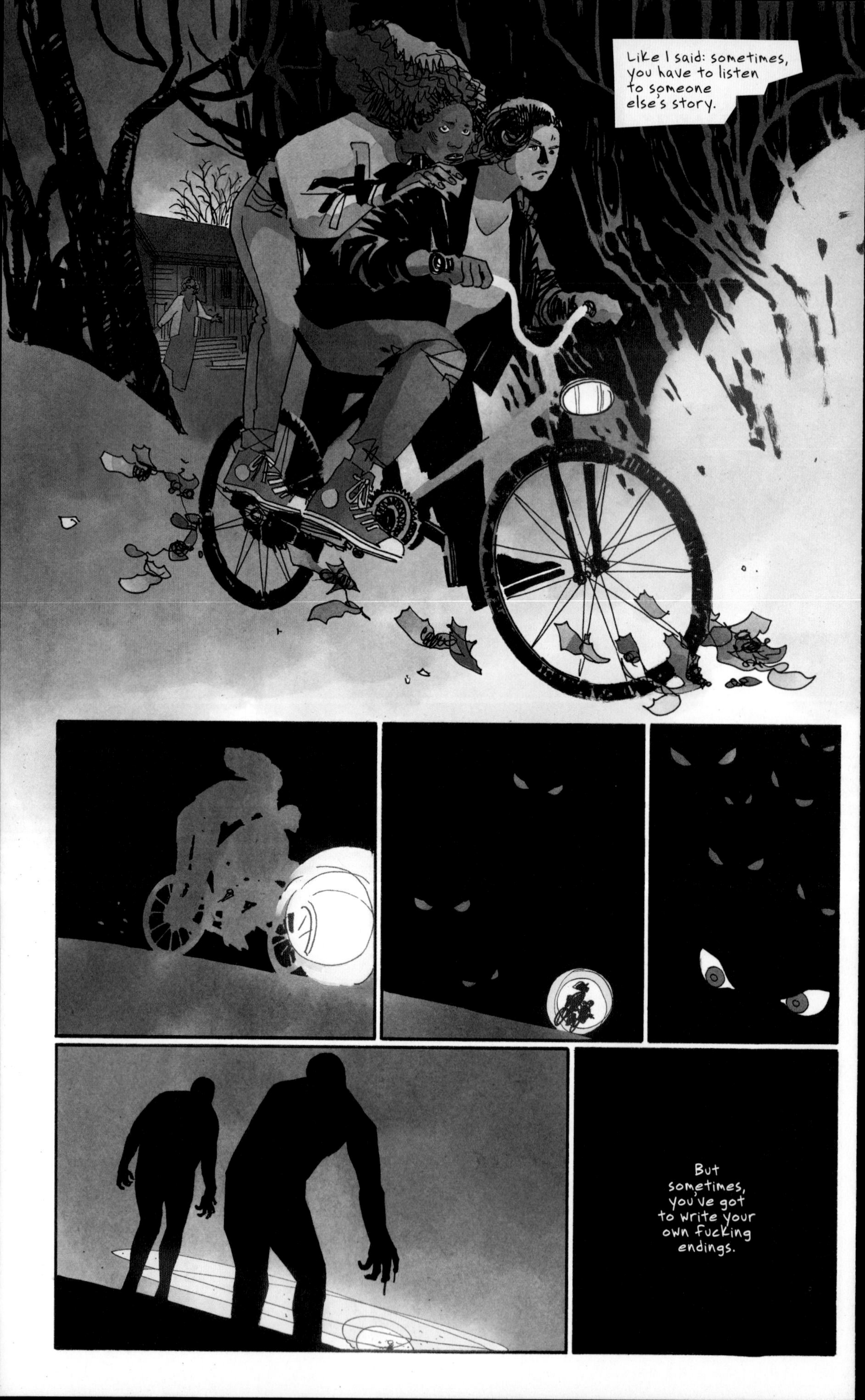
Like I said: sometimes, you have to listen to someone else's story.
But sometimes, you've got to write your own fucking endings.

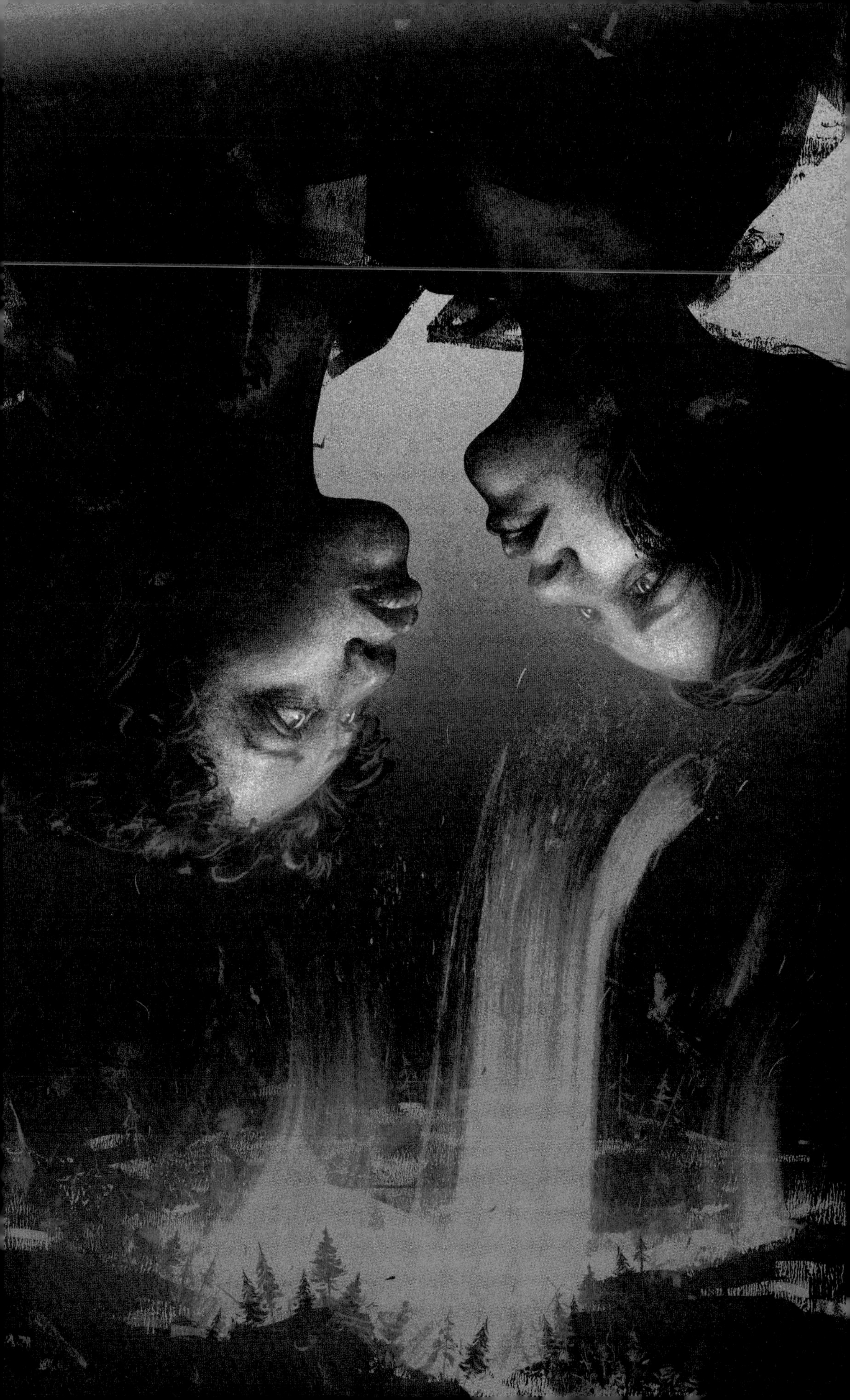

Bells to Rest, Lambs to Slaughter

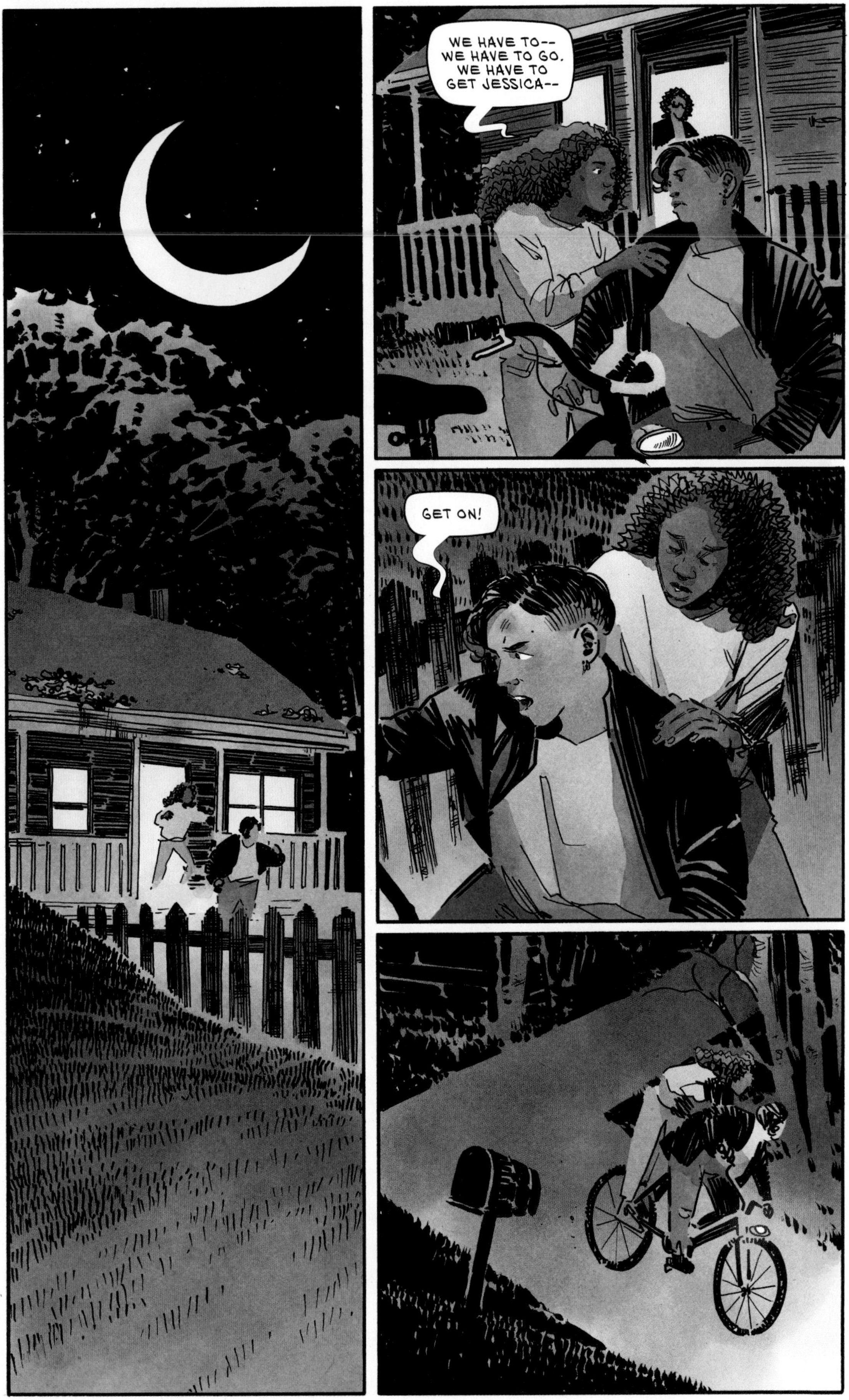
WE HAVE TO--
WE HAVE TO GO.
WE HAVE TO
GET JESSICA--
GET ON!

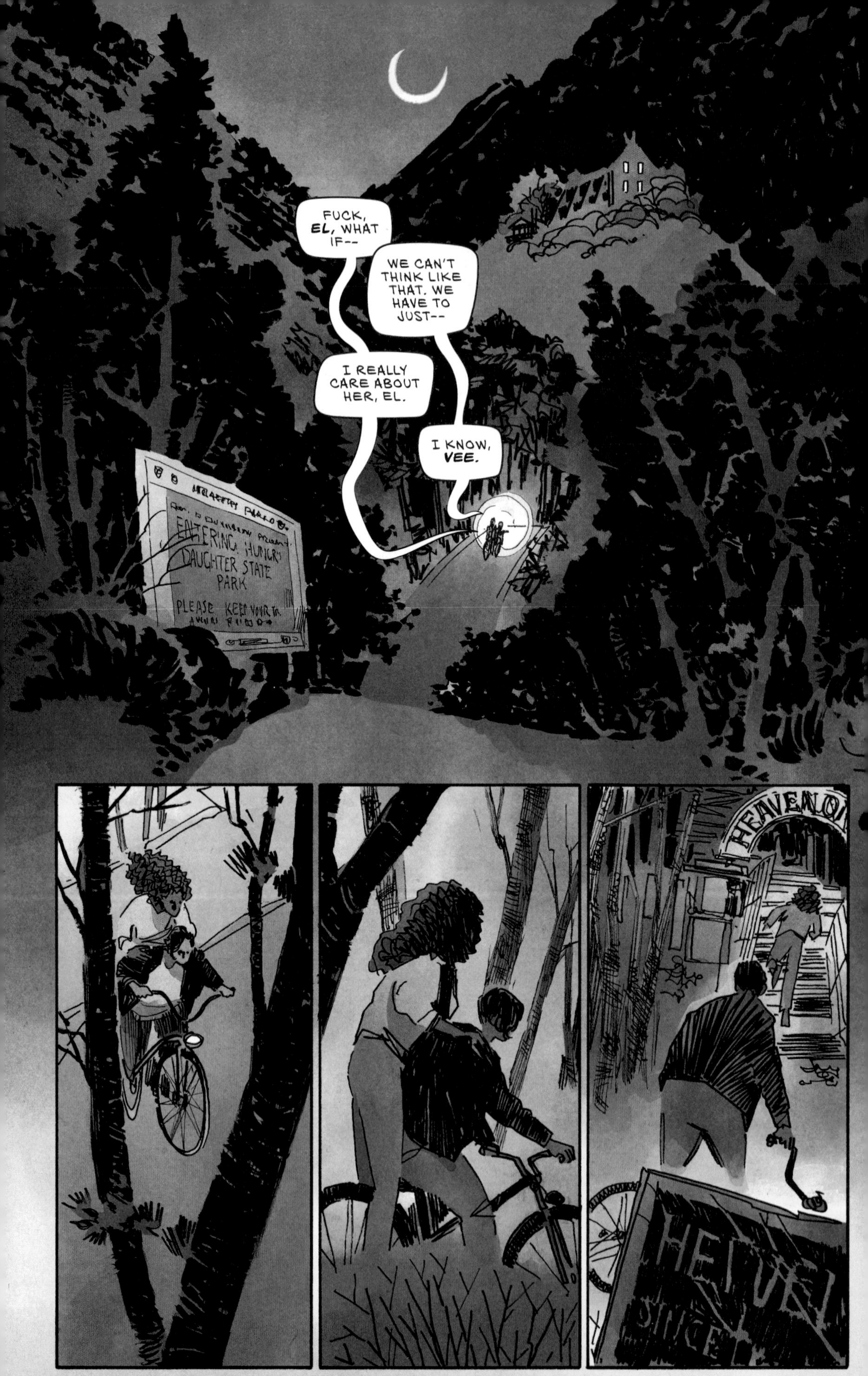
FUCK, **EL**, WHAT IF--
WE CAN'T THINK LIKE THAT. WE HAVE TO JUST--
I REALLY CARE ABOUT HER, EL.
I KNOW, **VEE.**
ENTERING HUNGRY DAUGHTER STATE PARK
PLEASE KEEP YOUR

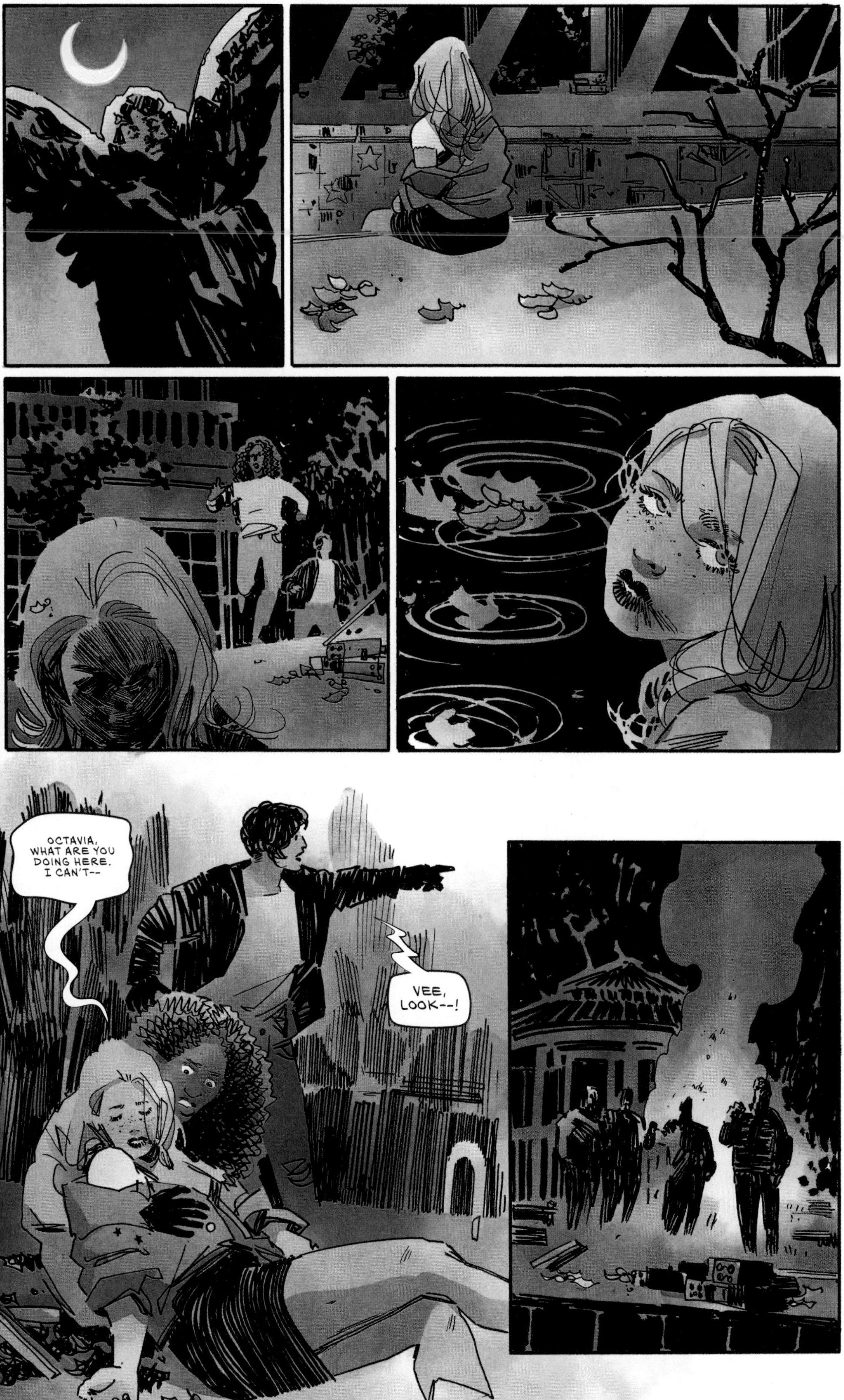
OCTAVIA, WHAT ARE YOU DOING HERE. I CAN'T--
VEE, LOOK--!

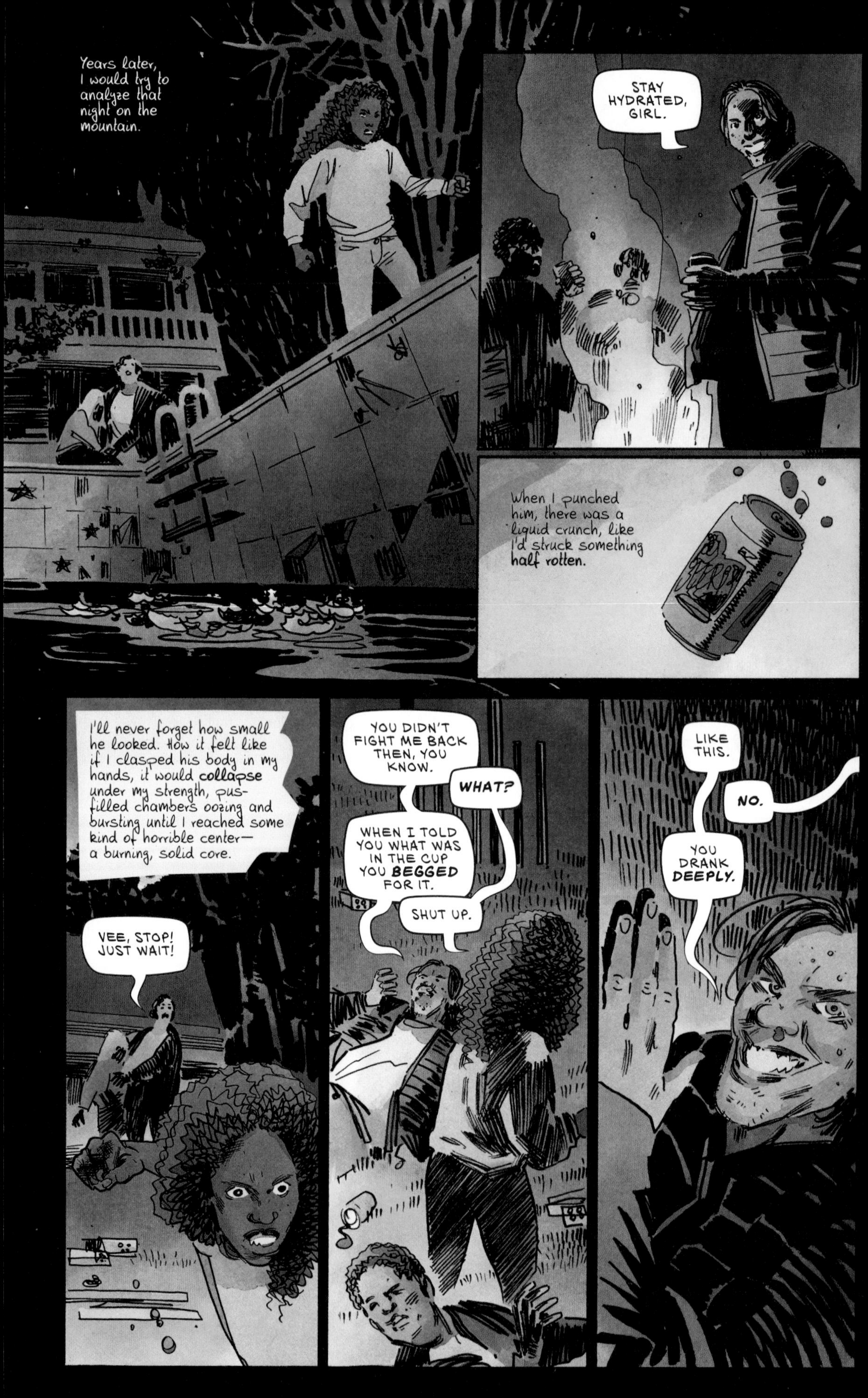
Years later, I would try to analyze that night on the mountain.
STAY HYDRATED, GIRL.
When I punched him, there was a liquid crunch, like I'd struck something **half rotten.**
I'll never forget how small he looked. How it felt like if I clasped his body in my hands, it would **collapse** under my strength, pus-filled chambers oozing and bursting until I reached some kind of horrible center— a burning, solid core.
VEE, STOP! JUST WAIT!
YOU DIDN'T FIGHT ME BACK THEN, YOU KNOW.
WHAT?
WHEN I TOLD YOU WHAT WAS IN THE CUP YOU **BEGGED** FOR IT.
SHUT UP.
LIKE THIS.
NO.
YOU DRANK **DEEPLY.**

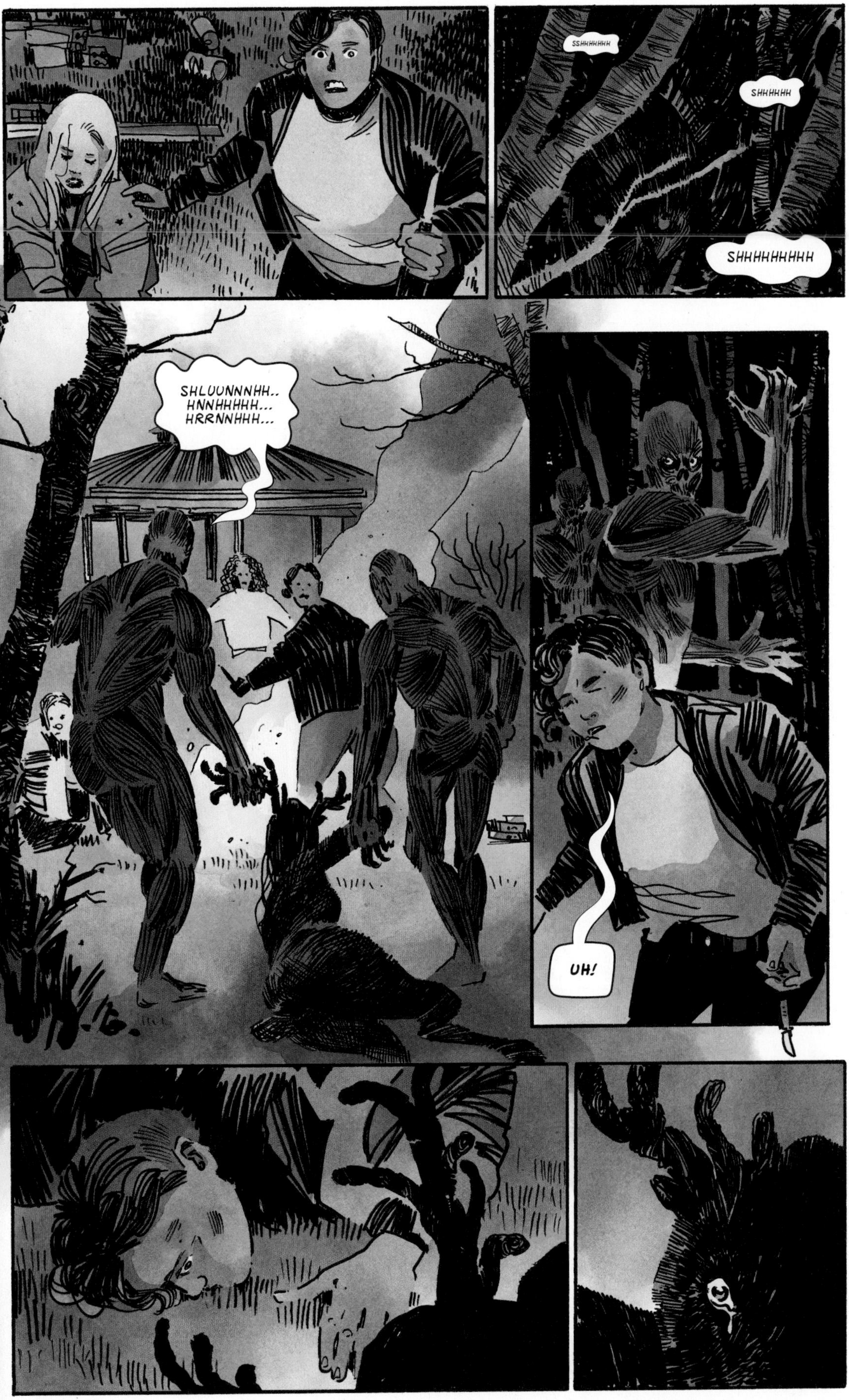
SSHHHHHHH
SHHHHHH
SHHHHHHHHH
SHLUUNNNHH..
HNNHHHHH...
HRRNNHHH...
UH!

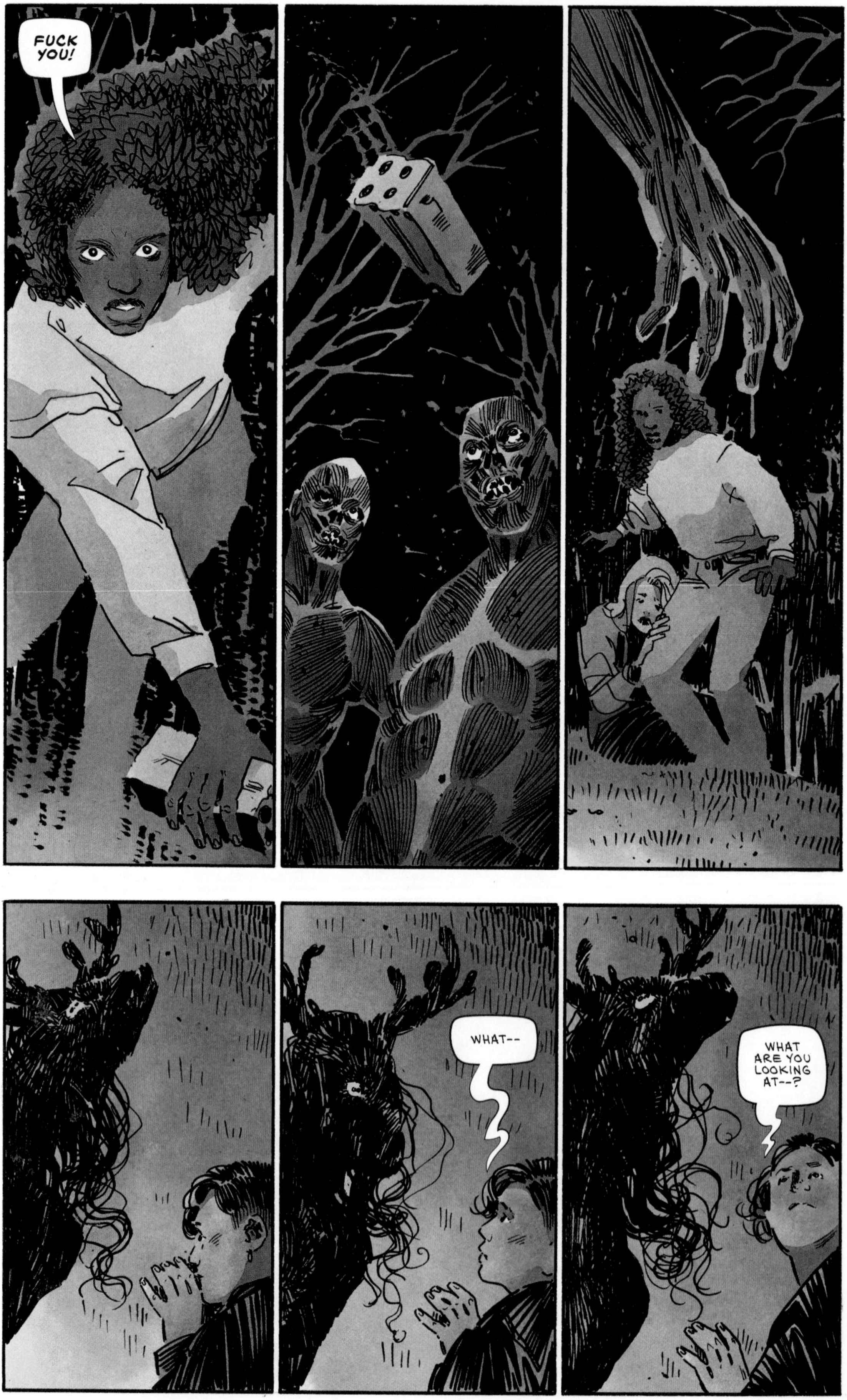
FUCK YOU!
WHAT--
WHAT ARE YOU LOOKING AT--?

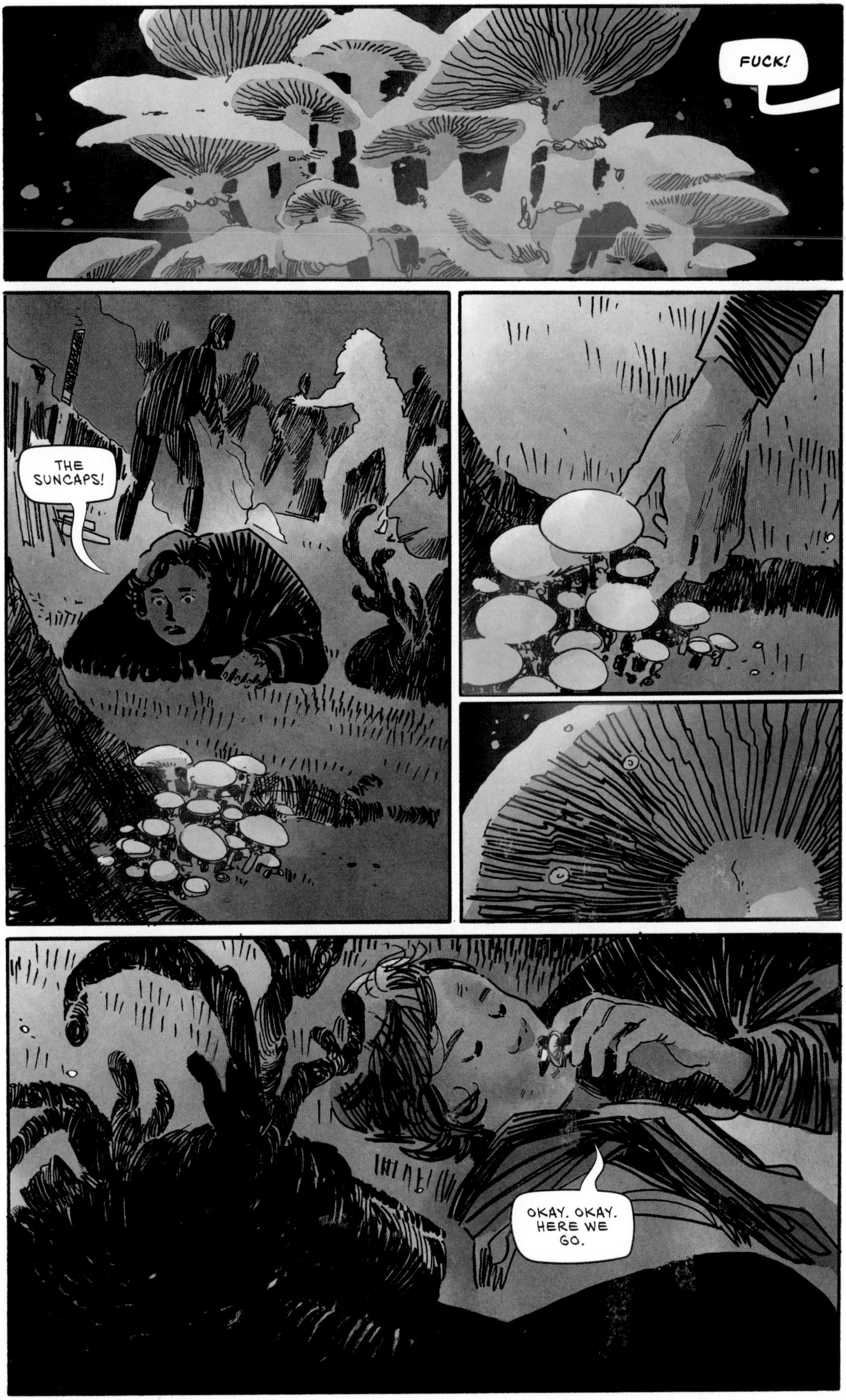
FUCK!
THE SUNCAPS!
OKAY. OKAY. HERE WE GO.

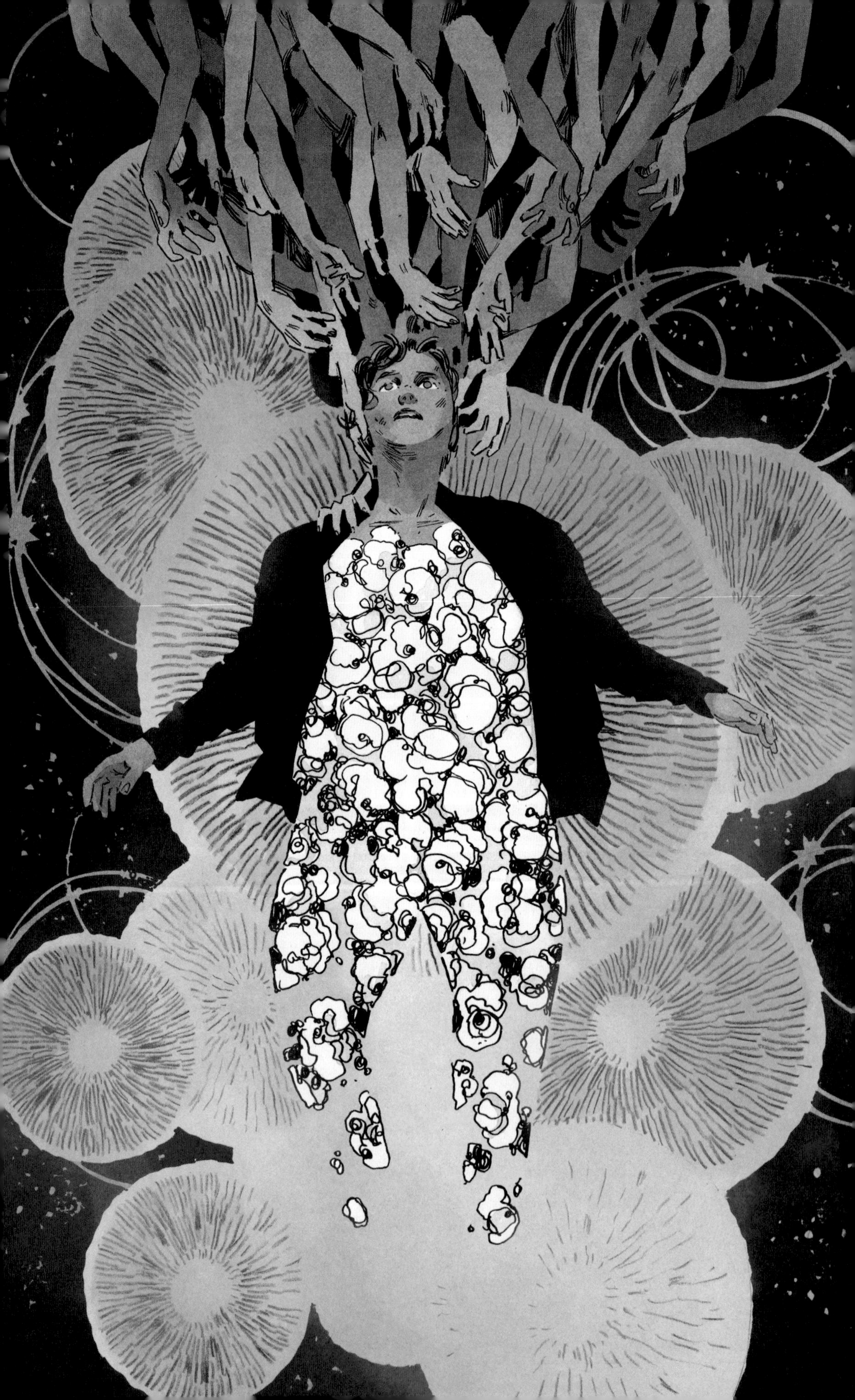

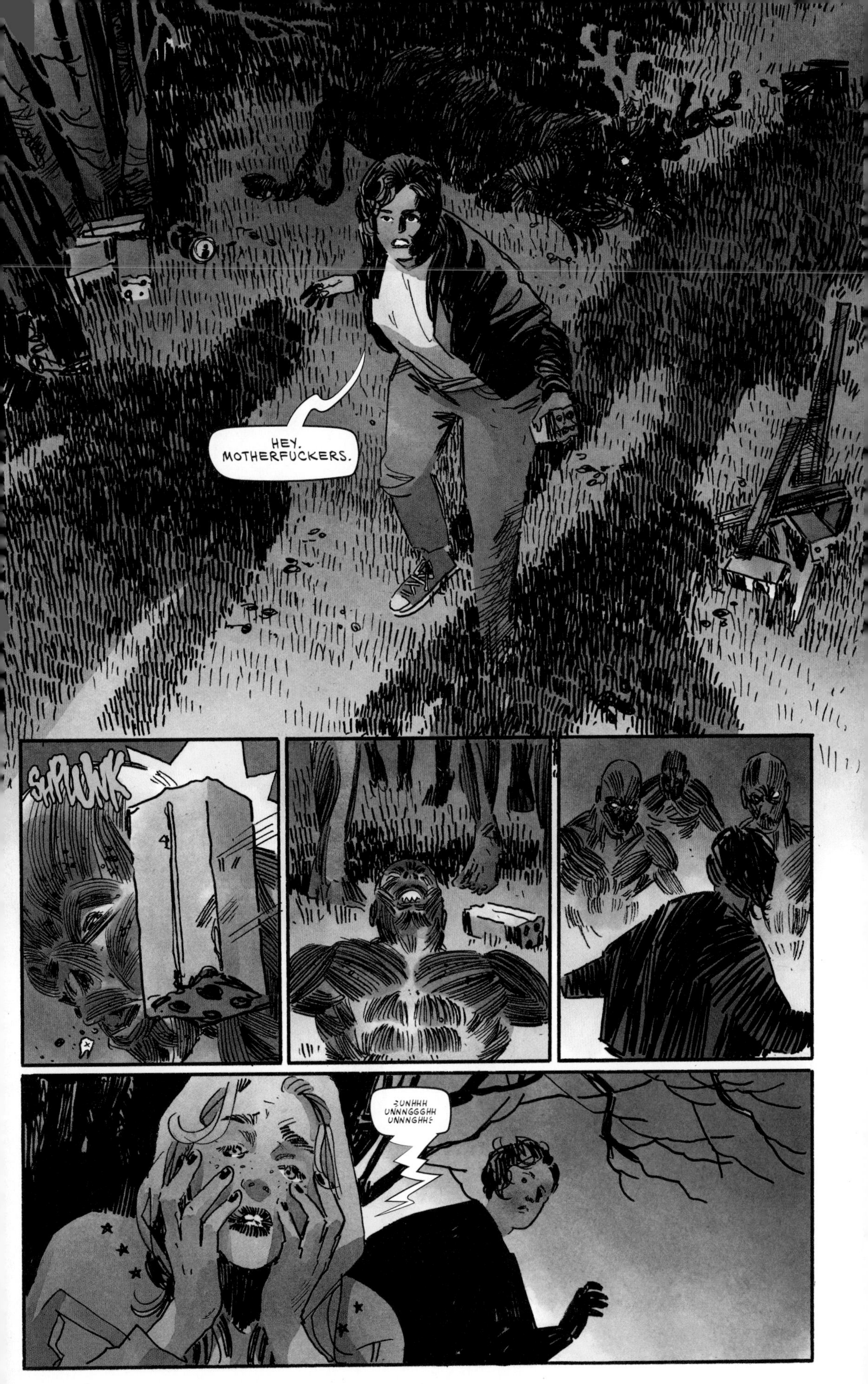
HEY. MOTHERFUCKERS.
SHPLONK
UNHHH UNNNGGGHH UNNNGHH

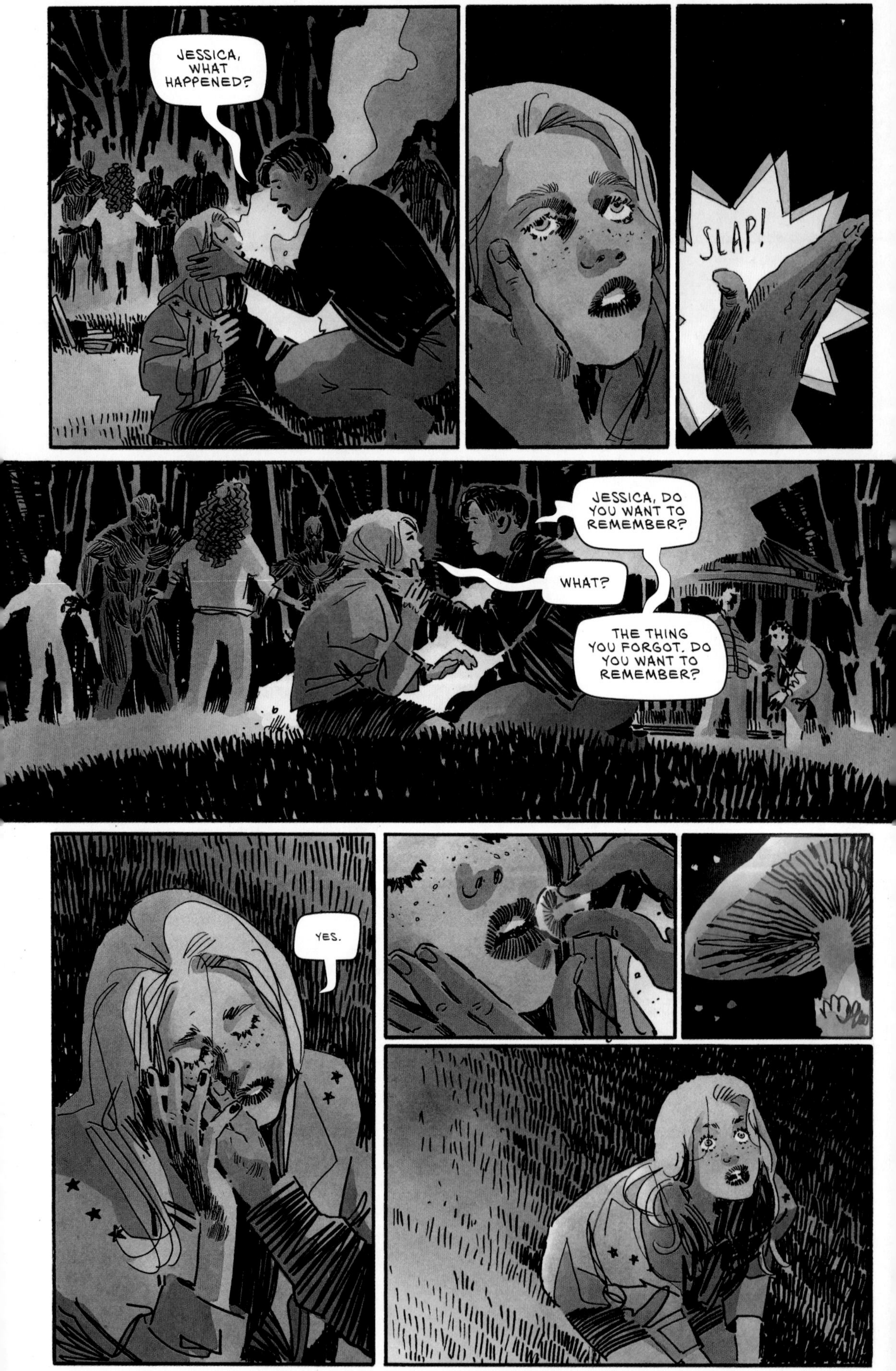
JESSICA, WHAT HAPPENED?
SLAP!
JESSICA, DO YOU WANT TO REMEMBER?
WHAT?
THE THING YOU FORGOT. DO YOU WANT TO REMEMBER?
YES.

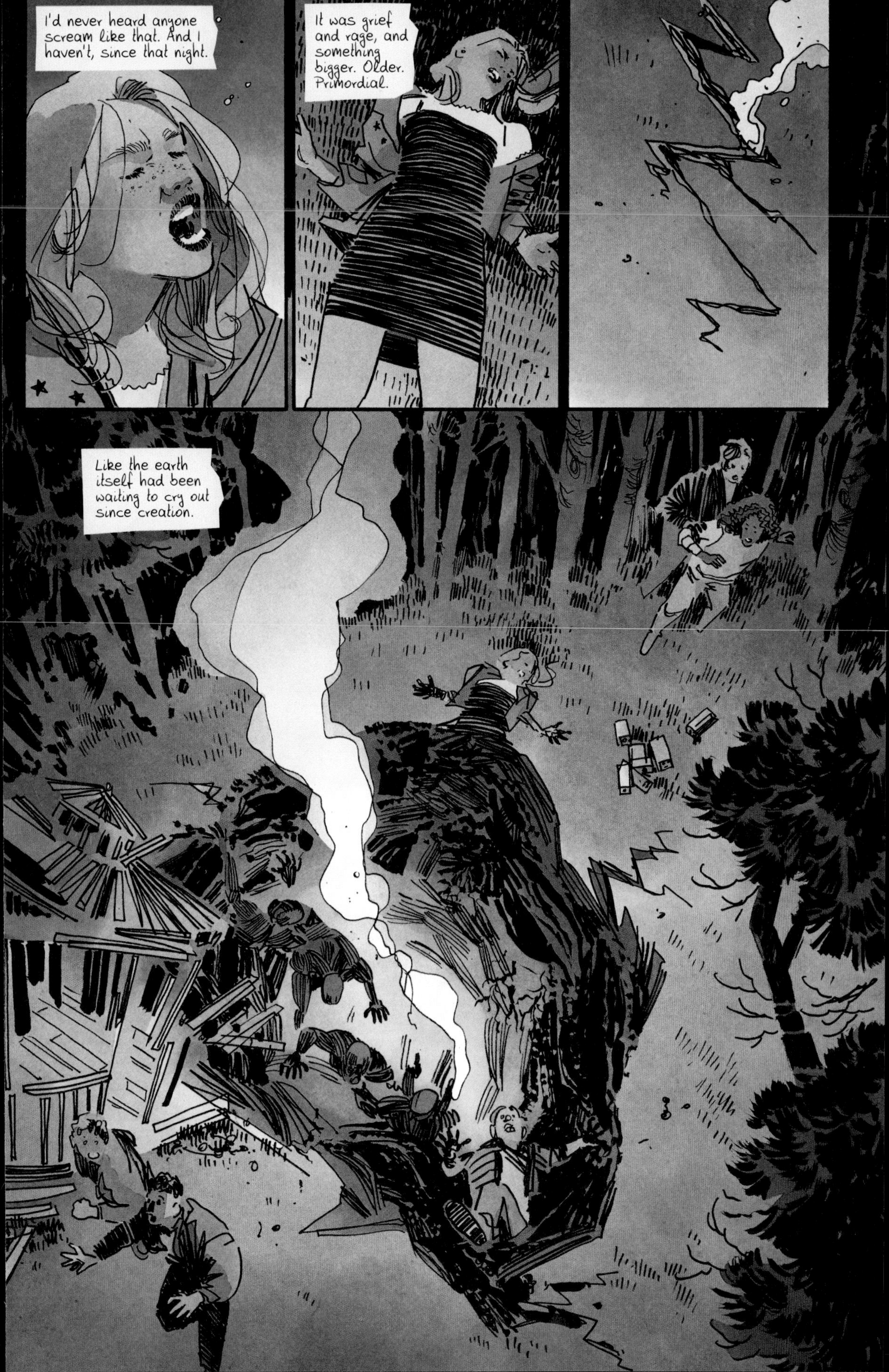
I'd never heard anyone scream like that. And I haven't, since that night.
It was grief and rage, and something bigger. Older. Primordial.
Like the earth itself had been waiting to cry out since creation.

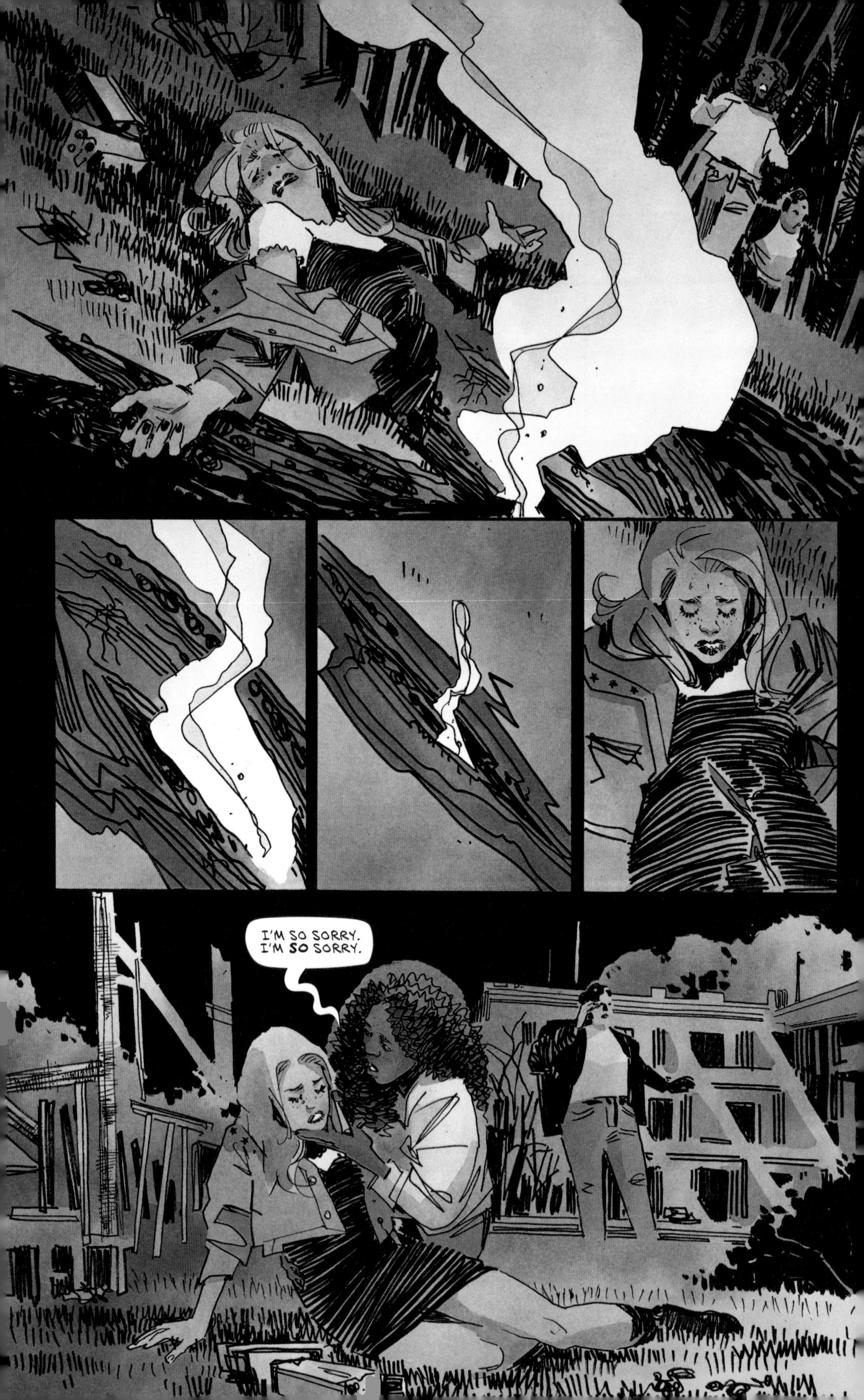
I'M SO SORRY.
I'M SO SORRY.

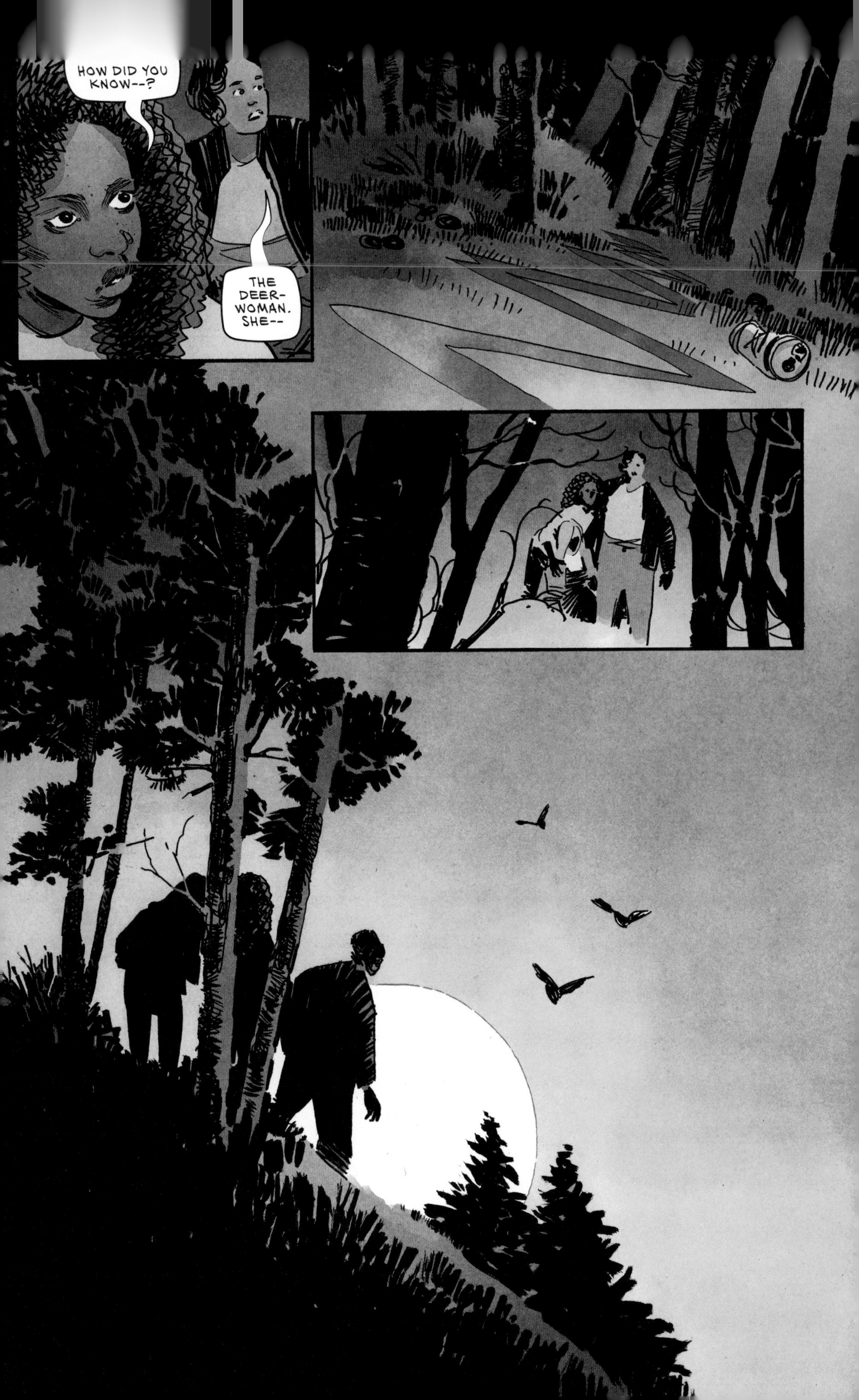
HOW DID YOU KNOW--?
THE DEER-WOMAN. SHE--

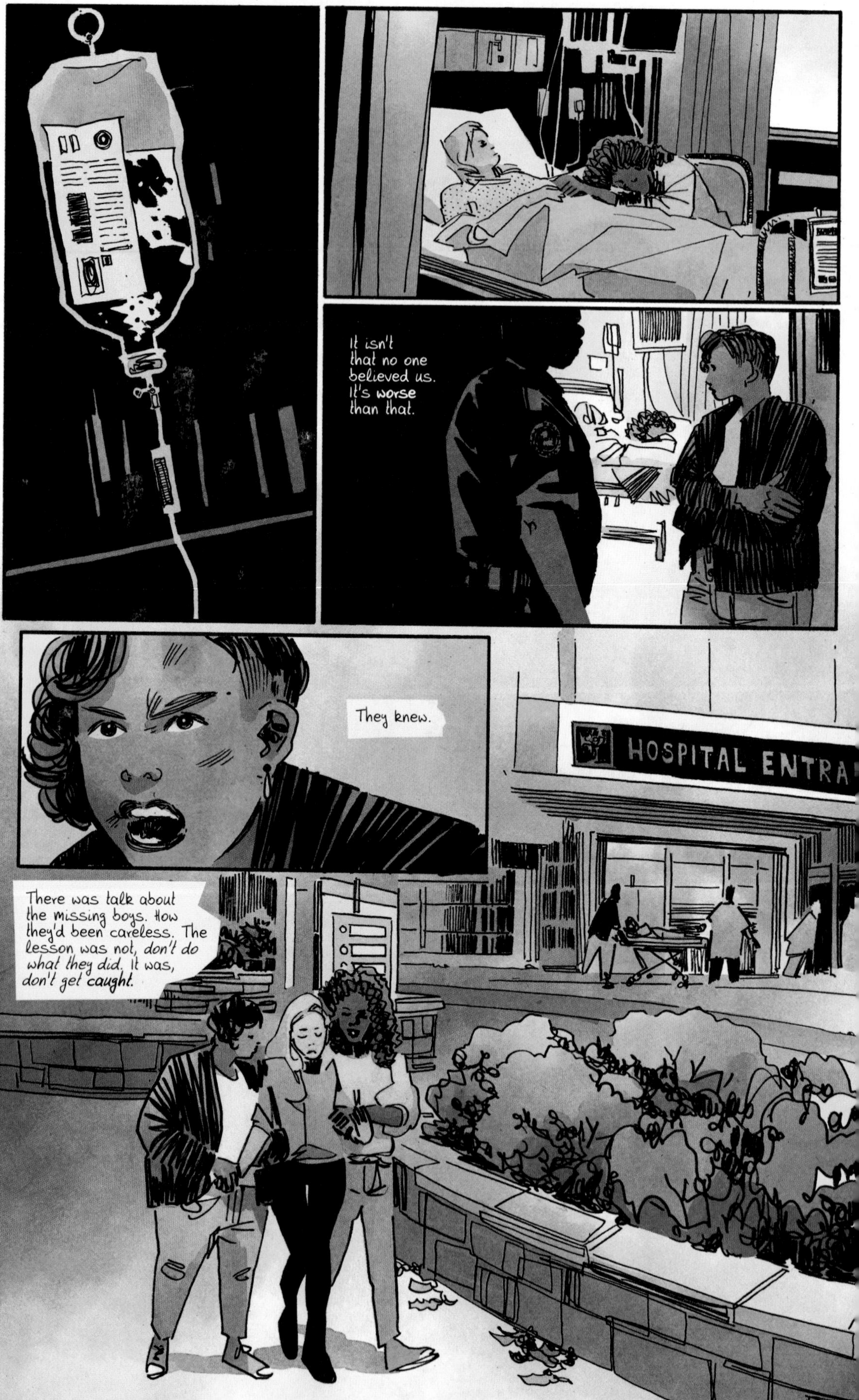
It isn't that no one believed us. It's **worse** than that.
They knew.
HOSPITAL ENTRA
There was talk about the missing boys. How they'd been careless. The lesson was not, *don't do what they did*. It was, *don't get* ***caught***.

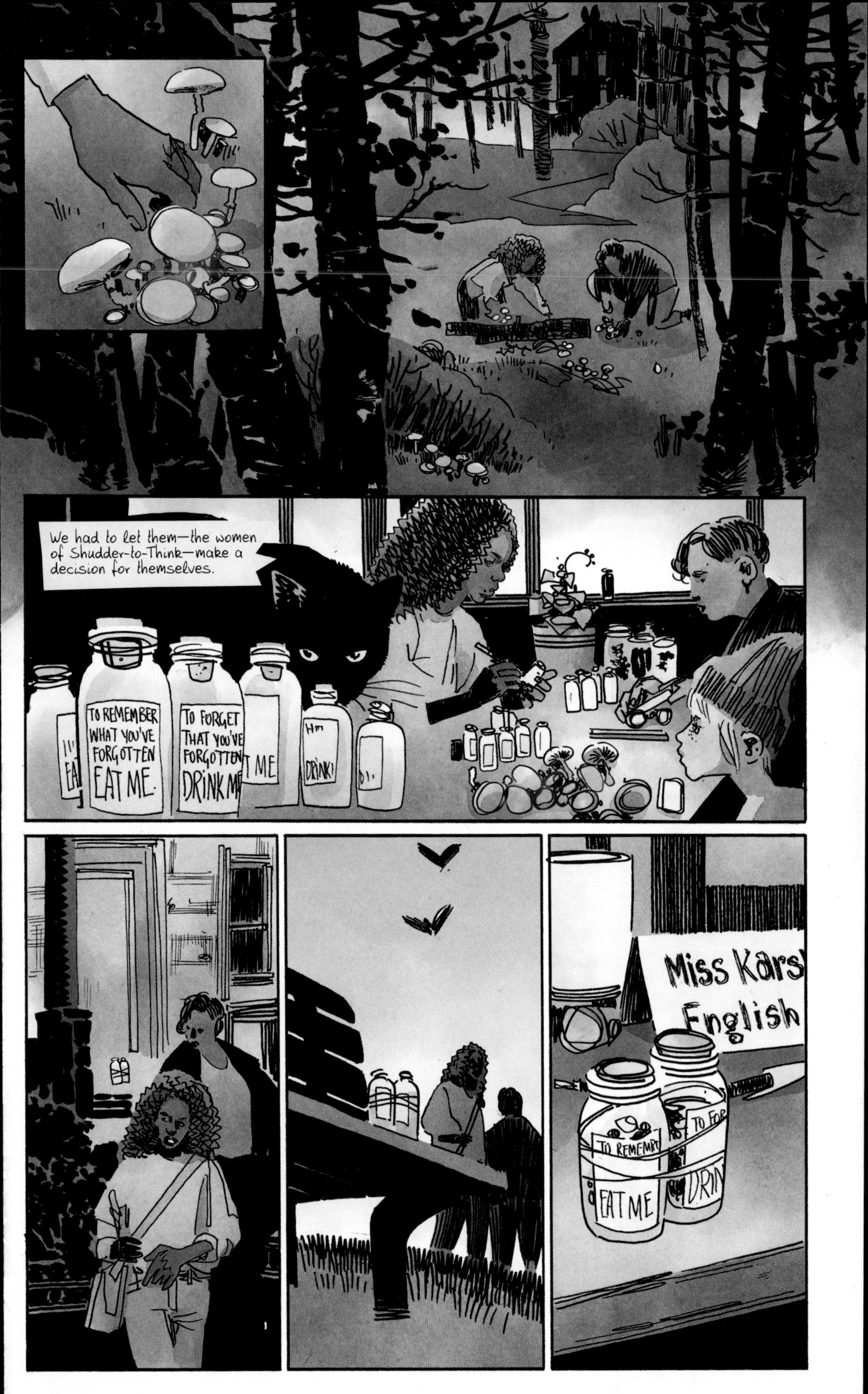
We had to let them—the women of Shudder-to-Think—make a decision for themselves.
TO REMEMBER WHAT YOU'VE FORGOTTEN EAT ME.
TO FORGET THAT YOU'VE FORGOTTEN DRINK ME
Miss Kars
English
TO REMEMB
EAT ME
TO FOR
DRIN

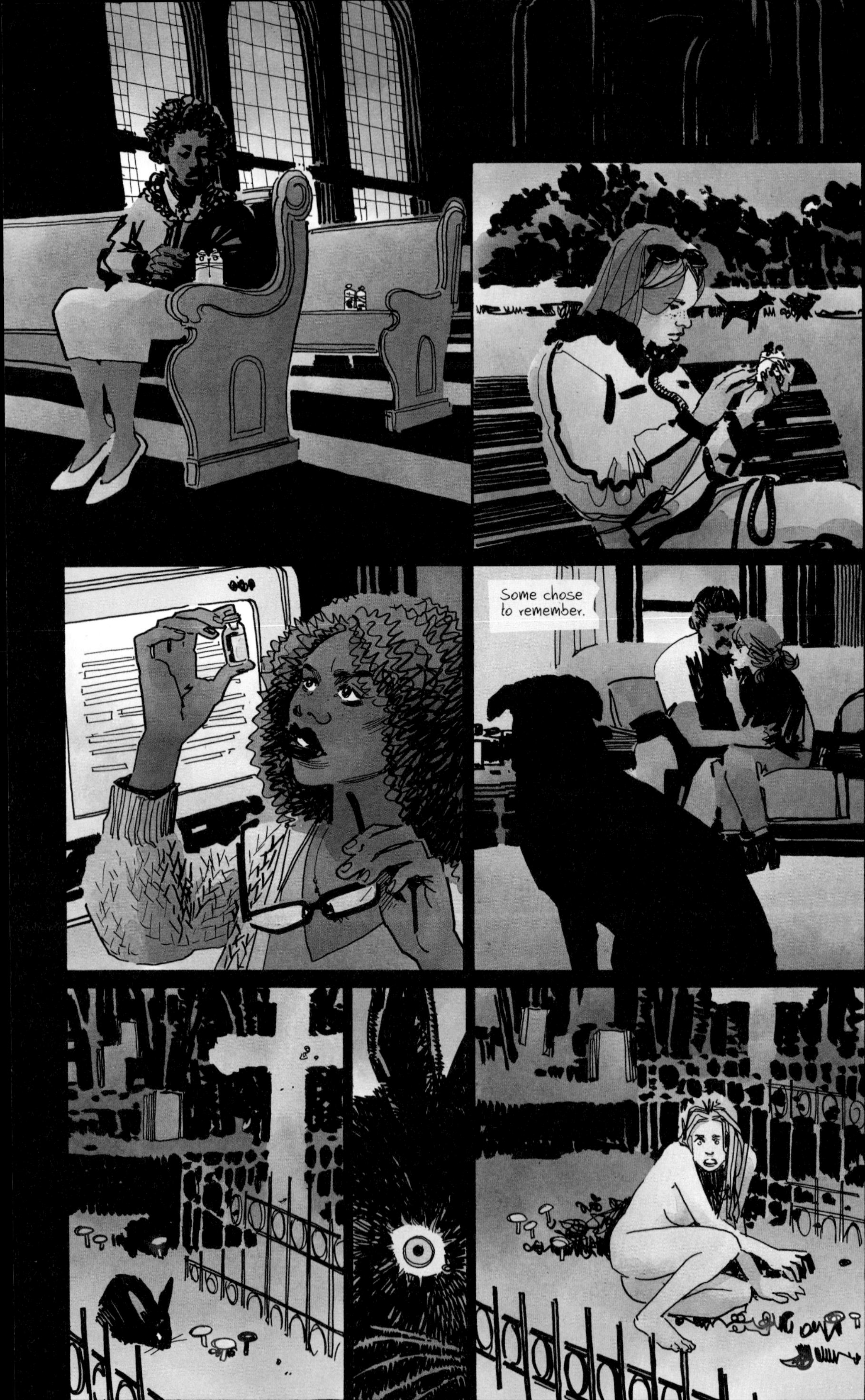
Some chose to remember.

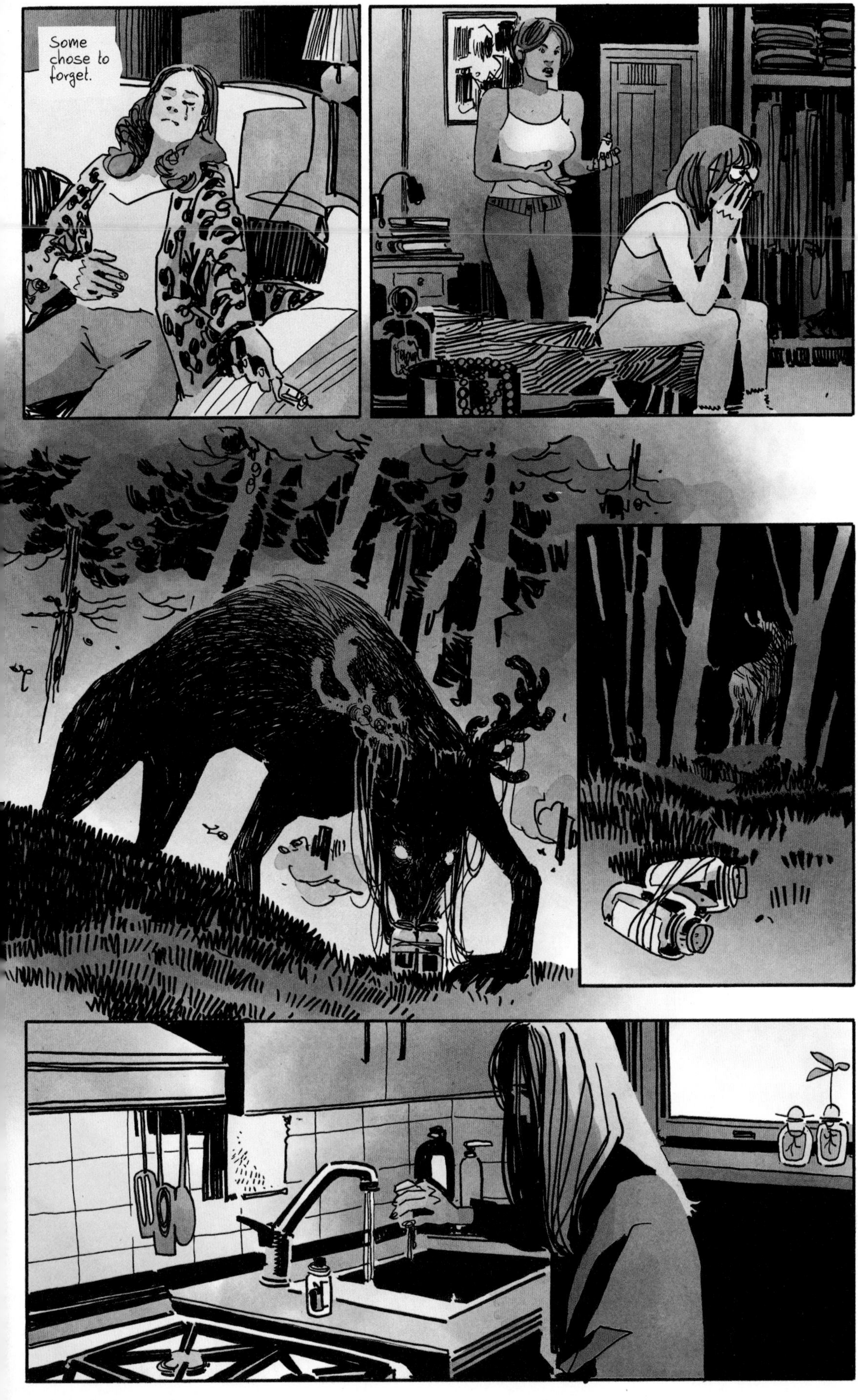
Some chose to forget.

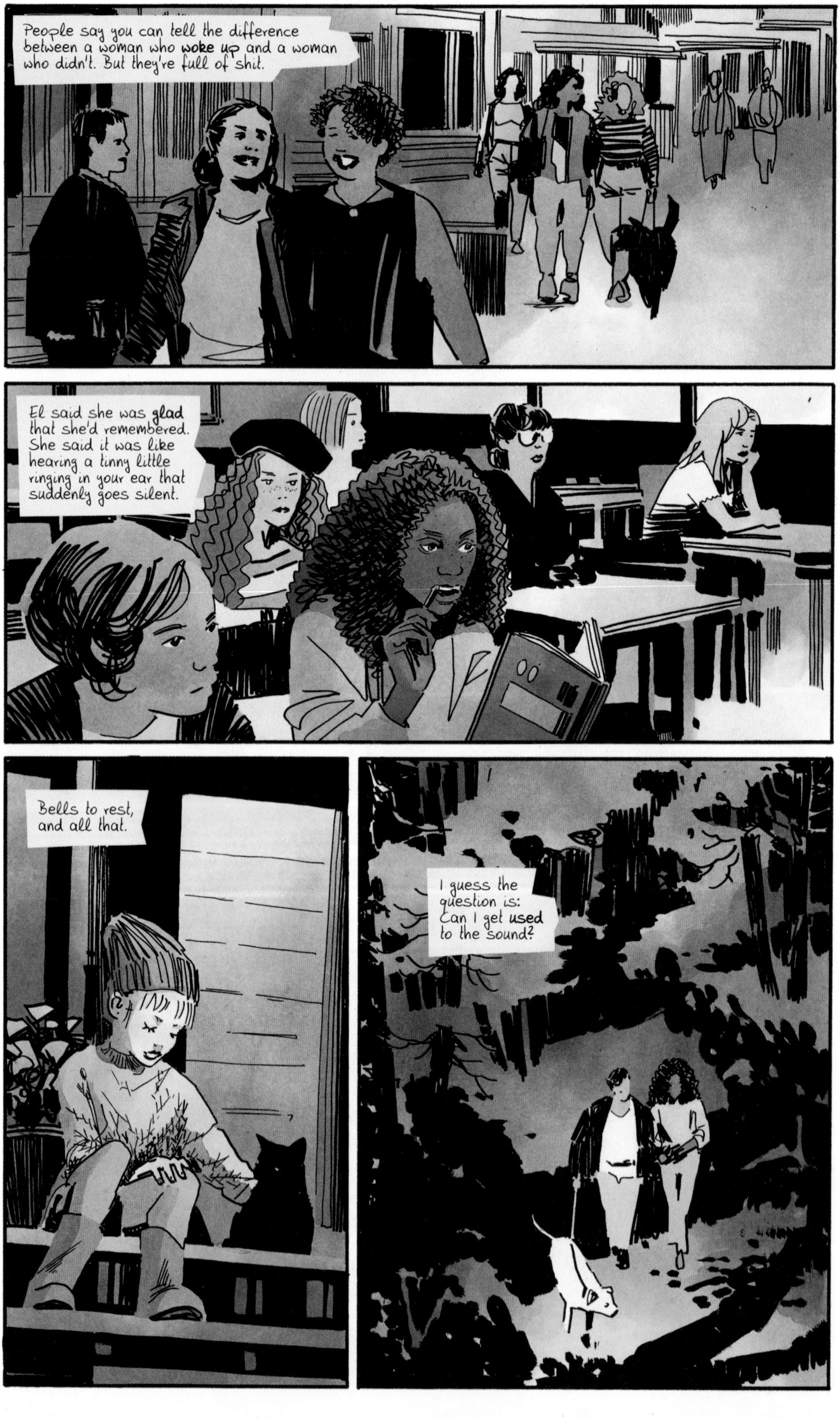
People say you can tell the difference between a woman who woke up and a woman who didn't. But they're full of shit.
El said she was glad that she'd remembered. She said it was like hearing a tinny little ringing in your ear that suddenly goes silent.
Bells to rest, and all that.
I guess the question is: Can I get used to the sound?

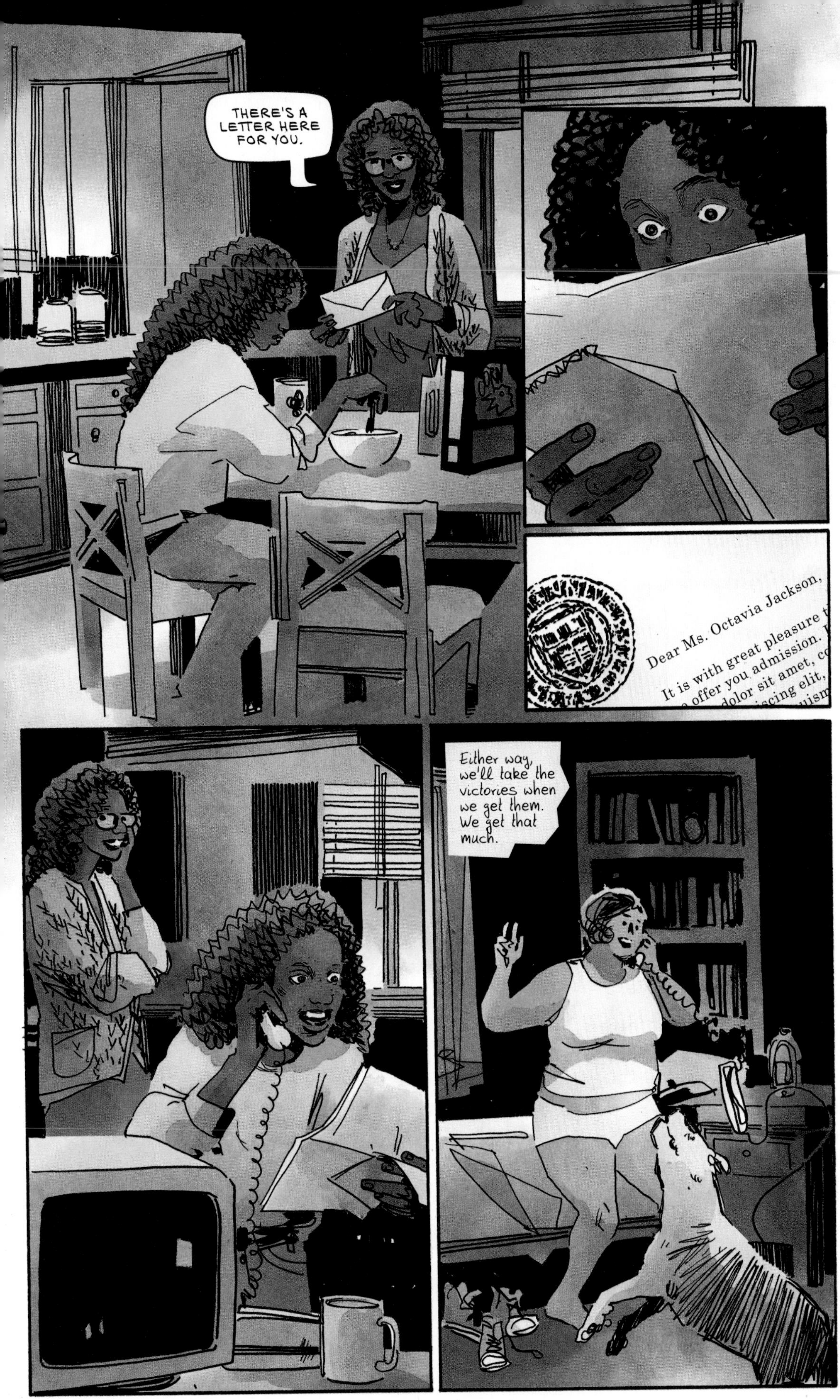
THERE'S A LETTER HERE FOR YOU.
Dear Ms. Octavia Jackson,
It is with great pleasure
offer you admission.
dolor sit amet,
Either way, we'll take the victories when we get them. We get that much.

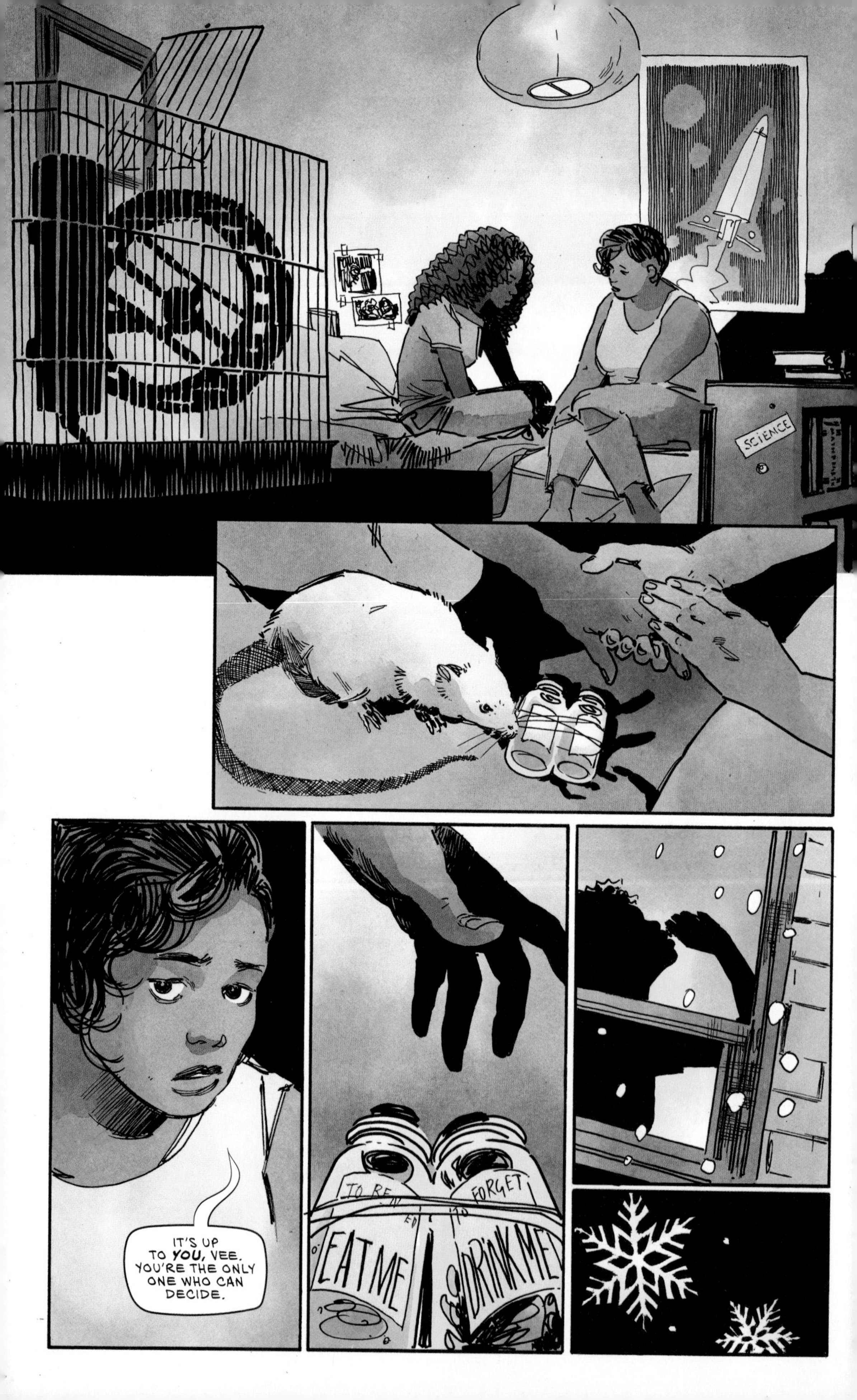
SCIENCE
IT'S UP TO YOU, VEE. YOU'RE THE ONLY ONE WHO CAN DECIDE.
FORGET
EAT ME
DRINK ME

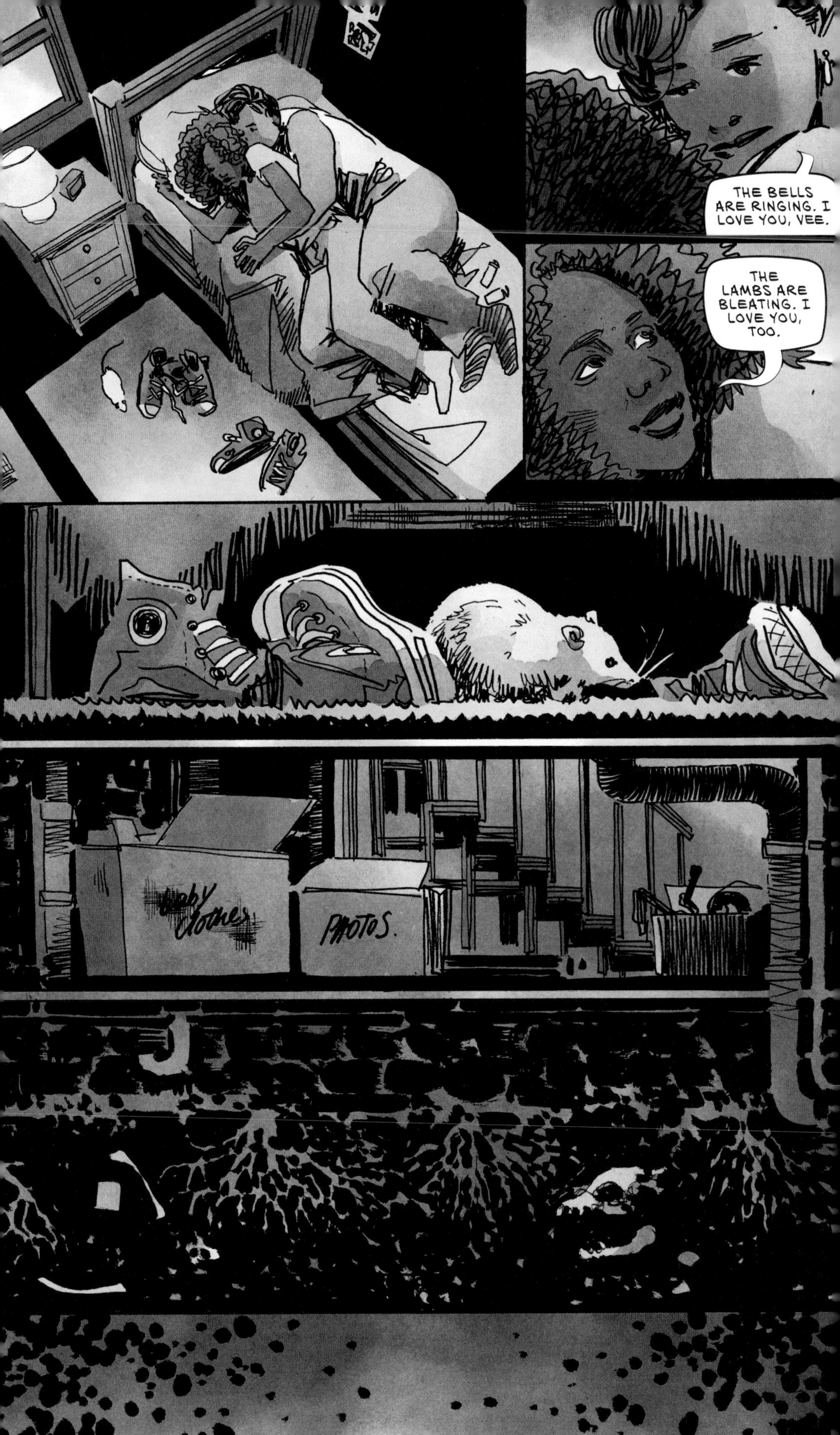
THE BELLS ARE RINGING. I LOVE YOU, VEE.
THE LAMBS ARE BLEATING. I LOVE YOU, TOO.
Baby Clothes
PHOTOS.

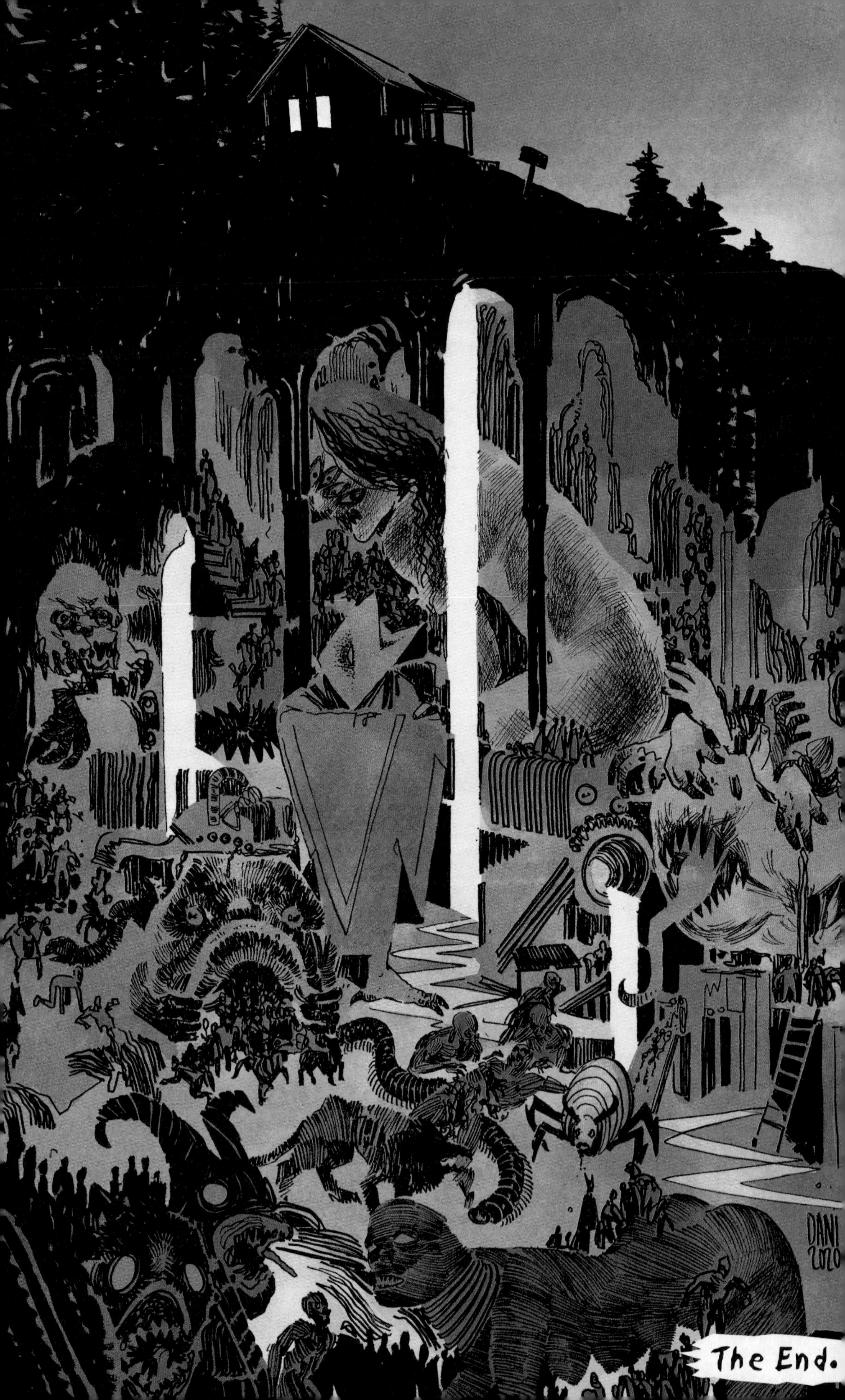
DANI 2020
The End.

Variant Covers

BY **JENNY FRISON**

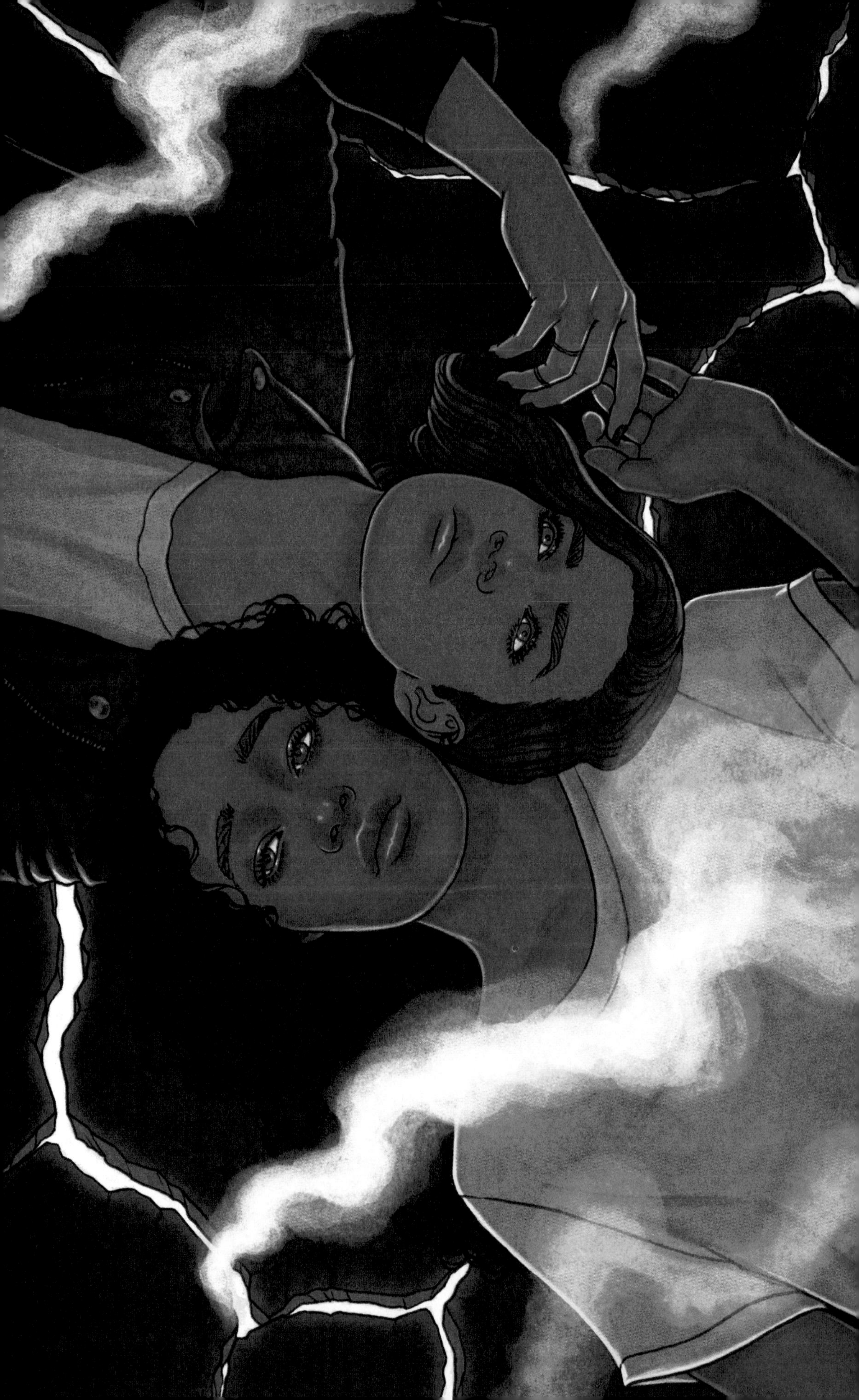

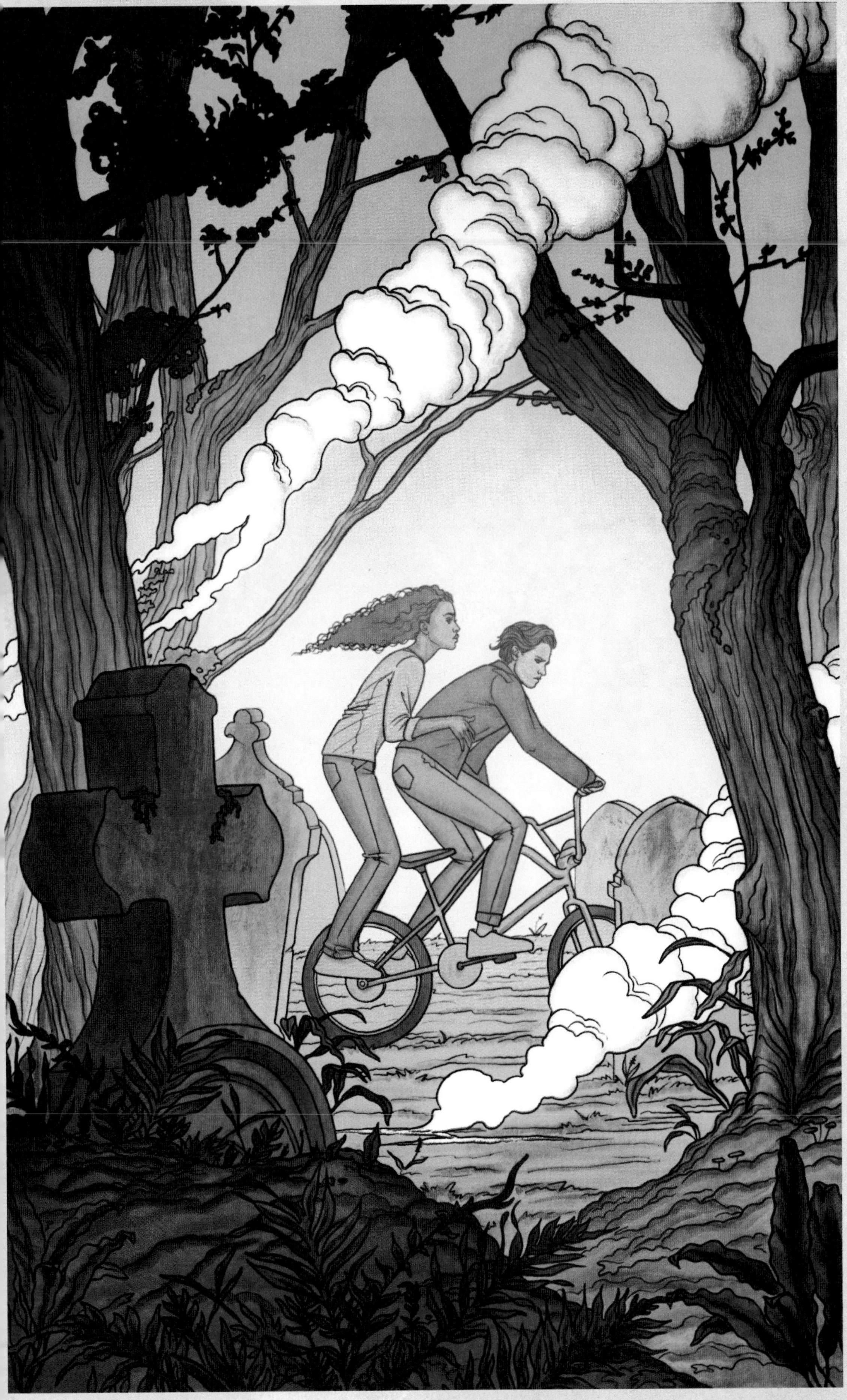

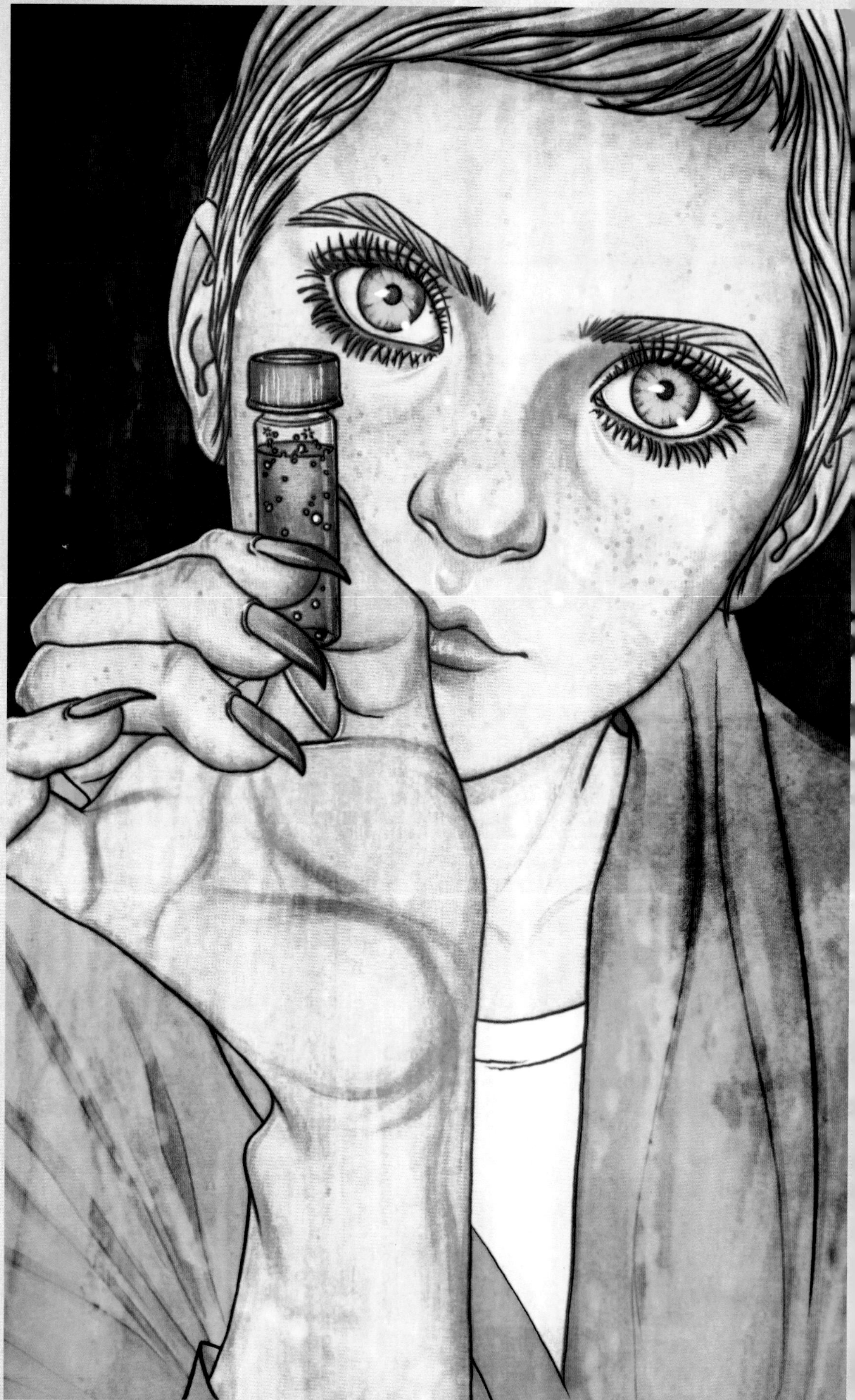

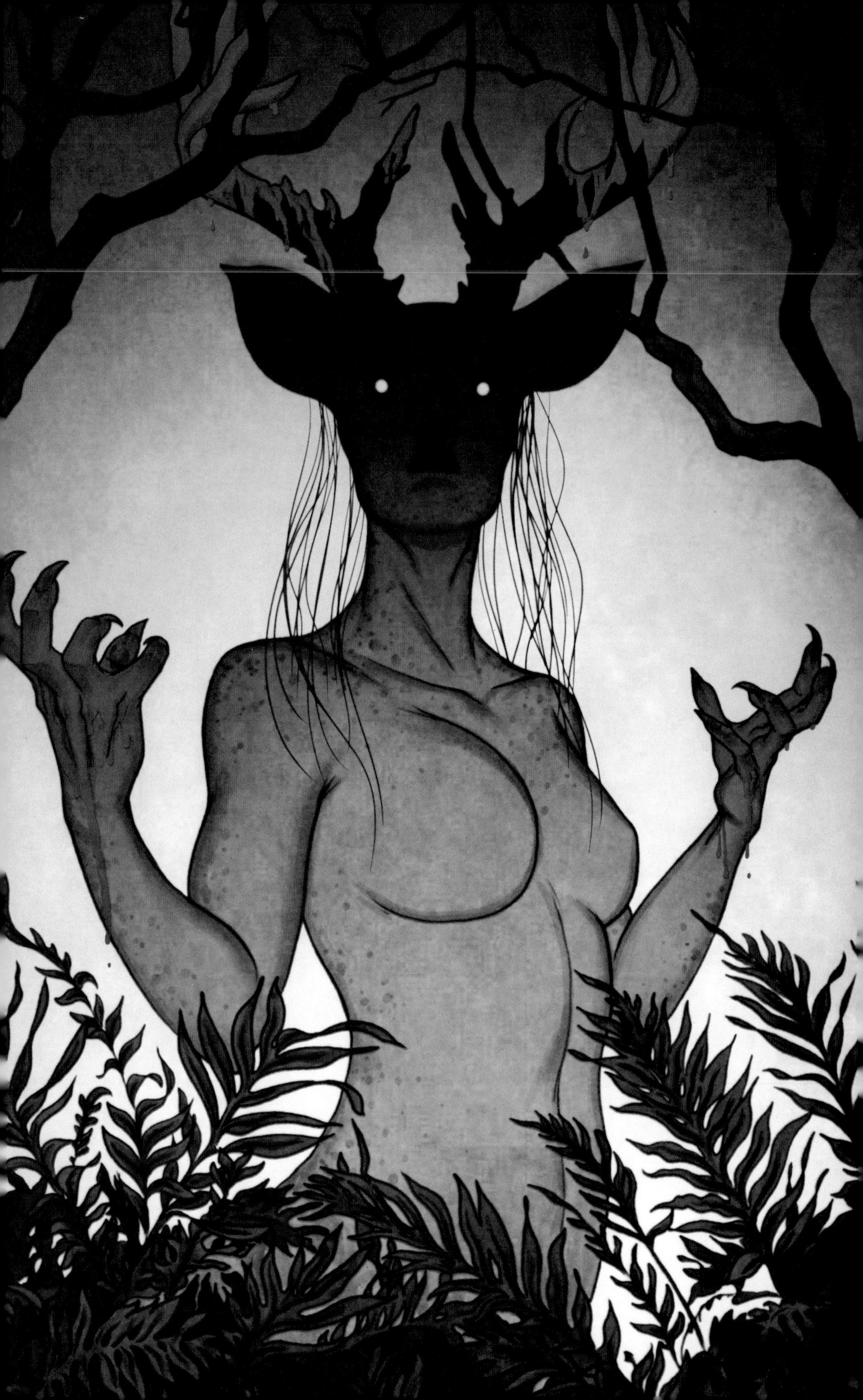

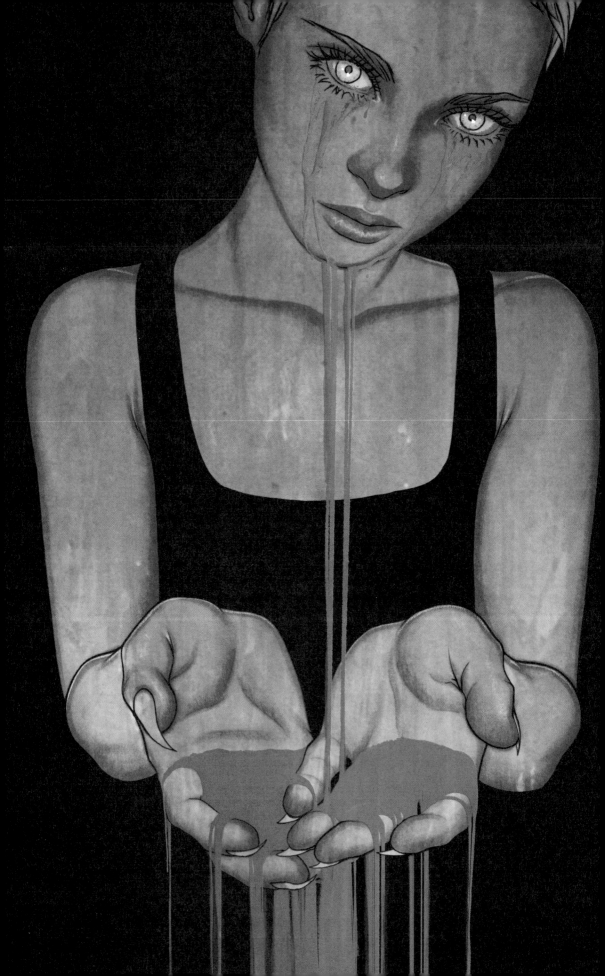

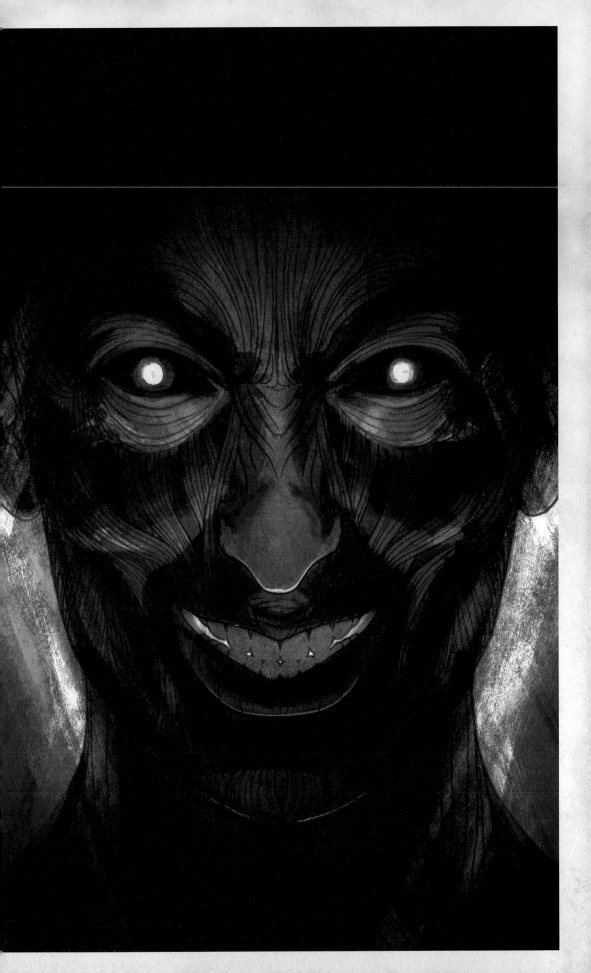

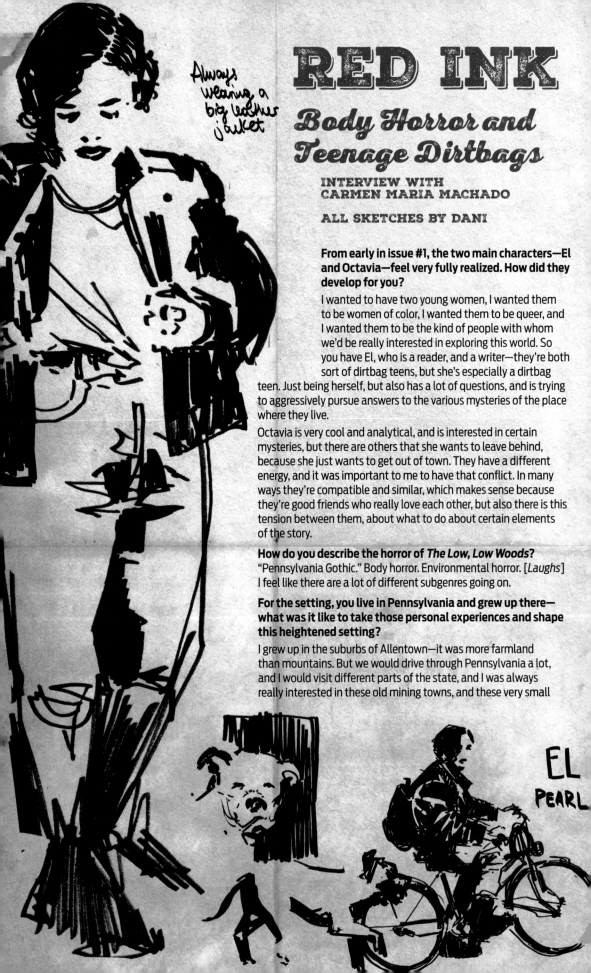

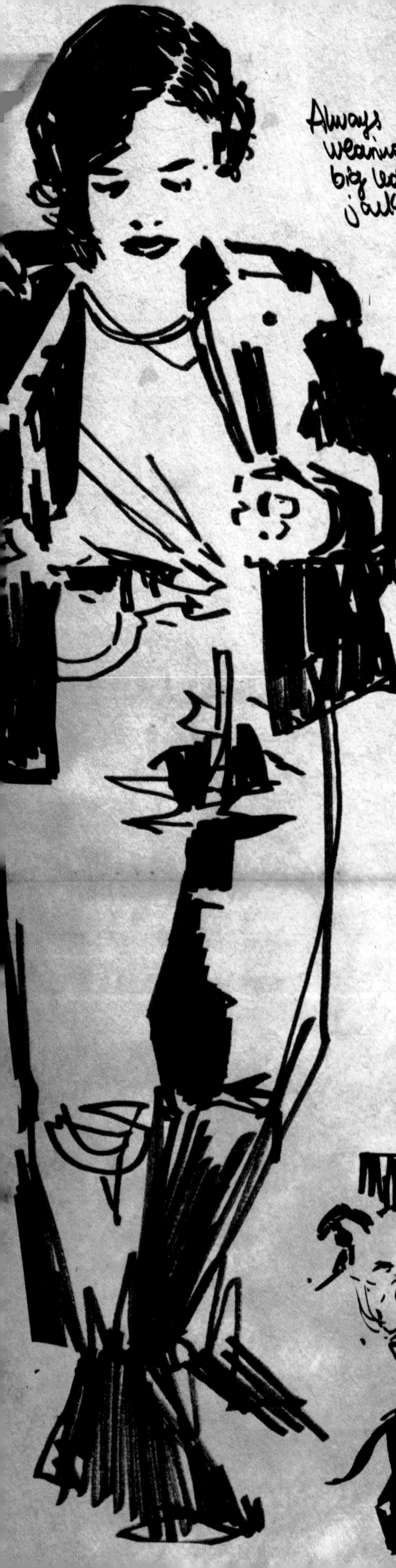
Always wearing a big leather jacket

RED INK

Body Horror and Teenage Dirtbags

INTERVIEW WITH CARMEN MARIA MACHADO

ALL SKETCHES BY DANI

From early in issue #1, the two main characters—El and Octavia—feel very fully realized. How did they develop for you?

I wanted to have two young women, I wanted them to be women of color, I wanted them to be queer, and I wanted them to be the kind of people with whom we'd be really interested in exploring this world. So you have El, who is a reader, and a writer—they're both sort of dirtbag teens, but she's especially a dirtbag teen. Just being herself, but also has a lot of questions, and is trying to aggressively pursue answers to the various mysteries of the place where they live.

Octavia is very cool and analytical, and is interested in certain mysteries, but there are others that she wants to leave behind, because she just wants to get out of town. They have a different energy, and it was important to me to have that conflict. In many ways they're compatible and similar, which makes sense because they're good friends who really love each other, but also there is this tension between them, about what to do about certain elements of the story.

How do you describe the horror of *The Low, Low Woods*?

"Pennsylvania Gothic." Body horror. Environmental horror. [*Laughs*] I feel like there are a lot of different subgenres going on.

For the setting, you live in Pennsylvania and grew up there—what was it like to take those personal experiences and shape this heightened setting?

I grew up in the suburbs of Allentown—it was more farmland than mountains. But we would drive through Pennsylvania a lot, and I would visit different parts of the state, and I was always really interested in these old mining towns, and these very small

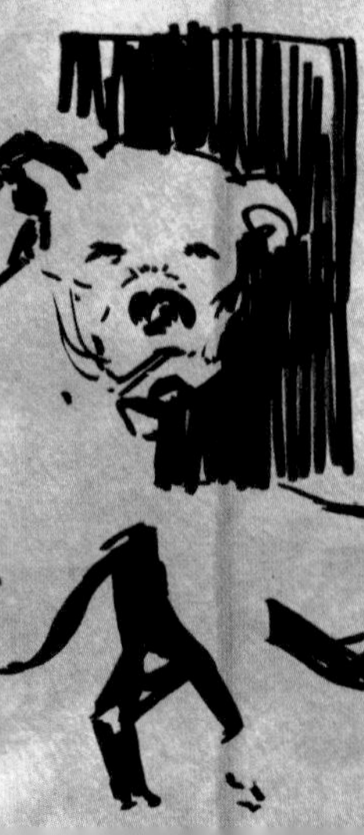

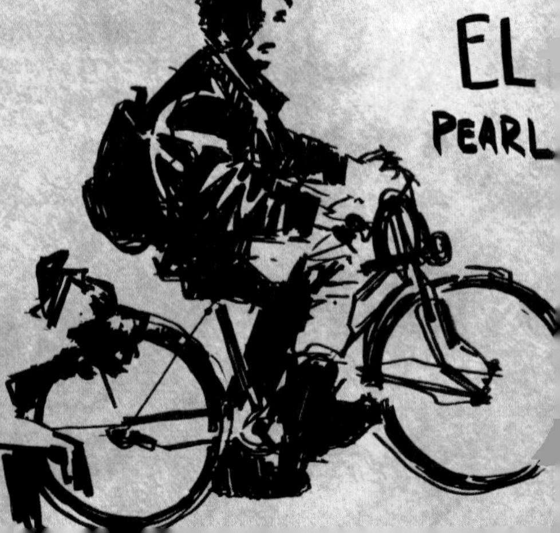
EL
PEARL

communities that had suffered a lot of economic loss, and the complicated relationship the state has with things like coal mining and fracking. The cool kids would go to Centralia and take photos of the smoke coming out of the ground—it was very goth, or something. [*Laughs*]

I liked the idea of setting it in something similar to Centralia, but I also wanted to have flexibility, and not stick to exactly that specific timeline and story.

Each Hill House Comics series is set in a different era, and this takes place in the mid-'90s. How did you land on that time period?

It was an era that I was alive for, but I was not a teenager for. I've had to ask some questions on Twitter—"If you were a teen in the '90s..." Close, but still a bit of a reach—exploring this time that I don't quite remember. I wanted it to be pre-cell phone, because I feel cell phones take the drama out of certain kinds of narratives.

Since this is your first comic book, what have you learned about how to tell a story—especially a horror story—that's unique to the medium?

A thing that I discovered when I was working on the first issue was thinking about perspective. In fiction you tell stories with perspective, but in this, I could have a person talking, and a voice narrating, and a visual perspective. It's way more complicated, but it also creates a lot more space for the tension of horror—visually, it gives you even more stuff to think about.

Speaking of visuals, what's excited you about working with Dani?

It's been amazing. I can't draw to save my life, so watching her transform my imagination into these physical images has been really, really incredible. "How does she do that? How is it even possible?"

What does it mean to you for *The Low, Low Woods* to be a part of Hill House Comics?

The really cool part is having a guide like Joe. Joe is not only brilliant at writing comics, but also he's a lovely, kind, generous human, who just gives really good writing advice. I've been overjoyed to have him as a part of this process, because he's done a lot for me, and gotten me to think in different ways about what I'm doing. I'm really grateful to him.

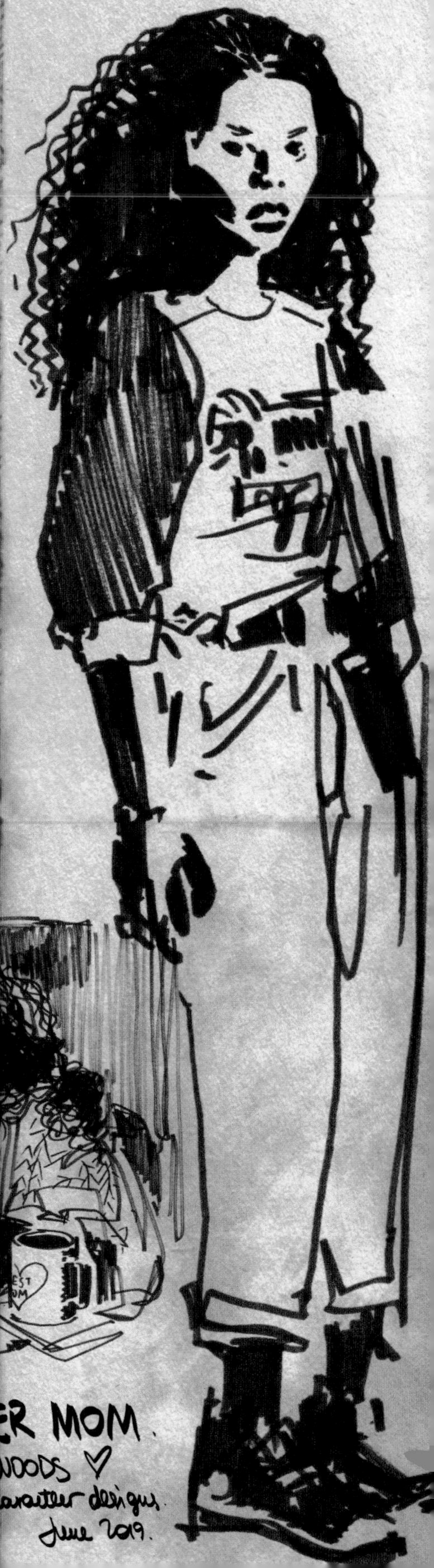

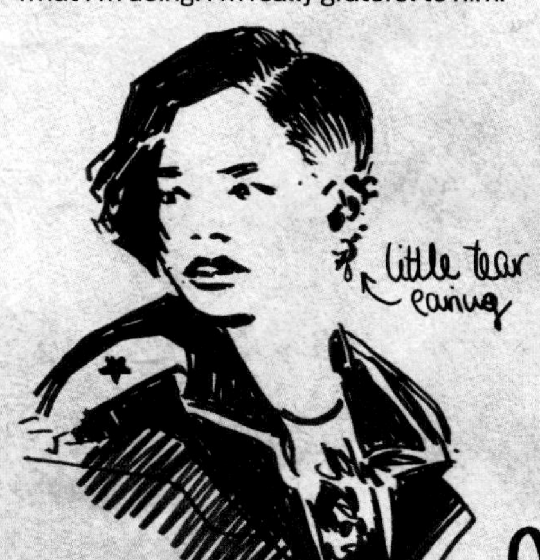
little tear earring

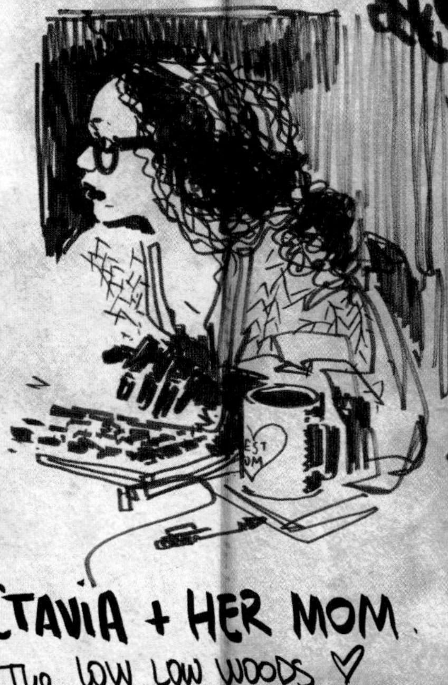
OCTAVIA + HER MOM.
The LOW, LOW WOODS ♥
DC character designs.
June 2019.

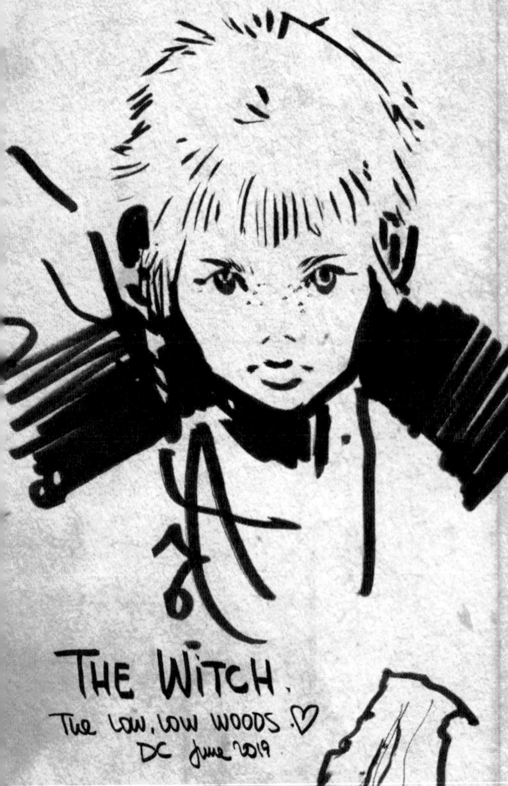
THE WITCH.
The Low, Low Woods ♡
DC June 2019

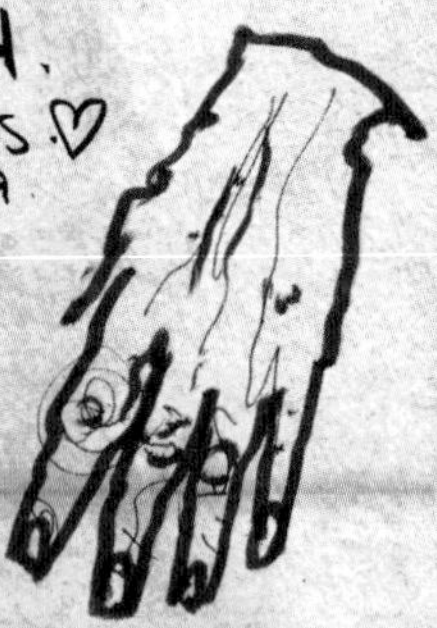

RED INK

INTERVIEW WITH DANI

What was it like bringing the profoundly unsettling town of Shudder-to-Think, Pennsylvania to life?

The whole experience was so pleasant and interesting for me. I hadn't worked on a book setting like this before, and I learned so many new things in the process while building the town and the place. Coming from Greece, I found out that I wasn't that well informed about small American mine towns, so I got through a lot of visual research and read about the situation in the script and various articles.

All of this stimulated the visuals of Shudder-to-Think, Pennsylvania!

Right from the first issue, El and Octavia feel like very real, grounded characters. How did they take shape for you?

They instantly felt like real people to me. Each of the girls has a unique personality and ways of dealing with their issues, so they had already taken a solid shape in my mind by the time I started drawing the actual pages.

During the time I was working on the book, I got to know them even better, and as a result I would draw specific mannerisms or facial expressions for each of the girls accordingly, and they would come so naturally to me—because of course this is how they would react!

While drawing them toward the end of the book, I thought, "Wow, this is actually the last time I'm going to draw El and Octavia," and I contemplated their whole journey a bit and felt so proud of them, and the people they are turning out to be.

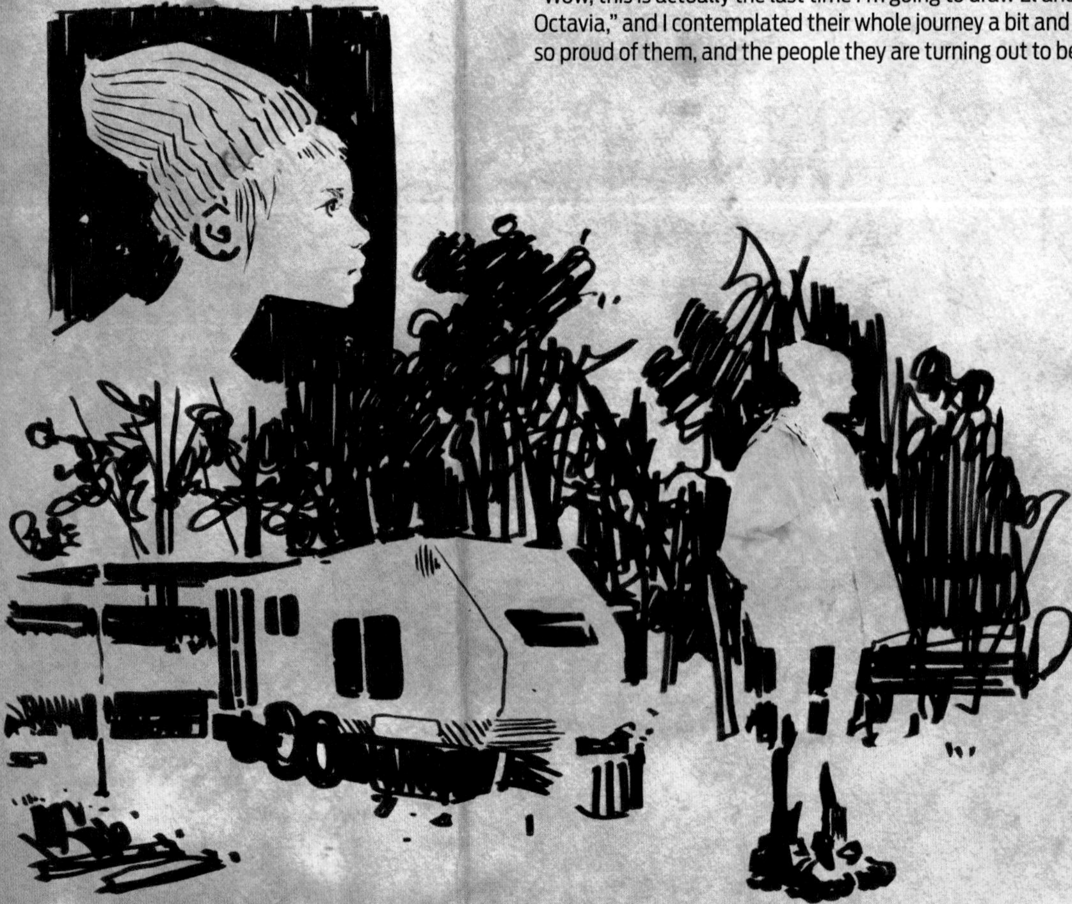

There are a lot of memorable—and memorably disturbing—visuals in *The Low, Low Woods* (the revelation of Jessica's mother in issue #3 will haunt readers for quite a while). What have been some of your favorite sequences to illustrate?

Everyone keeps mentioning the page with Jessica's mother, and honestly this is such a personal win for me! Figuring out how to visualize Carmen's phrase "sinkhole women" in a somehow creepy way was such a challenge for me.

I also really liked all the scenes where one of the girls would have a memory filling their head or a mushroom trip because I could get more creative.

Finally, I had hardly ever drawn a bicycle before *The Low, Low Woods*, and this book is *full* of scenes where the girls are riding El's bicycle. Can't say it was my favorite part, but I'm thankful for the challenge and practice!

What type of horror inspires you as an artist?

I like all types of horror, but mostly I prefer psychological horror. Of course, I will end up haunted by disturbing body horror images that will stay with me for the rest of my life and will eventually end up in parts of my art, but psychological horror ends up being more creative for me personally, as it will touch me internally.

For example, I saw *The Blair Witch Project* as a child (super young now that I'm thinking about it), and up to this day the most disturbing thing for me is still all the descriptions of the witch because it has created an image in my mind that I cannot fully grasp, but is extremely vivid, and this for me is terrifying. I'm sure it wouldn't have been the same if I had been given a clear image of the witch, and I've tried to apply the same logic with the Deer Woman in *The Low, Low Woods*. I had to draw her in scenes, obviously, but did my best to keep her just a shadow or a shape, so the reader can add the rest.

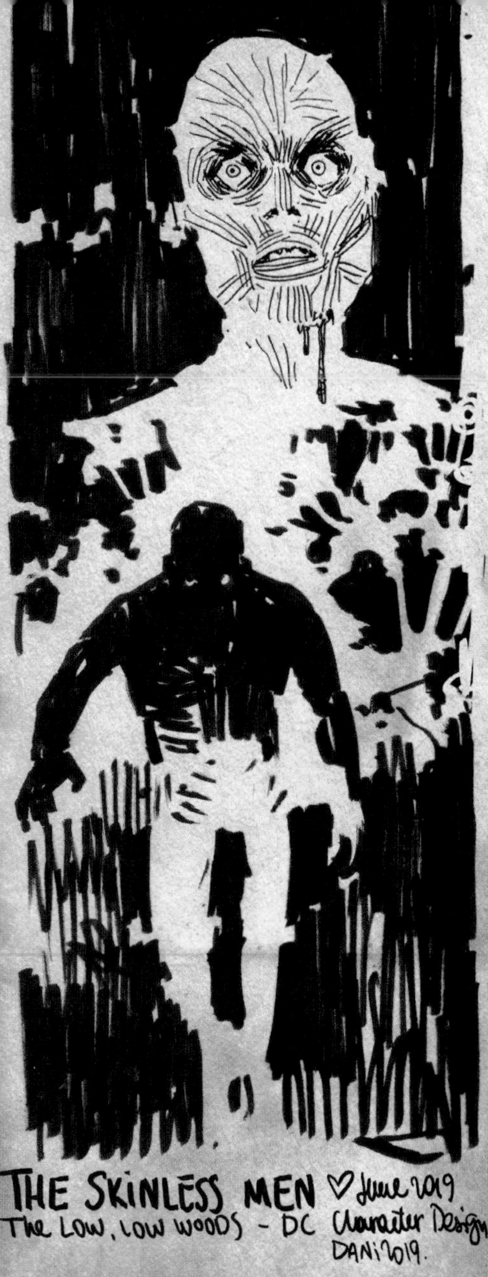
THE SKINLESS MEN ♡ June 2019
The Low, Low Woods - DC Character Design
DANI 2019.

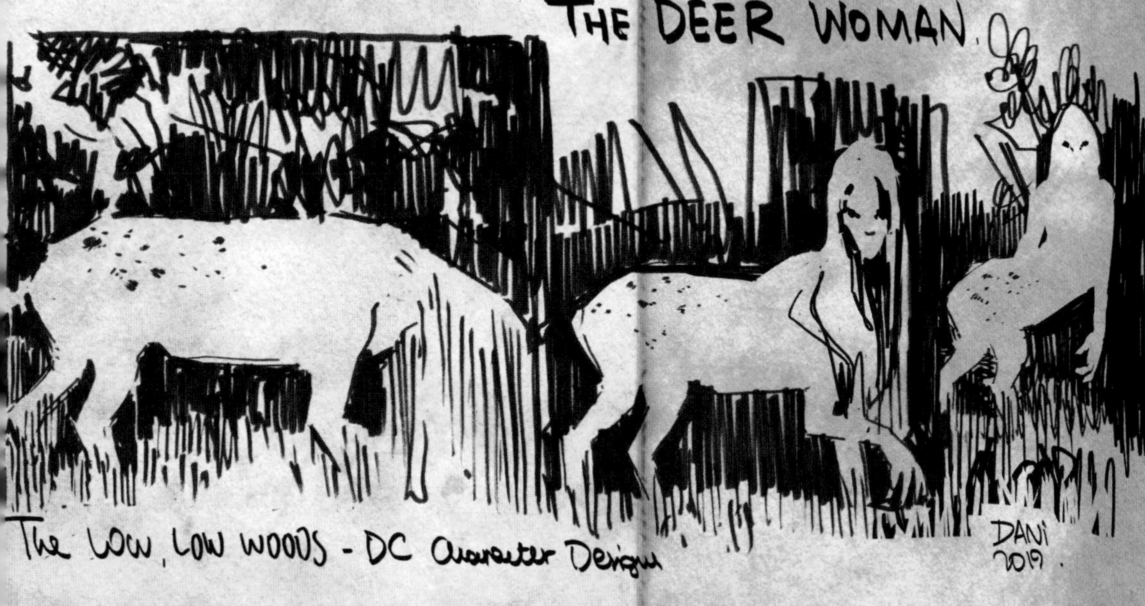
THE DEER WOMAN.
The Low, Low Woods - DC Character Design
DANI 2019

Carmen Maria Machado is the author of the bestselling memoir *In the Dream House* and the short story collection *Her Body and Other Parties*, which was a finalist for the National Book Award and the winner of the Shirley Jackson Award and the Lambda Literary Award for Lesbian Fiction. In 2018, the *New York Times* listed *Her Body and Other Parties* as a member of "The New Vanguard," one of "15 remarkable books by women that are shaping the way we read and write fiction in the 21st century." She lives in Philadelphia.

Dani was born in Athens, Greece, in 1992 and studied sculpture at the Athens School of Fine Arts. She has worked for *2000 AD*, IDW, Vault Comics, Legion M, Boom! Studios, Vertigo, Black Crown, and DC Hill House Comics, and is the artist behind the creator-owned series *Coffin Bound* from Image Comics, written by Dan Watters. She is also the creator of *Tales from the Strips*, a self-published series that won the Readers Choice Award at the 2015 Greek Comics Awards. She loves her cats and travelling around the world!

Tamra Bonvillain is an Eisner Award-nominated colorist who has worked on books for major comics companies such as DC, Marvel, Image, Dark Horse, Boom, and more. She currently lives in South Carolina.

Steve Wands is a comic book letterer, artist, and indie author. He's worked on top titles for Boom! Studios, Dark Horse, DC Comics, Image, Marvel, and Random House. He's the author of the *Stay Dead* series and co-author of *Trail of Blood* and *Feareater*. When not working, he spends time with his wife and sons in New Jersey.